theorizing gender

In memory of Ros Minsky

theorizing gender

Rachel Alsop,
Annette Fitzsimons
and
Kathleen Lennon

*With a guest chapter on psychoanalysis
by Ros Minsky*

polity

First published in 2002 by Polity Press in association with Blackwell
Publishing Ltd.

Reprinted 2003, 2005, 2006, 2007, 2008, 2009, 2011, 2012

Polity Press
65 Bridge Street
Cambridge CB2 1UR, UK

Polity Press
350 Main Street
Malden, MA 02148, USA

A catalogue record for this book is available from the British Library.

Library of Congress Cataloging-in-Publication Data
Alsop, Rachel.
    Theorizing gender / Rachel Alsop, Annette Fitzsimons, and Kathleen
Lennon ; with a guest chapter on psychoanalysis by Ros Minsky.
        p. cm.
Includes bibliographical references and index.
    ISBN 9-780-7456-1944-6
    1. Sex role. I. Fitzsimons, Annette. II. Lennon, Kathleen. III. Title.
HQ1075 .A435 2002
305.3—dc21   2001006332

Typeset in 10.5 on 12.5pt Bembo
by Graphicraft Limited, Hong Kong
Printed in Great Britain by the MPG Books Group

This book is printed on acid-free paper.

For further information on Polity, visit our website: www.politybooks.com

Contents

Acknowledgements

We would first of all like to acknowledge the contribution of Ros Minsky. We have all learnt a great deal from her work and were delighted when she agreed to contribute to this project. We were very sad to hear of her death before the book reached publication. Secondly we would like to thank each other. The mutual planning and execution of this book has benefited all of us. Thirdly we would like to thank participants in the Hull Centre for Gender Studies and also our graduate and undergraduate students for discussions over many years. Special thanks to Paul Gilbert, Minae Inahara, Gill Jagger, Lawrence Nixon, Michael Peckitt and Jay Prosser, for discussion, comments, references. Our editors from Polity have been supportive and very patient. The anonymous readers helped improve the book enormously.

Introduction

This book emerges out of more than ten years of teaching and re-
searching gender in an interdisciplinary way. In 1986 the Hull Centre
for Gender Studies was set up by academics of the universities of
Hull and Humberside and interested parties from the town. Over the
years it has hosted innumerable speakers from Britain and abroad
and spawned gender studies courses and modules at both institutions
as well as a journal on gender studies.[1] When the Centre was launched
the use of the term 'gender studies' was controversial, deemed by
some in women's studies as a political sell-out. (We are glad to report
that relations are now harmonious and the Centre hosted the Women's
Studies Network conference in 1998.) Our choice of title for the
Centre was prompted not by a desire for institutional disguise – but
by certain theoretical and practical concerns. The main theoretical
concern at the time was based simply on the conviction that it was
impossible to theorize women and the construction of femininity
without also theorizing men and the construction of masculinity. The
practical concerns arose from the involvement many of the founding
members had had with activist women's groups. A challenge in some
groups had been negotiating across divisions of class, sexuality and
cultural and national locations, among a myriad of other differences
leading often to uneasy compromises around the category 'woman'.
By focusing on the study of gender rather than the study of women
we hoped to be able to interrogate the ways in which constructions
of femininity and masculinity related to and were constituted by
other social divisions, without assuming the priority of gender over

other axes of social inequality. At that time there was also a men's group in Hull and many people wanted a forum in which we could listen to what they had to say. Then, about the time of the setting up of the Centre, there was a dispute in a local women's centre about the inclusion of transsexual women. The unease that many of us felt about their exclusion served to problematize further the use of the term 'woman'. Transsexual men and women have been regular contributors to the Centre since that time and we are very much indebted to them for their contributions, which have helped inform the approach to theorizing gender which is explored here.

This book aims to provide an examination of the different ways in which we can theorize gender. Through the analysis of different modes of theorizing our aim is to interrogate the processes whereby people generally become divided into the two categories, male and female, and to explore what the ensuing content of these categories is. As Scott (1988: 49) so succinctly remarks, '"man" and "woman" are at once empty and overflowing categories. Empty because they have no ultimate, transcendent meaning. Overflowing because, even when they appear to be fixed, they still contain within them altern- ative, denied, or suppressed definitions.' We suggest that we cannot simply take for granted what it is to be a man or a woman, or that the world is simply found with these divisions in it.

This project is thus distinct from accounts of gender which take the division of people into male and female groups for granted and which seek instead to explain the specific and unequal interrelations between these two groups socially. In this vein liberal feminists tra- ditionally have looked to a lack of equal opportunities for women as the root of inequality, Marxist feminists have identified the work- ings of capitalism as a prime cause of women's subordination, while radical feminists have explored the machinations of patriarchy in both personal and social relations. Such accounts share some common ground in that they tended to assume *a priori* that the human race is divided into the categories men and women. From this basis they then try to make sense of what difference gender makes in terms of social structure and norms of behaviour.

Although it is an oversimplification to suggest that none of the above accounts acknowledge or take into account the heterogeneity of women's experiences (Segal 1999) it is the critique from black and Third World feminists (among others) which brought to the fore the question of differences among women (and by implication differences among men), challenging as they did the false universalism of much white feminist criticism. These critiques called into question the terms 'woman' and 'man', so that it was no longer possible to take for granted what it was to be a man or a woman. In this book we aim to investigate just that. We are concerned with the myriad of things which it can be to be male or female and thereby with the processes by which we become *gendered* selves. Our discussion is informed by the constraint that an analysis of our gendered selves cannot be detached from other aspects of subjectivity and social positionality, such as race,[2] class, sexual orientation, able-bodiedness and so on. In so doing we wish to avoid an additive model of difference, which considers race, sexuality, class and so on in addition to gender, but instead to put forward an analysis which sees such categories of difference and inequality as mutually constitutive – to recognize that gendered categories are, for example, always raced, always class-specific.

In this book we are approaching the question of how we become male or female with the use of the term 'gender'. In this we are motivated by many of the concerns which led to the naming of the Centre, but our theoretical commitments to it have become more extensive. As we use the term it has several interconnected aspects. First, gender is a feature of subjectivity. We identify and make sense of ourselves as men and women or boys and girls. Secondly, gender refers to the cultural understandings and representations of what it is to be a man or a woman. For example, the belief that girls like sitting playing with dolls whereas boys like rough-and-tumble play has traditionally formed part of some cultures' understanding of gender difference in childhood. Thirdly, gender operates as a social variable, structuring the pathways of those so classified within society. In the field of work, for instance, there is still a tendency for men and women to be channelled into doing different jobs and by consequence to earn different rates of pay. All these three aspects of gender are interrelated and it is these interconnections we aim to explore through the course of this text.[3] For example, the division of labour within the public sphere (as in the home) is dependent upon our cultural understandings of men and women being different and thus more suited to different types of work. In turn how we make sense of ourselves as men and women is contingent upon the ways in which such cultural representations and social structures are gendered.

Often the theory that is explored brings into question the very language we are using to investigate. Although in the text we employ the term gender to refer to the production of male and female selves this does not mean that we either accept or endorse a simple sex–gender distinction or gender as a straightforward polarity between men/women and masculinity/femininity. Conventionally sex has been seen as distinct from gender in that sex has been taken to relate to a biological division between men and women and gender to refer to the social constructions masculine and feminine. In other words gender has been regarded as that which society makes out of biological sex difference. Our analysis of gender theory, however, also questions the rationale for splitting humans into male and female kinds and the limitations and boundaries the categories themselves produce.

The use of the term gender to conceptualize the production of masculinity and femininity is as controversial within feminist theory today as it was in the mid-1980s when the Centre was established. Gender has come under fire from within the feminist community for suggesting a false symmetry between men and women (Braidotti with Butler 1994), for being unable to convey inequality and power, and for being politically benign (Evans 1990). The main alternative to gender put forward to conceptualize the relations between men and women is that of sexual difference. Here the exchange between Rosi Braidotti and Judith Butler (1994) in *differences*, which is explored more fully in chapter 8, is useful in examining the merits and disadvantages of each term. For Braidotti the use of the term gender is at 'crisis-point in feminist theory', under attack, in her opinion, for its 'theoretical inadequacy and for its politically amorphous and unfocused nature' (1994: 36). She sees the term 'sexual difference' as able to convey the asymmetry between the sexes, and it allows space for women's redefinition of femininity, operating as the primary site of identification and resistance.

Our decision to take gender as our point of focus – to write a text entitled *Theorizing Gender* rather than one entitled *Theorizing Sexual Difference* – is rooted first and foremost in our questioning of the assertion prominent in the 'sexual difference' framework that sexual difference is foundational to identity. As Butler argues in response to Braidotti's defence of sexual difference, 'part of the suspicion toward the "sexual difference" framework is precisely that it tends to make sexual difference more hallowed, more fundamental, as a constituting difference of social life more important than other kinds of differences' (Braidotti with Butler 1994: 41). While acknowledging that gender can convey a false symmetry between men and women, it does at the same time release us from the idea that asymmetry between men and women is unavoidable.

We also challenge the argument that the use of gender as a concept to explore the production of masculine and feminine selves, and indeed the establishment of 'gender studies' as opposed to 'women's studies' (or 'feminist studies') within the academy is *necessarily* depoliticizing (Braidotti with Butler 1994; Evans 1990; Richardson and Robinson 1997). Evans, in a discussion of the shift from women's studies to gender studies in British academia, argues that 'gender studies' does not automatically invoke questions of power in the way that 'women's studies' does:

> it is acceptable . . . to study such things as gender and sexuality because they do not pose inherent questions about power and can take the form of descriptive accounts of aspects of social life. Without the integration of concepts of power and inequality, the world remains full of people who are just different in much the same way as the people in a children's encyclopaedia. (1990: 460)

While taking on board Evans's concerns, we suggest that an analysis of gender does not foreclose the possibility of a radical and transformative political agenda, and can in fact open up modes of resistance and transformation denied within a sexual difference framework.[4] The ways in which gender is conceptualized and deployed vary enormously between texts. As Hawkesworth (1997) illustrates in some depth, gender has a 'multiplicity of meaning' within feminist theory. The radical potential of gender (and indeed gender studies) depends therefore on the particular theoretical framework in which gender is conceptualized. This is not to dilute attention to the specific power relations in which *gendered* inequalities are constructed and embedded. Indeed our critique of the theories explored in this text is informed by a political and personal commitment to the reworking of gender in a more equitable, less oppressive manner. To this end we acknowledge that contemporarily relations between men and women are structured in a manner which tends to subordinate and devalue women. At the same time, however, we also recognize that current norms of gender marginalize many men and that cultural constructions of gender exclude and alienate those who do not fit neatly into the categories male/female. Although feminist analyses (in their many guises) feature widely within our analysis of gender theory, the theories with which we engage in this text also include the recent work on gender to emerge from queer analysis and transgender narratives. This is not in any way to set up gender studies in opposition to women's studies, to deny their considerable overlap or to dismiss out of hand the concept sexual difference in favour of gender.

While our discussion will take into account how debates within gender theory develop in relation to each other we wish to avoid an account which charts the development of theory primarily chronologically. As has been noted elsewhere (Segal 1999) there has been a tendency in so-called 'nineties feminism' to homogenize the past, failing to take adequate account of the diversity of ideas in early second-wave feminism or the specific context in which ideas were produced. 'Seventies feminism' has been uniformly castigated for being unable sufficiently to take account of differences among women, a propensity to universalize and a blind acceptance of the binary division male–female. While such criticisms hold some validity they ignore not only the heterogeneity of past (and present) theorizing but also the continuity of ideas over time. Instead this text is primarily divided into chapters which examine varying theoretical approaches to the study of gender, assessing how they complement, contradict and interconnect with each other.

In doing this our aim is twofold. First, we attempt to map out different ways in which gender has been theorized. Here the main approaches are naturalizing approaches, reliant on biology and psychology; psychoanalytic approaches; and social constructionist approaches. This last category is divided into those who prioritize material relations and those who place priority on the realm of language and discourse, the domain of the cultural meanings of gender. Again for those who place a premium on cultural meanings there is a division between theorists to whom gender is the central organizing concept and those who employ the notion of sexual difference. Our second aim is to evaluate these approaches and undermine the polarities which have been set up between them. Although there are inevitable tensions we none the less argue that we need to employ resources from psychoanalytic, materialist and discursive accounts to accommodate the complexities of gender and other aspects of identity. The focus throughout is with the shape of theory. There is therefore little reference to historical or empirical resources. We see our project as an evaluation and clarification of approaches to gender theory which could then inform empirical research within a gendered frame.

In the course of this discussion we look at particular theorists who exemplify particular approaches. This is not to say that such writers are necessarily the only theorists to develop such ideas. We have not had the space to consider comprehensively all the important contributors to the field of gender theory. Many we have not discussed are signalled in the references. Perhaps, however, we need to explain some of our decisions. The work of Judith Butler is given extensive attention. Partly this reflects the central position she has come to occupy in gender theory. She represents perhaps the most sophisticated development of discursive accounts of gender construction. Clearly, however, the amount of attention we pay to her work also reflects a judgement on our part as to the productiveness of her approach. The discussion of Butler, however, continually points to the need to supplement her account with insights from psychoanalytic and materialist theorists and the later chapters of the book attempt to weave these strands together in the discussions of sexuality, the body, transgendering and the politics of identity. There are some omissions which we particularly regret. The work of postcolonial feminists, including that of Gayatri Spivak, does not get as much attention as we would like, and of post-Lacanian French feminists we only discuss Irigaray in any detail. We can only plead time and space to explain but not to justify this.

We write this book not only as an aid for anyone studying gender and seeking to make sense of the different ways in which we can conceptualize how we become gendered selves, but also as a stimulus for debate. The development of our ideas as expressed in this text has occurred over time through our interactions and exchanges in both teaching and research and continues beyond the publication of this book. To this end we welcome constructive responses from readers. We aim throughout to make the work as accessible as possible, while recognizing the complexities of many of the ideas. We hope it will be of use to students from undergraduate level onwards, our own as well as others. Our past students have played a crucial role in informing the perspectives explored here.

The book is organized into ten chapters.[5] In chapter 1 we examine the ways in which gender divisions are naturalized in certain strands of theory. Sex difference research tends to assume a division of bodies into male and female and suggests that such a division generates distinct psychological and behavioural divisions between men and women. This chapter explores the problematic assumptions that

underpin such accounts. Through the work of writers such as Nelly
Oudshoorn and Anne Fausto-Sterling the *a priori* assumption that
there are two sexes, which preconditions naturalizing accounts of
gender, is interrogated.

In chapter 2, we move on to look at psychoanalytic accounts of
gender and the ways in which psychoanalysis has developed our
understanding of the unconscious dimensions of gender formation
and the importance of early interactions within the family on the
construction of our gender identities. This chapter discusses the
development of ideas on gender within psychoanalysis, taking into
account the contributions made by Freud, Lacan, the 'French feminists' (Cixous, Kristeva and Irigaray) and the object-relations school
of psychoanalysis (most notably, Chodorow). Here we are intro-
duced to the idea that our gendered subjectivities are unstable and
precarious, that our unconscious thoughts and desires are potentially
disruptive of our conscious actions. It also highlights the significance
of bodily difference in the process of subject formation, an issue to
which we return later.

In chapter 3 we begin our exploration of social constructionist
accounts of gender. Here our discussion centres on the debate between
materialist feminist and discursive accounts of gender as a means to
illustrate the different ways in which gender can be interpreted as
socially constructed. Whereas materialist feminist accounts look to
structural and material features and patterns to understand what it is
to be gendered, discursive accounts pay attention instead to the construction of meaning and significance in language and representation.
Looking in particular at the influence of Foucault's ideas on discourse,
and the appropriation of Foucault within feminism, this discussion
explores the idea that we make sense of ourselves as men and women
through the discourses on gender we encounter. We note that while
earlier materialist feminist accounts placed emphasis on our positioning within social institutions and structures to explain gender they
paid less attention to gender as an aspect of subjectivity, a move
made prominent within discursive accounts. We conclude by looking at the ways in which later materialist feminists, most notably
Hennessy, have sought to integrate attention to language, culture
and meaning within the materialist framework. This chapter introduces the importance of the recognition of difference among women
within feminist thought and the impact of it on feminist accounts of
gender. Through analysis of the concept of patriarchy the chapter

highlights the problems of defining women and men as collective, internally homogeneous groups with shared interests and needs, and considers the necessary modes of theorising needed to accommodate difference. The discussion resists totalizing theories of gender and the polarization of debates around the material and the discursive. Instead, we argue for contextual analysis which pays attention to the interweaving of discursive and materialist accounts.

In chapter 4 we move on to a specific consideration of the work of Judith Butler. Butler's account forms the limit of social constructionism. For Butler there is no real authentic gender; instead the performance constitutes the real. There is therefore no necessary link between masculinity and femininity and 'male' and 'female' bodies. For her it is the demands of the heterosexual imperative which force a cultural division into male and female. The critique of Butler begins an exploration of the limitations of her analysis, questioning, in particular, the place of the body within her work and the types of political action to which her theory gives rise. These issues are taken up again in subsequent chapters.

Chapter 5 explores in particular the interconnections between the categories of gender and sexuality. Through a discussion of the debate between Gayle Rubin and Judith Butler we consider whether sexuality should be in relation to a distinct category of analysis seen as both subjectivity and political collectivities. We conclude that, although these categories are discursively interdependent, there may be purposes for which they require separate analysis.

Chapter 6 takes as a case study the recent work to emerge on men and masculinities, looking in particular at the ways in which discourse theory and psychoanalysis as well as naturalizing accounts have been employed to analyse masculinities. This chapter assesses what this body of work contributes to our understanding of gender, exploring in some detail the construction of and interrelationship of hegemonic and subordinate masculinities, the interconnections between masculinity and homophobia and men's contradictory relationship to power.

Chapter 7 deals with the question of the body and the different ways in which theories tackle the issue of corporeality. After exploring the idea of a docile body as outlined in Foucault's work and its implications for understanding gender, the discussion questions the way in which Butler's account of gender, as influenced by Foucault, deals with the issue of bodily materiality. Butler's argument that materiality is a discursive effect is interrogated through the work of disability theorists, which questions the limitations of such a socially constructed view of the body. The chapter then provides an account of the role of the body utilizing a concept of bodily imaginaries, derived from both psychoanalytic and phenomenological thought. In this way the emotional salience of our relationship to our bodily identities is made evident.

The insistence within Butler's account that sexual difference is constructed culturally (that our understanding of biological sex differences is mediated via culture) is interrogated further in chapter 8 through an analysis of sexual difference theory. Irigaray's analysis of sexual difference and her project to develop different imaginaries of the body, ones which allow femininity to be lived in a less damaging way, is explored in some detail. But, while the work of Irigaray is given particular attention, the discussion is mindful of the varying accounts of sexual difference put forward by theorists in this field (Braidotti, Gatens, Grosz). Here we explore further the debates within feminist thought on the use of the term sexual difference over the term gender, looking in particular at the interchange between Braidotti and Butler.

In chapter 9 we consider the debates on transgendering and transsexuality, and the recent work that has emerged from queer theorists, taking as a thread through the chapter the notions of 'borderlands' and 'home'. This chapter outlines the different readings of transgendering and transsexuality for gender. We consider the challenge made by transgendering to the categorization of gender into male–female, and the limitations and boundaries constructed via such gender categories. By destabilizing the links between sex and gender, queer strategies open up the possibility for multiple and indeterminate sex–gender–sexual positionings. On the other hand, transgendering that seeks bodily modification raises questions again about the significance of the sexed body for gender identity. Through the work of Jay Prosser on transsexuality we consider the claim that queer is unable to account for transsexuals' desire for sexual embodiment. Prosser, using the concepts of borderlands and home to explore the contradictions raised by transgendering, makes a contrast between those who seek to live in the borderlands (where gender categories are destabilized and gender divisions are blurred) and those who seek a gendered 'home' (however mythical this home actually is). His claim in his earlier work that we need narratives that make sense of our lives challenges the idea central to queer theory that identity is simply performative. In this chapter the exploration of identity in terms of 'home' and 'borderlands' makes connections between the usefulness of these terms in understanding gender to their use within the work of postcolonial writers. It concludes that we require gender categories not only to construct our identities performatively but also to make sense of our experiences.

In our final chapter we consider the political implications of maintaining or deconstructing clearly defined gender categories. In this discussion we assess the possibilities and limitations of identity politics as well as the political potential of Butler's performative account of gender. In our analysis of the possibilities of gender politics we argue for a distinction between the political groupings with which we reflexively engage and our own complex subjective identities. Our analysis of the tensions between identity and queer politics highlights another key tension taken up previously in the text, the tension between material and discursive accounts of gender. The final section of this chapter considers the ways in which the book has attempted to resist such polarities, the usefulness of interweaving different strands of theory rather than setting them up in opposition, and the limitations of this endeavour.

Natural Women and Men

Brando's Own Story

I have always been lucky with women. There have been many of them in my life, though I hardly ever spent more than a couple of minutes with any of them. I've had far too many affairs to think of myself as a normal rational man. . . . I have 11 children and I'm delighted about that. As I grew older and pursued one exotic dark skinned woman after another I couldn't help but wonder if I wasn't trying to replace Ermi, my governess, whose soft dusky skin has seldom been far from my mind since I was seven. She was the ideal embedded in the emotional concrete of my soul. Once I lost her, I suppose I spent most of the rest of my life trying to find her. . . . Along with my mother, Ermi may also have had a lot to do with my refusal – or was it my inability to trust women after I grew up. . . . My mother abandoned me for a bottle when I was little more than an infant . . . then Ermi deserted me. . . . After that I always wanted several women in my life at the same time. . . . I enjoyed the women's company, but a man called Harvey was always standing in the corner, an invisible rabbit called a relationship. All but a few women wanted me to promise their love would be returned in equal measure, and that it would be forever and undying. Sometimes I told them what they wanted to hear, but I have always thought that the concepts of monogamy, fidelity and everlasting love were contrary to man's fundamental nature. Our adolescent childish myths tell us what love ought to be, and so do the songs we sing. . . . *I love you, you love me* . . . *I'm going to love you till I die, and you die and we're together in heaven* . . . I don't think I was constructed to be monogamous. I don't think it's the nature of any man to be monogamous. Chimps, our closest relatives, are not monogamous, nor the gorillas or baboons. Human nature is no more monogamous than theirs. In every human culture men are propelled by genetically ordained impulses over which they have no control to distribute their seed into as many females as possible. Sex is the primal force of our and every other species. Our strongest urge of all is to replicate our genes and perpetuate our species. We are helpless against it and are programmed to do as we do. Our genetic composition makes our sexual behaviour irresistible. We are driven by a force we know not of to make love, procreate and reproduce. (Brando and Lindsey 1994)

Brando, in trying to make sense of the life he has lived as a man, in particular the form his relations with women have taken, appeals to a variety of explanations. He concludes with an appeal to biological nature. It is not in the nature of man to be monogamous. It is against his fundamental nature. This appeal is legitimated by reference to the non-human animals such as gorillas and baboons, and to the genetically ordained impulses which form the subject matter of contemporary sociobiology. However, it sits in some tension with the explanations, which Brando mentions earlier. In his opening remarks he claims that he is not a normal rational man because he has had too many affairs. Here the notion of normal masculinity is tied, not to biological nature, but to a psychological characteristic of rationality, which is claimed to attach to normal masculinity. He explains his behaviour by a lack of such normal masculinity. In contrast to general explanations appealing to the presence or absence of the characteristics of normal masculinity, Brando also refers to his family history, attending to early emotional attachments to explain the objects of his adult desire. Yet another form of explanation surfaces when he discusses what the women he met wanted from him. Their desire for a promise of undying love, which he occasionally placated them with, came, he claimed, from social myths, like the songs we sing, from which we learn what love ought to be.

The concern of this book is to explain how we end up as gendered human beings, with a categorization as men or women, which we may be happy or unhappy with, but which in any case is one of the defining features of our subjectivity. What we are exploring, in exploring gender, is the binary division of people into male and female, a categorization which becomes fundamental to people's sense of their identity and carries with it associated expectations of patterns of behaviour. The division into male and female bodies yields an expected division into masculine and feminine people – where masculinity is a set of psychological and behavioural traits which are considered particularly appropriate to bodies classified as male, and femininity traits considered appropriate to those classified as female. In investigating how we end up as men and women we are therefore investigating a phenomenon that has bodily, psychological and behavioural features. While exploring this we will consider all the explanations which Brando has helped himself to. Sex differences might be natural, a result of early relations within the family or woven from the social context. This chapter is an exploration of the first option, the suggestion that sex differences are, in some sense, natural.

Natural States of Affairs

What does it mean to claim that a certain state of affairs is natural or unnatural? We are familiar with appeals to nature in a whole range of settings. It's a claim that we often hear. 'It's unnatural to see a man doing the ironing'; 'it's natural for women to want to have children and want to care for them, unnatural for them to leave them'; 'it's only natural for dogs to want to dig holes in the garden'; 'it's natural for adolescent boys to think about sex every few minutes'. Heterosexual sex is often thought of as a natural urge, consequent on 'chemistry' between people, anchored maybe in instincts to reproduce. At the same time same-sex desire is often viewed as unnatural, a perversion of a natural order as a result of a diseased body or mind.[1]

The appeal to nature is commonly an appeal to a certain kind of givenness, an appeal to a world which has a structure and order independent of our interactions with it, a structure which we cannot modify and which conditions our lives and agency. This is illustrated most clearly if we think of the concept of a natural kind. The philosopher John Locke (1690) claimed that there were two ways in which we could classify the world. First, we could classify into natural kinds, categories which 'carved nature and its joints' and enabled us to see the order and regularity which was simply given with the world. Such kinds had essential properties, characteristics which were found in all instances of the kind and which dictated how it behaved and interacted with other bits of the world. So water is made up of hydrogen and oxygen atoms. This is its essential feature, so all samples of water have it. Moreover, this essential feature explains how water interacts with other kinds of thing in the world. If the categories of men and women are natural categories in this sense, then there will be sets of characteristics which are essential to men and which explain their ways of interacting in the world and distinct sets of essential characteristics of women which explain their way of interacting in the world. Our job will be to find out what these essential properties are and how they work. On this picture the world exists quite independently of us as knowing subjects, already divided up into distinct kinds of thing: atoms and electrons, trees and flowers, animals and people, women and men. Our job as knowledge collectors is to find names or labels for these different kinds of thing and find out what their essential properties are and how these essential properties govern their interactions with other things in the world. In contemporary thinking about natural kinds these categories and the essential properties that mark them are ones which it is the particular task of science to uncover.

People who accept that the world is divided up into natural kinds like this usually also accept that there are other forms of classification which reflect, not nature in a direct way, but our interests and purposes in dealing with it. This was Locke's second way of classifying the world. So chairs and computers, romantic landscapes and monetary systems are kinds of thing which are grouped together for our convenience, with defining characteristics fixed by our decisions over language use rather than discovered by an investigation of the natural world. Instead of real essences to be discovered, they have only nominal ones, ones we have assigned to them. We have constructed the kind or grouping for our purposes. We can divide objects into tables and chairs and indeed produce them to fit into these categories. But if our purposes change then so might our classifications and then we might regroup: as hard or soft, big or small, etc. And we wouldn't be getting anything wrong about 'nature' if we did so. If the classification into 'women' and 'men' is of this sort then we won't grasp what is involved in being a man or a woman by looking at nature but by looking at our social practices. Moreover, these social practices can change and thereby we can change the content of these categories or give them up altogether.

One of the questions which, therefore, has been highly contested is whether 'men' and 'women' are natural kinds with real essences which explain their mode of interaction with the rest of the world, or whether they are constructed kinds, constructed for our purposes, whose defining characteristics are an effect of our social practices. Brando above is certainly drawn by the view that they are natural kinds, though he seems to have several distinct views as to what constitutes the essence of masculinity. Is it rationality, or the genetically ordained impulse to spread seed as widely as possible, that distinguishes men from other kinds of thing (women, for example)? In this chapter we will be discussing whether 'woman' and 'man' are natural categories. We will return in chapter 3 to consider that they might rather be social ones constructed out of our social practices. In between, in chapter 2, we will discuss psychoanalysis, which has both naturalizing and social constructionist aspects.

Male and Female in Western Thought

The essence of a thing is supposed to be what makes it the thing it is, what remains unchanged while the thing exists. There is a long tradition which regards the division of people into male and female and of associated traits into masculine and feminine as being natural, simply a reflection of the order of things. Before it was regarded as particularly the task of scientists to discover the essential features of natural kinds, philosophers and theologians pronounced on the distinctive features of human beings and in particular that in virtue of which they were divided into two kinds, male and female. These pronouncements were viewed as simply descriptions of divisions which were there in the world for anyone to see.

In an important book, first published in 1984, Genevieve Lloyd traced the history of 'male' and 'female' in Western philosophy (Lloyd 1993). The discussion of what is involved in being female or male was subject to shifts and changes, but certain common themes emerged. Crucially what was involved in being male was tied to being a rational and autonomous agent, characteristics which were taken themselves to mark off human beings from the animal world (though, throughout the history of philosophy, what exactly this rationality consisted in was subject to differing accounts). What was involved in being female, however, was in contrast to this. The female was seen as more closely anchored to the physical part of existence, consequent on her reproductive role. She was associated with the physical senses and the world of physical nature in a way that was sometimes celebrated and sometimes denigrated, but either way posed a threat and an obstacle to the development and exercise of rationality which was distinctive of the male. In Lloyd's account, 'rational knowledge has been construed as a transcending, transformation or control of natural forces; and the feminine has been associated with what rational knowledge transcends, dominates or simply leaves behind' (1993: 4).

The dichotomy between male as rational and capable of universally valid thought and female as emotional and tethered to the particularity of her body and situation is one that is still evident in patterns of thought today. Looking back at the history of these accounts, however, it is important to note that the kind of maleness which is being defined is not entirely universal, in the sense that, although it is supposed to capture what is essential to maleness, it is an essence which many biological males were themselves not considered capable of achieving. Slaves, non-Europeans and members of the lower classes were also regarded as deficient in rationality, anchored in the sensuous and unable to rise above their animal natures. These earlier philosophical accounts therefore shared a feature of later scientific ones – that of trying to explain not only gender differences but also other social divisions by an appeal to the different natures of those who occupied different social positions. Such views served to justify social inequalities as well as the colonialist enterprise of bringing 'order' and 'civilization' to non-European parts of the world.

These exclusions make clear what kind of definition of maleness was at issue here. For being male was defined in terms of an aspirational *ideal* which characterized what men should be. The definitions of female were different in this regard. Being female was treated much more as a biological kind. This anchorage in biology restricted woman's nature. Some men also were constrained, but in so far as they were unable to transcend their physical natures they were thereby less male.

Sex Differences as Natural Kinds

With the ascendancy of science as the exemplar of knowledge the task of providing an account of maleness and femaleness became increasingly viewed as a scientific rather than a philosophical one. Here again the model of sexed kinds as natural kinds with real essences awaiting discovery and description continued to hold sway. Sex difference research has been a continuously thriving area for the last two hundred years. This work has been founded on a set of assumptions. The first is that the division of bodies into male and female is a natural division, part of the order of the world. If we did not recognize it then there would be facts about the world conditioning our existence that we would be unable to recognize and explain. Secondly, although the visible bodily differences are fairly reliable markers of maleness and femaleness, particularly the presence or absence of a penis, these surface bodily differences are a manifestation of inner characteristics which serve to fix us as male or female. (After all, men whose penises are removed are still men, as are women without wombs or breasts.) These underlying features which make us male or female are matters of dispute, but it has most commonly been assumed that they fix not only the obvious bodily distinctions, but also sets of associated psychological and behavioural dispositions which are regarded as constituting masculinity and femininity. Here there need be no assumption that we all manifest our masculinity and femininity in the same way – only that there are some underlying determinants, which are different for men and women, that are conditioning our response to our environments. There is, of course, disagreement as to what range of responses are conditioned by sex differences in this way. Recurring themes concern greater aggression and competitiveness in men and nurturing qualities in women; greater spatial and abstract reasoning abilities in men and greater linguistic skills in women. (More recently it has been suggested that the reason boys underachieve in schools is because teaching methods now emphasize co-operation and care whereas male brains respond better to methods based on competition and aggression.)

For thousands of years male and female bodies were thought of as fundamentally similar. Women were thought to have the same genitals as men, only hidden inside the body. In the eighteenth century, however, there was increasing emphasis on bodily differences between the sexes. The concentration on genital sexual difference and secondary sex characteristics such as breasts and facial hair became expanded so that more and more parts of the body were seen as sexualized. One nineteenth-century biologist saw opposite kinds of processes at the level of cells, with the result that 'males are more active, energetic, eager, passionate and variable . . . females more passive, conservative, sluggish and stable. The more active males, with a consequently wider range of experience, may have bigger brains and more intelligence; but the females, especially as mothers, have indubitably a larger and more habitual share of the altruistic emotions' (E. Martin 1987: 33). By the late nineteenth century male and female bodies were seen as opposites, and the female body became a central focus of medical attention. First the uterus and then the ovaries were regarded as the seat of femininity. But early in the twentieth century the essence of femininity came to be located, not in an organ, but in chemical substances: sex hormones (Oudshoorn 1994). This is now one of the dominant modes of thinking about the biology of sex differences, with women's bodies seen as particularly dominated by the balance or imbalance of hormones, a 'fact' used to justify exclusion from important roles in public life: 'If you had an investment in a bank you wouldn't want the president of the bank making a loan under those raging hormonal influences. Suppose we had as president in the White House a menopausal woman president?' (Rose, Lewontin and Kamin 1984: 133–4.) (This is a particularly telling quotation in the light of the scandals surrounding Bill Clinton in 1998.) It is not only in accounts of the female biology that hormones have been given a determining role, however. In the mid-seventies Steven Goldberg wrote *The Inevitability of Patriarchy*, arguing that men have a greater tendency to dominate than women do (Goldberg 1973). This tendency is a result of male hormones, in particular testosterone, whose presence is claimed to produce changes in brain mechanisms with long-lasting effects.

There are important parallels in the way sexual difference and racial difference have been treated. In the nineteenth century racial categories were viewed as natural kinds, with distinct physiological and psychological characteristics. 'Race meant accumulated cultural differences carried somehow in the blood' (Stocking 1993: 6). Such a conception of race then informed the development of eugenics policies right through to the middle of the twentieth century. Analogies were drawn between women and non-European peoples in terms of physiological characteristics such as the shape of their skull, and psychological characteristics. Sander Gilman (1985) has drawn attention to the way in which scientific work in the nineteenth century interwove conceptions of both women and colonized people as inherently primitive. Darwin commented, 'some at least of those mental traits in which women may excel are traits characteristic of the lower races', and the craniologist F. Pruner argued, 'The Negro resembles the

female in his love of children, his family and his cabin' (quoted in
Rose, Lewontin and Kamin 1984: 143).

Unlike sexual difference, however, scientists no longer treat racial
difference as a biological natural kind. The direction of genetic theory
since 1900 eroded its basis, although it took until nearly mid-century
before race disappeared from the theories of biological scientists.
(It is still, of course, treated as a natural kind by many in everyday
discourse and see Haraway 1997: part 3, ch. 4, for its re-emergence in
the human genome project.)

Recent Work

It is not possible here to give a comprehensive review of the biological and psychological research into sex differences and there are
some really excellent texts, which provide a critical review of this
work, from biologists, psychologists and historians of science (Bleier
1984; Fausto-Sterling 1992). It is, however, worth looking at two
currently active research areas to give a sense of the kinds of difficulties surrounding this kind of research.

Selfish genes

We can start by looking at the contemporary theory that is echoed
in Brando's conclusions. This is the view found in the work of
sociobiologists that our genes programme our behaviour. Genetic
similarities, which had been taken to explain physical similarities
among relatives and to explain the recurrence of certain illnesses in
families, are now viewed in a much more problematic way to be the
basis of complex behavioural traits such as 'Shyness, alcoholism or
criminality' (Fausto-Sterling 1992: 62). Unsurprisingly, the behaviour
of men and women has been seen to be the result of the fact that, in
crucial respects, the genes of men and women are different: 'In addition to twenty two pairs of chromosomes called autosomes, females
have two X chromosomes. Males on the other hand, supplement
their twenty two autosomes with one X and one Y chromosome'
(1992: 19). (These chromosomal differences do not always correspond
to observable sexual difference: see below.) Central to the framework of sociobiology is an adaptation of the argument from natural
selection. It is assumed sexual differences have evolved through natural

selection to the maximal advantages of both sexes. One example of this is the 'selfish gene' hypothesis, which Brando refers to. Our genetic constitution is such as to maximize the chances of our genes surviving. For men with plentiful sperm this is best achieved by spreading their seeds into as many fertile wombs as possible. Women, with fewer eggs, need rather to nurture the fertilized ones which they come across and to persuade men, against their interests, to help them in this nurturing path. So a conflict of interests between the sexes is genetically programmed.

Another example of such a genetic story is given in Rose, Lewontin and Kamin (1984). Male dominance is seen as evolving from the dependency of the human infant on human care. If early societies depended on the hunting of large animals, women would be disadvantaged while pregnant or feeding, and the baby would be in danger if women engaged in these tasks. So skills increasing spatial-temporal co-ordination would be selectively favoured in men and increased nurturative abilities favoured in women. Consequently a division of labour would become genetically fixed. (However, as the authors point out, it is quite uncertain how important hunting was to the survival of early groups, with evidence suggesting that gathering provided most of the diet. Moreover, with spaced-out births women seemed to be disadvantaged for only small periods.) Such socio-biological stories, stories attempting to ground social behaviour in a genetic determinism, are reinforced by animal studies showing that male/female differences are found in non-human societies in ways that supposedly parallel those found in human ones.

This range of theories has been used to explain not only sexual differences but also antagonistic behaviour between peoples who view themselves as different. So, even while the old racism, which envisaged a natural division into distinct races, was disappearing, a new theory was evolving to justify as natural antagonistic behaviour to those who we perceive as unlike us. The story is started by ethologists studying animal behaviour. They argued that there is an innate tendency to form groups and to engage in altruistic behaviour in relation to that group and aggressive behaviour to anything perceived as different: 'man is a tribal animal and the great super tribes will always be in competition with each other' (Barker 1981: 82). This is a consequence of needing to deal with the aggression, which might threaten the social cohesion necessary for survival, by redirecting it elsewhere. This view was challenged by sociobiologists for whom living things behave in such a way as to maximize their own fitness and for whom there is apparently no place for altruism even within the limited scope of the in-group. However, *kin* altruism would be consistent with sociobiological premises, for this would foster the survival of shared genes. But how are we to recognize kin relatedness?

> . . . genetic relatedness often declines dramatically beyond the social group . . . and significantly aggressiveness increases in turn. Hostility towards outsiders is characteristic of both human and non-human animals. Physical similarity is also a function of genetic relatedness and human racial prejudice, directed against humans who look different could well have its roots in this tendency to distinguish in group from out group. (1981: 97)

In this way racism is seen as rooted in the genes.

This range of theories in which a genetic base is seen as determining social organization has, however, been profoundly criticized by other biologists. There are several issues here. At the level of animal studies there has been debate about the way in which animal groups are looked at through the structuring lens of human society and the supposed discoveries then used to justify as natural the very social order from which they began. The entry of new animal observers, such as women, into the field has also resulted in different kinds of observations being made. Of this more below. At the more general level there is scepticism that complex social behaviour could simply be programmed in. This is especially the case since what patterns of behaviour would maximize the chances of genes surviving is highly contextual. It depends on the environment in which the organism is placed. And in the case of human societies there is simply no continuity of environment. Moreover, it has been argued that such pictures misunderstand the way in which genes work: 'a proper understanding of brain development suggests that while genetic information plays a key role in the unfolding of many details of the brain structure extensive development of nervous connections occurs after birth influenced profoundly by individual experience' (Fausto-Sterling 1992: 77); 'complex traits arise not simply (from genetic information) but also from the intrusion from the external environment and chance variations in development' (1992: 88). It is therefore just not possible simply from genetic modifications to read off complex patterns of behaviour.

Brains

The hunt to discover sex differences in the brains of men and women and between white men and those of supposed 'other races' began early in the nineteenth century when such supposed differences were linked to psychological characteristics such as intelligence, maturity, rationality, sensuality, childlike natures and so on. Most of these claims died a death earlier last century. Two of them, however, have recently been revived: the idea that brain size differs in males and females and in people of higher and lower intelligence, and the idea that the region connecting the two hemispheres is different in men and women. These have been joined by the suggestion that the hypothalamus is sexually dimorphic – and, it has been suggested, also differs in heterosexuals and homosexuals. This revival has come via developments in views about the ways in which hormones work. When they were first discovered, scientists imagined that there were separate male and female hormones, but it later emerged that males had female hormones and vice versa. Nowadays it is thought that males and females are constituted by different combinations of the same hormones. Increasingly it is thought that hormones affect all parts of the body, including the brain. Much has been made of research which suggests that pre-natal hormones affect the development of brains (Money and Ehrhardt 1972). The brain then fixes the different dispositions of man and woman.

Fausto-Sterling evaluates the research relating to brain size to find that 'the average male/female difference in brain weight for all ages is 9.8%. When charted as a function of either height or weight however the difference in adults virtually disappears' (1992: 244). Moreover, the reports of links between brain size and intelligence that used very small sample sizes found a barely significant correlation and failed to investigate whether class and nutritional status were parallel when the brain was growing. This doesn't prevent numerous reports of the supposed findings in both scientific magazines and the popular press. More attention is currently concentrated on the nerve fibres connecting the right and left hemispheres. Here the studies suggest some difference in shape between males and females, though it does not show up until well after birth and it is impossible to know whether experiential differences, biological differences or both contributed to the final result. Moreover, any functional consequences which such shape differences, if they exist, are supposed to have, remains quite murky. The research into differences in the hypothalamus has more than one laboratory reporting a difference in volume in the hypo-thalamus of males and females, though the numbers used are very small: eleven in one study and six in another. Moreover, we are dealing with a region 'that varies by more than a tenfold within each sex' (1992: 244) and where the ranges for each overlap enormously. None the less the difference became a cover story for *Time* magazine on 20 January 1992.

When the direction of research moves into the area of sexuality the international publicity becomes even more intense. A report on the origins of male homosexuality by Dr Simon LeVay led to numerous articles and television appearances in America, Britain and elsewhere. LeVay's argument is now published in his book *Queer Science* (1996). From a study on male rhesus monkeys LeVay and co-workers found that hypothalamic injury decreased the frequency of what was char-acterized as male heterosexual sexual behaviour, mounting, ejaculat-ing, and so on, but not of masturbation. He concluded that these changes affected their heterosexual behaviour but not their sex drive. Assuming that the hypothalamus is sexually dimorphic (i.e. different in men and women), on the basis of data problematized above, he hypothesized that there would be parallels in the appropriate parts of the hypothalamus in heterosexual men and homosexual women and in those of heterosexual women and homosexual men. The thesis is that homosexual men have feminized hypothalami. LeVay supports this hypothesis in his book by quoting studies to suggest that homo-sexual men have as children engaged in gender-dysphoric behaviours – that is behaviour more commonly displayed by members of the opposite sex. Examination of the hypothalami of a small sample of (dead) gay and straight men yielded results that were singularly in-conclusive, with what small differences there were being in distribu-tion of sizes within the categories, rather than a distinction between them. The smallness of the categories, the fact that differences could be linked to other factors such as cause of death, differences in level of sexual activity, and so on, all render the suggested hypothesis highly questionable. Moreover, LeVay ignores evidence that human and animal sexual behaviours do not allow a neat division into homosexual and heterosexual. In his assumptions that gay men are likely to be feminized and lesbian women masculinized, he also seems to be assuming there is a mapping of people's sexuality and their characteristics as male and female which is very problematic. (The connection between sexuality, as it refers to the objects of desire and the kind of sexual practice which people engage in, and sexual difference, as in whether or not someone is male or female, is a complex one which we will discuss in more detail in later chapters.) All these are points to which we shall return.

The Sex/Gender Distinction

In our discussion so far the division between male and female has been considered as a division into natural kinds. We have been exploring models in which biological facts were supposed to yield underlying differences between male and female, which then fixed distinct psychological and behavioural dispositions. These did not fully determine behaviour but provided conditioning structures which were different in men and women. The problem was that when the evidence for these distinct traits of masculinity and femininity was examined it turned out to be unstable. Even if the division into male and female bodies based on reproductive role has a biological base, the repeated attempts over hundreds of years to derive from these differences psychological and behavioural ones has been difficult to ground. One issue is the way the categories of distinction show such a large area of overlap. Strength endurance, intelligence (however measured), spatial and linguistic abilities, and aggression (however measured) are all such that, even where there seems to be some weighting towards male or female (some men so far have faster marathon times), there are many members of the other category who outperform those in the group to which the trait is supposed to be attached. (Women marathon runners are clearly faster than most men are.) A second issue is that the attempts to find biological pathways, which are supposed to link such traits to biological sex, have yielded only the most slender of results based on very few cases. A third and crucial issue is that, where there is some correlation between dispositions and apparent biological sex, there are available other explanations as to why such correlation might exist, crucially to do with the individual and social life experiences of those who have been assigned to the categories male and female. The remarks made by Mill more than a hundred years ago are still apt here. Until we treat men and women the same socially then we have no way of telling what natural differences there may be between them (Mill 1869).

These sets of considerations led to the making of one of the most central distinctions in feminist gender theory: namely that between sex and gender. Sex differences, the division into male and female bodies, were seen as biological differences, which it was the domain of the biological sciences to investigate and define. Gender differences, however, behavioural and psychological traits associated with masculinity and femininity, were viewed as socially constructed. The sex/gender distinction became one of the most fundamental assumptions in feminist gender theory from the 1970s on. The distinction was fuelled by the recognition of the very different ways in which people with male or female bodies could display masculinity or femininity. Much of the evidence supporting the recognition of such diversity has come from anthropological studies. The important precursor of much of this work was the anthropologist Margaret Mead's investigations in non-Western societies in the 1930s and 1940s (Mead 1949a, 1949b). She studied men and women in three societies and concluded that, in the Arapesh, gender norms consisted of gentle and non-dominant men and women; in the Mundugumor, the norm was violent and aggressive men and women; and, in the Tchambuli, the norm involved dominant women and dependent men. She concluded: 'If those temperamental attitudes which we have traditionally regarded as feminine can so easily be set up as the masculine pattern in one tribe and in another be outlawed for the majority of women as well as for the majority of men, we no longer have any basis for regarding such aspects of behaviour as sex linked' (Mead 1949b).

Later anthropological work has importantly brought to notice that not only can gender roles vary across and within societies but they are also not necessarily tied to biologically male and female bodies. There are numerous cases where behaviour which is, within the culture, normally associated with a male/female body can be found in someone with a female/male body. The identity of these people as men or women is also adjusted, often by a designation which signifies that they are women, but without a female body, or vice versa (Herdt 1994). Within the West the insistence on the recognition of difference which has been at the forefront of much political activism since the 1980s has served to draw attention to the very different gender norms which operate within a society as well as across them. The masculinity displayed by a vice-chancellor skilfully eroding democratic constraints on university governance is a very different phenomenon from that shown in a Clint Eastwood movie. And, as the

American anti-slavery and women's suffrage campaigner Sojourner Truth made clear more than a hundred years ago at Seneca Falls, the norms of femininity for women vary profoundly with class and colour. Moreover the widespread phenomenon of cross-dressing, of explicitly feminine men and masculine women (of which more in later chapters), also serves to fuel the distinction between sex and gender and the view that in understanding the construction of gender we are understanding a social process and not a natural one (in the sense of natural that we have been employing in this chapter).

Men and women, or masculinity and femininity, as gender categories, came, then, to be seen as socially created kinds, categories not given by nature but geared to our purposes. The scope of the categories (i.e. who they apply to) and their content (i.e. what is required to be masculine or feminine) are therefore susceptible to modification and change.

Science as Culture

If the best-known response to scientific accounts of sex difference was the making of the sex/gender distinction, it was followed by work which challenged the supposed objectivity of science itself. Recognition was given to the fact that scientific theories reflect the culture from which they emerge and the subjectivity and positionality of those who produce them. On certain standard, and perhaps everyday, accounts of scientific activity, science is seen as simply reflecting the world which it is describing. According to this kind of picture scientific methodology itself guarantees objectivity. Central to this methodology is an empirical base with reference to which all hypotheses have to be defended; an insistence on public criteria for the assessment of evidence; and an experimental method which requires the repeatability of results. These are supposed to ensure that any particularities of the individual scientist or the specific culture from within which they are working are eradicated.

It has, however, been increasingly argued that science is a social product and reflects the culture from which it emerges. It is recognized that there are no brute facts, no unmediated access to the world. The concepts and frameworks of interpretations in terms of which we organize and interpret our observations mediate all our encounters. There are no raw facts, as it is often said. They all come to us cooked in some way. Consequently what scientists see when they interpret the results of their experiments is influenced by the framework of interpretation which they bring to them. If we think of those scientists testing the hypothesis that the skulls of women and non-European races were smaller than those of European men we could think that they deliberately falsified their results to fit their theory. Some probably did. For others, however, the theory they were keen to prove conditioned what they saw so that it appeared to fit in with it. Consequently they were unable to see the range and diversity which confronted later researchers without that range of presuppositions.[2] Donna Haraway gives excellent examples from the study of the big apes, primatology, to illustrate how what was observed in the apes' behaviour varied according to the agendas of the investigators. In many instances what is seen is a mirror image of patriarchal social ordering. With the entry of feminist primatologists into the field, however, the contributions of the female apes to the cohesion and survival of the group, together with their active sexual role and ability to orgasm, came into view (Haraway 1989).

It is important here not to view such mediated scientific knowledge simply as bad science, examples where scientists have let their objectivity be compromised. It is not so. This is a characteristic of all knowledge collecting. There is no way we can step outside our conceptual frameworks and engage with the world in an unmediated way. It does mean, however, that those frameworks cannot themselves be seen as simply given with nature. This conclusion is reinforced when we recognize the role that models and metaphors play in the construction of scientific theories. These metaphors draw on the resources and assumptions of the surrounding culture. An easy example here, which doesn't take much unpicking, comes from Emily Martin (in Fox Keller and Longino 1996: 103), who highlights the way in which conventional biological accounts of fertilization are laden with sexist metaphors. In this conventional account sperm are described as active, battling valiantly from vagina to the oviduct and penetrating the egg, thus engendering new life. In contrast the passive egg is shed by the ovary and swept down the Fallopian tubes to await its date with destiny! Given the biological reality, in which the egg's adhesive surface traps the sperm, Martin suggests that a more appropriate model is to regard sperm and egg as mutually interacting in a process marked by 'feedback loops' and 'flexible adaptation'. It is important to note here how integral the metaphors are to the articulations of the process, structuring our conceptions of the reality, and indeed what it is possible for us to observe. As noted by Fox Keller and Longino, 'metaphors guide the construction of similarities and differences – i.e. our very categories of analysis' (1996: 7). When Martin puts forward an alternative account of fertilization she does not do this simply by shedding metaphor and opting for 'literal' descriptions, but rather by employing new metaphors ('feedback loops'). It is not therefore possible to regard the gendered nature of much language and metaphor as a detachable extra, removable from the articulation of areas of knowledge, to leave an ungendered content intact. The content is tied necessarily to its mode of articulation.

If, however, we cannot retreat to an account of science as an unmediated representation of the world (a 'mirror of nature'), we can at least pay attention to the models that it is employing and scrutinize the cultural assumptions that lie behind them. The writings of Donna Haraway (1989, 1991a, 1991b, 1997) are centrally important in establishing not only the way culture mediates our understanding of nature, but also the impossibility of maintaining any dualism of 'nature' and 'culture'. The two are irrevocably intertwined. This makes the pretensions of sociobiologists to explain culture in terms of genes unviable, but it also makes unviable an attempt to see nature as *purely* a cultural product (see below). More complexly *we cannot disentangle* in our stories of the world the 'given', *nature*, from the 'constructed', *culture*. 'Nature and Culture are reworked; the one can no longer be the resource for appropriation or incorporation by the other' (Haraway 1991b: 151). Consequently the sex/gender distinction outlined in the previous section itself becomes problematized.

Gender Constructs Sex

The general reflections on the nature of scientific knowledge have a clear bearing on the history of theories of sex difference. It is not possible to see such results as there have been as simply reflecting the facts; for they have been organized and interpreted by scientists carrying cultural baggage with them. This recognition takes us a stage further than the point reached by those theorists who reacted to sex difference research by insisting on a distinction between sex and gender. For such theorists biological sex differences were accepted as part of what was simply given. What was challenged was the assumption that gender differences necessarily accompanied them.

However, it is possible to raise a further challenge. Sex differences are not simply given either. The biological theories, which purport to give an account of them, are the products of particular historical and culturally specific moments of production. This raises the prospect that cultural assumptions about gender differences condition biological theories about sex. Such a prospect has allowed biological accounts of sex differences to be revisited with an eye to where cultural assumptions about gender have influenced them. Of key importance in this regard has been the assumption that there are simply two sexes, male and female, a model which has come increasingly under challenge in recent work. Nelly Oudshoorn (1994) excavated the history of the theory whereby the essence of sex differences was seen as being fixed by hormones. As work progressed the original assumption that each sex was governed by its own hormones gave way to the recognition that 'male' and 'female' hormones are present in both sexes. Here was a possibility for dualistic notions of male and female to be abandoned. Given the cultural context, however, traditional classifications prevailed, yielding a theoretical framework within which the hormones work in distinct ways to produce two discreet categories. Where it is not possible to assign a body to one of these categories then something has gone wrong and this requires medical intervention to put it right.

Such assumptions have been challenged by, among others, Anne Fausto-Sterling (1993), who points out that the existence of intersex bodies has always been known. Hermaphrodites often featured in stories of human origins. She draws attention to the range of bodies which are included within this category. Bodies which possess the usual male (XY) or female (XX) chromosomal make-up can have a variety of external genitalia and secondary sex characteristics: 'the varieties are so diverse . . . that no classificatory scheme could do more than suggest the variety of sexual anatomy encountered in clinical practice' (1993: 22). Nor is the phenomenon as rare as we might suppose. Some have suggested that it may constitute as many as 4 per cent of all births. Most of these 'unruly' bodies are now treated by surgical intervention and by hormones at birth or sometimes at puberty and assigned to one of our prevailing sexual categories. Marianne Van den Wijngaard (1997) scrutinized the basis of the decisions made concerning which category the children were to be assigned to:

genetic sex appears to be an important criterion. For women it is decisive. Doctors usually 'make' a little girl when a child has two X chromosomes. When the child is a boy in genetic respects . . . , however, the size of the penis is decisive. If the penis is of a certain minimal size [to enable a normal sexual life in the male role], the team decides to help the child become a boy. If not a vagina is created and the child is 'made' into a girl.' (1997: 86–7)

In the making of the girl the creation of a penetrable vagina is considered central, but the 'deviant clitoris' looking like a penis is either removed or shortened with scant respect for its consequences for the sexual pleasure of the being made girl.

What the treatment of children classified as intersexed bodies signals is *not* that the biological classification into two sexes is that which nature dictates. It reflects instead a cultural need to reinforce and defend a gendered binary, a clear classification into male and female and a modification of bodies which appear to cross the divide. Such an insistence does not only inform the treatment of intersexed bodies. It also forces a *spurious assumption of homogeneity* within the categories of male and female themselves. The different markers of biological sex – genes (chromosomes), hormones, genitals, reproductive function, secondary sexual characteristics – do not all line up neatly together in the same way, even in cases where the label of intersex is not forced. Once we recognize the cultural anchorage of scientific inquiry we recognize that in searching for an explanation of sex differences biology itself becomes part of the contested zone.

The Politics of Naturalizing Accounts

It has commonly been assumed that the naturalizing approach to sex differences, which we have been discussing in this chapter, is a conservative one. Those who argue that nature fixes ranges of behaviour are likely to think that the current social order with its apparent inequalities is simply a reflection of that natural order. In this way direct links have been made between the scientific research and socially conservative policies. But we cannot assume that naturalizing discourses are necessarily linked to such politics. LeVay's work is an example here. In the campaign for gay and lesbian rights and more recently in the debates over the rights of transsexual people the argument from nature has been put to progressive use. If there is a difference in the brains of homosexual and/or transsexual people, it is argued that they constitute a natural kind. Their behaviour is not the result of a deviant or sinful lifestyle choice but a manifestation of a natural disposition. LeVay (1996) contends that where people hold these beliefs they are more likely to support anti-discriminatory legislation. We should none the less be aware that even in this case naturalizing beliefs have been employed differently. For, as LeVay himself documents, many of those originally exploring a biological basis for homosexuality did so because they wanted to find a medical cure for it.

It is more difficult to see how naturalizing moves can be used in a progressive way in the case of gender. If gendered identities are given, then the challenge to existing social inequalities appears to be undermined, since these will be viewed simply as a reflection of the natural order. There are, however, theories within which naturalizing moves around gender can be progressive. In some versions of radical feminism there is an appeal to what are regarded as natural characteristics of women which would prevail if they were not subject to the domination of the patriarchal order. These characteristics are viewed as a cause for celebration rather than denigration. There is no consensus over exactly what this underlying female nature might consist in, but characteristics such as sensuality and fecundity, emotional understanding, intuitive knowledge, and an embedded and caring relation with the rest of the natural world often feature. These so-called natural characteristics can then be put to progressive political use, particularly, for example, in the women's peace movement and the feminist ecology movement. In political protests like that at Greenham Common, a women's peace camp in the 1980s opposing American cruise missiles based in Britain, women exploited their role in reproduction and care and their embeddedness in and protectiveness towards the natural world to highlight the damage wrought by an aggressive and mechanistic masculinity, the consequence of which had been the production of weapons of mass destruction. Here aggressive and mechanistic masculinity was sometimes viewed in essentialist ways. In a similar way some eco-politics sees previously excluded female values as a site for renewing our relationship with the rest of the natural world.

It is important to note, however, that the same political practices can be engaged in by women with very different metaphysical views.

Many participants at Greenham Common were exploiting politically what were *socially viewed as* the appropriate roles for women. Moreover, the links between feminism and ecology can be seen as deriving in part from values which women in traditional roles hold as a result of the particular social and cultural positions they occupy and labours which they have been called on to perform. These values they might share with men who have performed similar labours.

There are dangers, which have become all too evident within political feminism, of marrying activism to views about the natural characteristics of men and women. For how are we to ascertain what the essential traits of femininity are, or would be once the mantle of patriarchy has been shaken off? The dangers of looking at the local and mistaking it for the universal have become very clear here. From the early 1980s the issue of difference within the category 'women' has become central to feminism. Women in different situations reveal different characteristics and have different political priorities. The attempt to identify certain traits and accompanying forms as activism appropriate to female nature is to ignore these differences and treat the experiences of a restricted group as if they represented the manifestation of universal traits of a natural kind (see chapter 3). The debates within the peace movement make this clear. Can we argue that women are 'naturally' pacifist? Can we construe, for example, women's involvement in militarism, the giving out of white feathers in the First World War, the inauguration of the Falklands War, the condoning of the bombing of Iraq, and so on, as simply a result of patriarchal domination? We might like to think so in these cases. But what then are we to say of women fighters in the Sandinista armies, or those risking their lives opposing apartheid? Women's involvement in armed struggle would be justified in these latter instances by the distinctiveness of the situation, by what is needed to achieve their goals in ensuring a better life for future generations. What these examples illustrate is the shakiness of claims that a characteristic is a part of our nature and the difficulties of providing any grounding for it. Many of the characteristics which it has been argued constitute women's nature, even when celebrated, have been connected with maternity. Not only does this marginalize the lives of women who are not mothers, it also ignores the ambiguities in the experiences of those that are. These experiences of mothering can be very different in different material circumstances. Moreover, in linking nurturing roles to women we seem to justify current social arrangements in which such roles are left to them, to the detriment of their participation in other aspects of social life.

The dangers of a false universalism attaching even to the naturalism employed for progressive purposes are linked to a further danger. To accept the naturalizing talk is to reinforce the dichotomies of the conservative thought around sex differences. If behavioural traits associated with masculinity and femininity are a consequence of biological differences between male and female then this must be believed to explain much of the current social order, with all its inequalities, and to restrict the possibilities of radical social change. Most feminists therefore oppose naturalizing explanations of gender differences.

The Naturalizing Trick

There are some ways in which my body responds to the world which are independent of my understanding – my heartbeat, the operation of my reflexes, the movements of my lungs, etc. (though it is possible for more of these to be modifiable in the light of the subject's self-understanding than we may sometimes think). There are other ranges of behaviour, however, where our engagement in the world is dependent on our understanding and conceptualizations of the situations in which we are placed. For that range of activities, our intentional acts, there are no brute causal relations between the movements of our body and the world. Our behaviour is instead mediated through the interpretative frameworks in terms of which we experience our world. Even acts to satisfy what might be regarded as basic needs such as hunger depend crucially on what we perceive as food, and equally what we perceive as good food or delicious food. This depends on modes of experiencing the world mediated through conceptualization and understanding (Taylor 1985). The role of understanding provides an insurmountable obstacle to attempts to explain actions purely in terms of biological processes. Our identities as subjects in the world are dependent on our understanding of those identities; on the salience and significance those identities have for us. It is only thus that our identities can impact on our behaviour. Perhaps some examples can make this clear. Whether or not I menstruate does not in a direct way depend on my understanding of menstruation. For some young women the events occur out of the blue. What responses I have to it, how I behave in relation to it, does, however, depend on my understanding of it; including whether I celebrate it or keep it hidden. Whether or not I have a vagina and breasts is commonly something which is independent of my understanding. What does affect my behaviour is the significance which these have for me.

All this has a clear impact on the way we can understand our identities as women and men. The way in which our being male or female can impact on our intentional acts depends on the understanding of what it is to be male or female. Masculinity and femininity as aspects of the identities of subjects and agents are constituted in part by those subjects' understandings of what it is to be masculine and feminine. In giving accounts of gendered identities we therefore have to pay attention to these interpretations.

Our ways of seeing the world are not, of course, entirely individual. We are initiated during our lives into patterns of conceptualization, ways of seeing and understanding which make it possible for us to become subjects and agents in the world. The specific kind of significance and salience which our world has for us is learned in a social context and anchored in shared practices, which structure our responses. We eat with a knife and fork or with our hands or with chopsticks. Certain kinds of food are recognized as good. We go into public toilets marked 'men' or 'women', see some animals as pets and take them into our homes. Initiation into ways of conceiving the world is an ongoing process, not one that comes to an end in childhood. It is a process which is fluid and susceptible to change. None the less many of our conceptual frameworks have become completely habitual. They constitute a framework of interpretation without any awareness on our part that a process of interpretation has gone on. They have become, we might say, *second nature* to us. Where this is the case, our ways of looking at the world strike us as entirely natural, fixed only by how the world is, without the intervention of organizing subjects. We cannot conceive of any other way in which it could be understood. This, which we might term the naturalizing trick, is clearly at work in many people's response to sex and gender. It's natural for a man to want to compete, feel responsible for his family, enjoy a night out with the lads, get turned on by largish bare breasts. It's natural for girls to like cuddly toys or be close to their mothers. Where ways of seeing have become second nature in this way then it requires particular strategies to unseat them, to bring back into view the mediated nature of our relationship with the world. We shall be discussing some of these strategies in later chapters.

To insist on the role that understanding plays in our behavioural response to the world is an *anti-naturalizing* move. It is in opposition to the view that we can expect an explanation of our gendered identities from within the resources of the biological sciences. There is, however, an important point to be noted here. Those scientific accounts which we have been looking at themselves form an important way of understanding sex differences, which, to different degrees, are made available to people as a way of understanding their own identities. The naturalizing scientific modes of understanding can become widespread, forming the framework in terms of which people conceptualize their world. These naturalizing accounts can themselves produce a naturalizing effect, which it can prove difficult to unsettle.

What about the Body?

The arguments of the last sections have been anti-naturalist ones. They oppose the idea that we can provide an adequate understanding of gendered identities by an appeal to nature. The concept of nature as we have been applying it here captures what is in some sense given, rather than humanly created; that which, on some accounts of the biological and natural sciences, it is their job simply to describe.

The resistance to naturalizing accounts of sex/gender differences has been threefold. First, that the putative accounts which have been offered have been flawed, even by the standards of conventional science. Secondly, science itself reflects the culture which produces it and in this case cultural assumptions about gender have been seen to influence scientific accounts of sex. Thirdly, gendered identities manifest themselves in behaviours which are mediated by understanding and therefore cannot be reduced to the mere effects of biology.

The concept of nature as simply that which is given, which served as our starting point, seems, however, to be itself undermined by the second and third of these arguments. For they both rely on the recognition that we have no direct and unmediated knowledge of the world. In fact we have no coherent idea of what such knowledge would be. Science itself is one of our projects and its account of the world is mediated also by frameworks of understanding. But, we might ask, what has happened to the world in all this? Can we make no sense of there being something fixed and given, which constrains the possibility of action? In relation to accounts that are offered of gender such a query is often focused on the body. Surely there are facts about my body, which bear some relation to my identity as male or female. Doesn't the possibility of childbearing, the monthly cycle, etc., play any role at all? Aren't these simply givens which our frameworks of understanding have somehow to accommodate?

There are several important points that need clarifying here. The first is that anti-naturalism does not require us to give up any idea that the world/our bodies can set constraints on what it is possible to do or think. To insist on the mediated nature of all knowledge is to deny that nature simply offers herself to us ready categorized. It is to recognize that our account of what we take to be nature emerges from a complex interaction of scientific investigations and cultural metaphors and the networks of social power which condition the availability of theory (see the discussion of Haraway on p. 28 above). This, however, is not to deny that there is something independent of our conceptualizations which sets constraints on what can be said about it. What we cannot do is disentangle the bit which is given from our ways of thinking about it. What we have to recognize here is captured by Donna Haraway in following way:

> the practices of the sciences force one to accept two simultaneous, apparently incompatible truths. One is the historical contingency of what counts as nature for us; the thoroughgoing artifactuality of a scientific object of knowledge that makes it inescapably and radically contingent . . . and simultaneously scientific discourses make claims . . . physically . . . they have a sort of reality to them which is inescapable. No scientific account escapes being story laden, but it is equally true that stories are not all equal here. Radical Relativism just won't do. (1991a: 2)

Haraway herself often characterizes this world which we are providing our accounts of as a coyote or trickster, always escaping from our best attempts to understand it, something in excess of anything our conceptual schemes can grasp: 'the real world is not the world of our best physics but the world that defeats any physics that would be final, that would desire to be the last word' (1991a: 6).

In taking an anti-naturalist stance in relation to the formation of sexed identities, then, we do not have to deny that our biological bodies may have a role to play. We do have to recognize, however, that we have no uncontested and unmediated account of the characteristics of these bodies. Moreover, such bodies, while constraining the possibilities for action (we cannot, after all, fly unaided), can provide an explanation of our gendered behaviours only in terms of the meaning and significance which are attached to them. These are points to which we shall return, most particularly in chapter 7.

Psychoanalysis and Gender

Most areas of knowledge take gendered identity to consist primarily of consciousness, that is, the thinking, rational dimension of who we are. In contrast, psychoanalysis takes a more complex view of identity as something which is fundamentally divided into consciousness and what it perceives as the unconscious or hidden aspects of identity which influence our actions throughout our lives without our conscious awareness. This suggests that psychoanalytic insights may allow us to explore the unconscious as well as conscious aspects of our gendered existence, the psychical as well as social dimensions of identity.

Sigmund Freud invented the theory and practice of psychoanalysis and in his work, which spans nearly fifty years, he suggests that we are never in a position to know the whole 'truth' about ourselves or the world of culture we produce. He argues that this is because of the existence of a largely unknowable unconscious dimension in us all, which creates a split in who we are. This is a rift between a consciousness which is knowable through language and a hidden, wordless unconscious. He sees the unconscious as 'another scene' of our being which is radically split off from the conscious, rational part of who we are with its own symbolic language of condensed and displaced meanings. We can see these in slips of the tongue and pen, in hesitations and other kinds of bungled speech and actions, but most easily in the vivid language of dreams. For Freud, our gendered identity is unconsciously constructed in early childhood.

In this chapter we shall begin by looking at Freudian theory, starting with Freud's theory of the construction of 'masculinity' and

'femininity' and moving on to Lacan's influential redevelopment of
Freud's ideas within the context of language. Following a discussion
of Lacan's work, we shall suggest how the object-relations strand of
psychoanalytic theory can help us analyse gender and the subordination
of women.

If some psychoanalytic ideas strike us as rather bizarre and inaccessible, we may need to remember that they refer to the ways in
which the infant or very young child attempts to make sense of itself
and the world through unconscious phantasy. Psychoanalysis suggests
phantasy precedes rational thought.

Freud

Freud's theory, taken as a whole, suggests that from our earliest
childhood we are impelled by a variety of biological drives. But,
contrary to the view taken by numerous writers,[1] that his theory of
identity is simply one of biological determinism, Freud focuses, in
a much more complicated way, on how we construct ourselves and
our culture out of what we unconsciously 'make' of our earliest
bodily experiences and, crucially, the passionate emotional entanglements which arise out of these experiences within our particular historically and culturally situated families.

Freud's theory allows us to begin to imagine how we create and
live out our gendered identities as 'masculine' and 'feminine', men and
women, in culture, to a greater or lesser extent divided within ourselves, as a result of these experiences. The unthought and unconscious
part of who we are together with the part of us which can be expressed
within language or consciousness are always embedded together
within the contingencies of history and place. Since Freud's theory
grew out of European culture as a whole, we should remember it is
likely to apply particularly to individuals brought up in that culture,
and within the family structures on which his studies were based.

Sexuality and Infantile Sexuality

Freud's focus was primarily on what we 'make' imaginatively of
bodily drives and sensations rather than on relationships. (The latter
forms the basis of the object-relations-based psychoanalytic theory

which came after him.) In giving an account of what we make imaginatively of our bodily sensations, as a consequence of our familial
interactions, Freud makes central use of the Greek myth of Oedipus.
Freud argued that not only is all identity fundamentally split into
consciousness and the unconscious, but the unconscious, sexuality
and the body are intrinsically interwoven. He thought the central
moment which achieved the vital conjunction of these different dimensions is the Oedipal crisis, which occurs when the child is between
three and five years old. This is the moment when we emerge from
our phantasies around the body of the mother into fully fledged
human beings. Before this time, we shared a fused identity with the
mother which is initially supported by primitive sensations of pleasure associated with what Freud called 'component instincts' or drives
connected with particular areas of our bodies – mouth, anus and penis
or clitoris. At first, Freud, for whom sexuality means something
much more far-reaching than what most of us mean by this term,
described these drives and their potential for pleasure as infantile forms
of sexuality because they are associated with both pleasure and our
earliest sense of having an existence or identity (Minsky 1996: 31–3).
In the *Three Essays on the Theory of Sexuality*, Freud systematically
describes these overlapping drives (Freud 1905). Oral sexual pleasure
is associated first with the baby's sucking or 'incorporation' of both
milk and the comforting idea of the breast (and later fingers and other
more controllable objects). Anal sexual pleasure is derived from the
satisfaction connected with the control involved in 'holding on' and
'letting go' of faeces (control we could never have over our mother's
breast). Voyeuristic pleasure deriving from what Freud called the
scopophilic drive is associated with the control involved in secretly
looking at other people's bodies as objects of curiosity, initially at
the mother's body. Phallic pleasure is connected particularly with
masturbation in the context of phantasies of having total control and
dominion of the mother, whose care is associated with so much
pleasure that we imagine the power of our love can captivate her for
ever. In thinking about Freud's theory of infantile sexuality, it is very
important to remember that the different oral, anal, scopophilic and
phallic forms of bodily pleasure, like adult sexuality, yield not only
pleasure but also a crucial sense of having an existence, of feeling
alive, that is of having an identity.

For Freud it is the Oedipal crisis that allows us to make the transition from our merged, narcissistic identity with the mother (based

on a self as a reflection of her) into human beings capable of being able to lead a relatively creative, self-reflecting, autonomous existence. It makes possible our separation from the mother as our first lover and our entry into culture and the world beyond her body.

The Oedipal Crisis

Freud argues that we are precipitated into the Oedipal crisis by 'falling in love' with the mother, who has cast a spell over us through her care and love and all the touching, wiping, stroking and hugging this entails. But this new stance in relation to the mother – now phantasized as a potential lover we can steal for ourselves from our father and, if possible, from our siblings and anyone else – coincides with another tumultuous discovery in the child's so far body-preoccupied experience: the discovery of sexual difference. For Freud, largely on the basis of what his many female patients told him, the child's first awareness of sexual difference is based on the visual perception of the presence or absence of the penis on the bodies of those around it among whom it must eventually find its place. However, it is at the moment of discovery of bodily difference based on the presence or absence of the penis that Freud introduces the most dynamic concept in his theory of the construction of gendered identity, the castration complex and the role of the symbolic father.

At this point let us look at the experience of the boy and girl separately. In the context of both his guilt in relation to his father – who is perceived as a rival for his mother, since his initial identification with the mother involved a passive sexual stance in relation to the father – and his supposed perception of the mother's or girl's lack of a penis, the boy falls prey to the terrifying idea that girls are different because they have been castrated and that therefore he may fall victim to the same fate. This, he phantasizes, is likely to be at the hands of his father as a result of his sexual ambitions to steal away his mother. It is important to understand that, for Freud, the small boy's fear of castration is experienced symbolically and not only as the threat of being physically mutilated. At the symbolic level, castration anxiety is the threat of the extinction of his fragile and emergent sense of identity which at that time centres around the pleasure derived from his penis. Castration anxiety threatens the small boy with a potentially overwhelming catastrophe, that of psychical annihilation.

It is also claimed to threaten those adults who remain in a state of residual, unresolved castration anxiety. As Freud recognized, large numbers of us emerge from the Oedipal crisis with infantile conflicts which for a variety of complicated emotional reasons have not been fully resolved.

Desperate to avoid potential annihilation, the small boy, Freud argues, is finally persuaded by his castration anxiety to give up his mother and reconcile himself to the deferment of his phantasies about her until he is an adult and can find a woman of his own as a substitute. From this moment on, if all goes smoothly, the small boy gives up both his earliest identification with his mother and his desire for her and at the same time makes an alternative identification with his father. This is someone of the same sex, that is someone with a body like his own who may be able to fill the void left by the loss of his mother. Although Freud does not elaborate on this aspect of the boy's experience, if his Oedipal crisis is resolved successfully, in order to achieve his cultural 'masculinity', and the power this confers, the boy has to lose his mother in two ways – both as his first source of identity and as his first love-object (phantasized lover). In her place, he identifies with his father, although highly ambivalently, because he has to internalize someone who is both loved and feared at one and the same time. The internalized father continues to inspire murderous feelings and guilt, but now the boy is under surveillance from within rather than from outside. In this sense the small boy's new identity is composed of a potentially divisive mixture: both himself as potential victim and his father as potential executioner. Henceforth, the father exists in the psyche of the boy as what Freud describes as the superego, as an internal representative of the external laws of culture and moral authority, not least the law forbidding incest and the law of who belongs to who within families. It is through the child's crucial identification with the cultural 'masculinity' of the symbolic father, someone beyond the enticements of the mother's body and being, that culture makes its unconscious impact on the child's identity through its entry into the symbolic world of language. For Freud, this entry into the laws and values of culture, involving the repression of the desire for the mother, represents the child's entry into its humanity, its vital transition from phantasy to reality and the setting of boundaries on its desire. But, crucially, it eventually also offers us the only opportunity, emotionally, of 'growing up' through gaining access to the creative possibilities of language and symbolization (see Minsky 1996: 42–5).

   It is at this crucial and emotionally fraught time, Freud argues, that the unconscious is formed out of the repression of the boy's love for and loss of the mother. The formation of the unconscious allows the pain of this loss to be concealed from consciousness but results in a divided subject. This means that consciousness, what we think we know about ourselves and the world, is always vulnerable to sabotage from the sudden eruption of hidden desires and loss. If the boy is unable to identify sufficiently with the father for him to feel able to separate from the mother, Freud maintains, he will continue to be dominated by phantasy involving possession of the mother and castration anxiety which will inhibit his ability to cope with the demands of reality and relationships. What Freud does not emphasize is that early separation from the emotional bodily world of the mother might also entail the boy being permanently cut off also from this vital dimension of himself. The small boy has to survive the double loss of both his identification with his mother and his first love-object. The symbolic power of the penis/phallus (phallus is the term used to capture the symbolic meaning of the penis) as the apparent linchpin of cultural 'masculinity', and the pleasure and sense of identity it offers, seems to provide the only hope of compensation for his loss. In this sense, unconsciously, the penis/phallus, paradoxically, symbolizes both power and loss and symbolic castration. This is in dramatic contrast to the girl's predicament if she manages to emerge successfully from her Oedipal crisis. For many boys, in the context of their lingering castration phantasy, 'femininity' is inevitably viewed as a position of loss and castration and therefore one of inferiority even though in their earliest identification with the mother they were a part of this 'femininity'. For some theorists this rejection of 'femininity' may go a long way to explain some men's mixture ·of longing for and fear of women and their need to dominate and control them (see chapter 6 on masculinities for further discussion of this).

   In his lecture 'Femininity' (Freud 1933) Freud describes how at the beginning of her Oedipal crisis the girl, also passionately in love with the mother, discovers sexual difference and, according to Freud, perceives herself as lacking in relation to the boy's penis (and, retrospectively, understands the cultural inferiority this implies). In spite of the pleasure involved in her own version of masturbation in relation to the mother based on her clitoris, she angrily rejects her mother for not giving her a penis which she desires in someone else. Recognizing difference and the power of the penis/phallus over her mother's desire, she subsequently rejects her clitoris as second best. This means she gives up the active, 'masculine' dimension of her sexuality in favour of the passive 'feminine' form associated with the vagina which Freud believes she discovers only later in puberty. It is important to emphasize here that her anger with her mother seems to be primarily provoked by her mother's apparent wish (in the child's phantasy) to remain with her father or a substitute rather than the little girl herself. This is at the root of what Freud, controversially, describes as penis envy, the female version of castration anxiety – wanting to have, be, what the mother desires rather than what she is. Apparently the mother is not interested in bodies like that of her daughter but only, it seems to the little girl, in those of the opposite sex. She, like the little boy, rejects 'femininity' as a desirable state to be in. So it is the fact that the mother is always female and that her assumed heterosexual desire is for a body which is different from rather than like her own, together with the assault on the little girl's narcissism, which provokes the rejection of 'femininity' in the unconscious of the little girl as well as the boy. But, according to Freud, the girl never completely gives up some vestiges of what he called her penis envy, that is her early homosexual love for the mother. He believed that most women, although most of them are heterosexual and eventually have children, never completely give up their yearning to be what their mother wanted, that is a man. This is why Freud thought that, importantly, although both men and women are bisexual (small Oedipal boys fall in love with their fathers as well as their mothers), because of the prevalence of penis envy, women were particularly so.

For Freud, it is penis envy which achieves what he thought was impossible to accomplish without it – the girl's crossing over from her homosexual love for her mother as the primary object of her affections to her heterosexual desire for her father, and eventually other men. Freud rejects biological explanations for this change of heart, suggesting that there is very little reason why the girl, now sexually self-sufficient with her clitoris, should ever be drawn towards her father except, initially, as the one evidently favoured by her mother and therefore perhaps the most promising source of access to a penis through an identification with him. Eventually, when this unrealistic project fails, Freud argues that the girl abandons this temporary identification with her father and falls in love with him. Now she phantasizes having a baby with him instead of her mother while at the same time making a secondary identification with her mother.

This, for Freud, achieves a successful outcome for the girl's Oedipal crisis, not least because it entails abandoning phantasy for reality. Realistically, she abandons the phantasy of being what the mother wanted for being like her. This means that as an adult woman she will be unlikely to be undermined by neurotic symptoms caused by an unconscious sense of lack coming from within rather than from external, male-dominated culture.

Bisexuality and the Rejection of 'Femininity'

Contrary to what is often thought to be Freud's emphasis on biological drives, his central concepts of the unconscious and bisexuality may be seen as radically freeing sexuality and gender from a dependence on biology. (However, he wisely never entirely rules out what he calls 'constitutional' factors.) Freud suggests that gender arises out of what the child 'makes' unconsciously of its passionate sexual/emotional entanglements with both its parents in early childhood in the context of cultural constraints symbolized by the father. These initially result from the child's drives but are transformed into unconscious symbolic meanings in the mind of adult men and women which have a dramatic bearing on who they are able to be. Although Freud spent his lifetime trying to discover how the traditional gender identities of 'masculinity' and 'femininity' come into existence, he ended up concluding that, since most children identify with both parents, the pure categories of gender and sexuality rarely exist. Even when they appear to be pure it is only because unacceptable dimensions of gender have been firmly repressed into the unconscious, that is, lingering penis envy or 'masculinity' in girls and castration anxiety or 'femininity' in boys. So if Freud's preferred views and feelings about gender, and the form of sexuality which accompanies it, seem, at times, ambivalent, defensive and over-influenced by the cultural assumptions of his time, the overriding impact of his theory is that the pure, biologically determined binary identities of 'masculinity' and 'femininity', heterosexuality and homosexuality historically purveyed by culture, are largely non-existent because children of both sexes are bisexual. They both fall in love with and identify with both parents and, to differing extents depending on family dynamics, subsequently express or repress those desires and identifications as adults in culture. So, in Freud's theory, what culture calls 'masculinity' and 'femininity' emerge as forms of identity which refuse to be confined inside the boundaries of male and female bodies leaving men and women as inherently bisexual mixtures of gender. Each of us is a product of a range of desires and identifications which make us different individuals across the dualistic divisions of 'masculinity' and 'femininity'.

Freud's theory also suggests why, within culture, traditional gender categories are so often allied with superiority and inferiority which have such a surprising capacity to masquerade as natural and 'given' properties of men and women. Freud's theory powerfully suggests that this is because they match up with many children's earliest unconscious phantasies in relation to their parents and their emotionally driven hierarchical perception of sexual difference. In other words, in these early childhood phantasies, having a penis seems, incontrovertibly, to symbolize the mother's desire and acceptance (making it superior), while the lack of one symbolizes her rejection (making her inferior). Here it is important to understand the central role psychoanalytic theory gives to sexual difference in the formation of identity or subjectivity. Freud assumes, for either biological or cultural reasons, that it is sexual difference which will be most salient to the small child. The boy does not judge himself to be like the mother because he shares with her his black skin. Rather his body is judged as like the father, in having a penis which, being primarily associated with pleasurable sensation, crucially confers a sense of having an existence and therefore a primitive sense of identity. This bit of his anatomy, because its meaning is so integral to his sense of having an identity, becomes destiny. So, from within a psychoanalytic perspective, our sexual identity, mediated by pleasurable sensation in relation to the mother, constitutes us as subjects in a way that our ethnicity or class do not. Before we go on there is a further point we need to understand. For Freud, successful gendering (in social terms) requires the achievement of heterosexual desire. Our gendered and sexual identities are supposed to form an intertwined unity (but see below for his discussion of homosexuality).

Freud maintained, controversially, that conventional gender positions provide the best defence the individual has against painful and inhibiting neurotic symptoms because they fit with the requirements of culture; they are therefore more comfortable to live with. But Freud took the view that it was largely cultural prohibition in the form of the internalized father which causes our need for the repression of unacceptable desires (the girl's 'masculine' identification with the

father and desire for the mother and the boy's 'feminine' identification with the mother and desire for the father and every position in
between).

So Freud's theory suggests that the ideals of gender within patriarchal societies consist of splitting human attributes potentially common to all of us into two complementary ways of being human, one
of which is apparently universally valued more than the other. Each
sex then represses the culturally unacceptable dimension of their identity which then forms the basis of their unconscious.

Homosexual and Lesbian Sexuality

As we have seen, in Freud's theory gender depends primarily on the
unconscious identifications we make with a parent or parents within
a complex field of desire for both parents during early childhood. This
means that we are all potentially bisexual and Freud thought that, in
circumstances where there were no opportunities for sexual relationships with the opposite sex, most individuals would make what he
calls a homosexual choice of love-object. Freud's early views on homosexuality or what he termed 'inversion' clearly repudiate the idea
prevalent at the time that inversion in men or women had any link
with degeneracy. On the contrary he insists that homosexuals are
frequently indistinguishable from heterosexuals in every other way and
are frequently particularly intellectually talented and ethical in their
behaviour. (He believed that love of the same sex often expressed
itself in the public domain as social concern.) He emphasizes that
male homosexuality was widespread in the ancient world and that, as
practised in ancient Greece, it was crucially linked with bisexuality.

There are, however, aspects of Freud's theory which are more
problematic. Freud also argues that it is men's bisexual nature which
frequently determines the choice of a male partner who, often in a
compromise between a man and a woman, combines the characteristics of both sexes. The object of love may appear culturally 'feminine' in gender but must have masculine genitals. Freud, in 1908, in
'The Sexual Theories of Children', calls this kind of object choice the
'woman with a penis' (1908, PFL 7: 194). Here, Freud suggests that
this results from the child's fixation with an early childhood sexual
theory which attributes to everyone, including women, the possession
of a penis and which then overrides the discovery of sexual difference.

In the last section of 'A case of homosexuality in a woman' Freud (1920b) emphasizes that gender never dictates sexuality and the choice of love-object. He argues that a predominantly 'masculine', active man may still be homosexual in respect of his object, preferring a 'feminine' man to a woman. A 'feminine' man who we might expect to choose a male lover may in fact be heterosexual and be no more prone to homosexuality than an average 'masculine' man. Freud thought exactly the same was true of women.

Freud argued that psychoanalytic investigation had revealed two fundamental facts about what he saw as the complexity of homosexuality. In men, it was often a question of the interrelation between two variables: a strong fixation on the mother and, in addition to the man's manifest heterosexuality, a substantial quantity of homosexuality which can be found in all heterosexual people. He thought these vary independently and have manifold permutations. However, Freud never regarded this analysis of a homosexual scenario as complete. He also suggests that, in the context of a mother fixation, jealousy of siblings sometimes culminating in death wishes could be repressed and transformed so that the siblings become the first, narcissistic homosexual love-objects. Both the affectionate and hostile feelings of identification arise as reactive formations against the repressed aggressive impulses.

If we turn now to what Freud called female homosexuality we can draw particularly on two papers, 'A case of female paranoia' (1915) and 'A case of homosexuality in a woman' (1920b). In these two papers Freud suggests that female homosexuality rests on an early Oedipal fixation on the mother, rejection by the father and what he calls a 'masculinity complex' which he thought was only to be found regularly in women. Controversially, in 'A case of homosexuality in a woman', he sees the homosexual desires of an eighteen-year-old female patient as the direct result of an adolescent replaying of her Oedipal phantasy of rejection by her father in favour of her mother in early childhood. Freud argues that evidence of this complex emerged in her analysis with him in the form of her memories of being a tomboy who enjoyed 'romping' and 'fighting' but most significantly in her envy of her older brother's penis when she discovered it. Freud goes on, very controversially, to include as further evidence of her 'masculinity' her feminist belief that girls should enjoy the same freedom as boys and her rebellion against the lot of women generally!

Feminist Criticisms of Freud

Some feminists have argued that Freud's work is biologically deter-
minist, patriarchal, phallocentric, and inattentive to the unequal power
relationships between men and women; and that it emphasizes the role
of the father, the phallus and sexuality to the exclusion of the role
and importance of the mother. Critics (Firestone 1979; Millett 1970)
argue that Freud's construction of gender and the inherent inequality
within his categories of 'masculine' and 'feminine' seem to centre
obsessively around the father and the phallus and the idea that, as
Freud himself infamously wrote, 'Anatomy is destiny' (1973: 7. 320).
They have questioned why the child should initially assume that
everyone, including the mother, has a penis and why this bit of the
anatomy should provoke envy. Feminists have also pointed out that
Freud's scenario makes central a certain form of nuclear family. They
argue that there is no research to date to suggest that children brought
up from birth in single-parent households or by lesbian or gay
couples are differently gendered. There has also been resistance to
his account of femininity, which Freud admitted remained somewhat
of an enigma to him. This is reflected in his accounts of lesbianism,
including his reading of the case history above. Diana Fuss, for example, asks: 'Why is it presumed from the outset that the desire for
the mother is a displaced articulation of unfulfilled desire for the father,
and not the other way round?' (Fuss 1989: 63). Unsurprisingly, feminists have also resisted Freud's equation of feminism in general with a
'masculinity complex'.

Many feminists argue, as did the psychoanalyst Karen Horney
much earlier in the twentieth century, that women's subordination
and powerlessness in relation to men is the result of the social construction of femininity rather than unconscious phantasies centring
around the difference between male and female anatomy (Horney
1967). However, as Juliette Mitchell emphasizes (Mitchell 1974),
penis envy is a laughable idea only if we understand it literally and
fail to understand that it refers symbolically to the child's unconscious
envy of the power that the penis/phallus has over the mother; the
mother apparently desires to stay with the father or a man, rather
than with the little girl who unconsciously thought she had the
monopoly of her mother's love. Freud's work, despite his claim that
'anatomy is destiny', powerfully suggests that our gender cannot be

read off from our anatomies and frequently crosses the boundaries of the body because few of us resolve our Oedipal crisis unproblematically. His work as a whole argues that most of us emerge from this crisis with bisexual gendered and sexed identities composed of a complicated mixture of 'masculinity' and 'femininity' and 'activity' and 'passivity' because of our particular and varying degrees of identification and love for both parents. On the other hand, using the insights offered by his work, Freud's sometimes ambivalent and patriarchal attitude towards women and what may have been his own compensatory over-valuation of the penis was perhaps a defensive way of protecting himself from anxieties (frequently shared by other men) about the authenticity of his own 'masculinity' (Minsky 1996: 72–4). Mitchell's suggestion that we interpret Freud's 'penis envy' in a symbolic way has been influenced by the work of a later psychoanalyst to whom we now turn, Jacques Lacan. The focus we find in Lacan on the world of language and culture serves to answer the anxieties of those who feel that in Freud's account the process of gendering is tied too closely to particular structures of relations within the family.

Lacan and the Shift to Language

In a striking refiguration of Freud's concepts, Lacan makes a dramatic link between the bodily, sexual world of the Oedipal crisis and the cultural world of language which includes the reassuring bodies of knowledge it makes possible. For Lacan, in the same way that, as small children, we come to understand the meanings of the phallus as the first sign of (sexual) difference, of exclusion (from our parents' relationship) and of absence (our separation from the mother), we gradually come to grasp the binary divisions of meanings in language also based on difference, exclusion and absence. The phallus is therefore a kind of pilot-boat signifier leading into language which we understand as a system also based on difference (words only have meaning because they are different from others), exclusion (one word's meaning excludes others) and absence (words stand in for immediate experience and the loss of the mother). This lays the ground for Lacan's view that rational thinking and the subjectivity it creates through language are effectively phallic (because grounded on the phallus as the first sign of difference) and therefore 'masculine'. The 'feminine' in language therefore becomes what is absent and lacking because the desire for the mother is repressed and women lack the powerful phallic sign. Women, therefore, although they may use language, are alienated from it because they represent the lack of meaning and subjectivity in culture and can exist only in the spaces between the rational categories in language through which they sculpt out a meaningful, though unpredictable, existence. In this sense, 'masculinity' and 'femininity' emerge as unequal and complimentary in language, prefiguring traditional gender categories.

Lacan's theory is carved out of three over-arching structural categories or 'orders': the real, the imaginary and the symbolic. The real lies outside signification as the realm of impossible plenitude and bliss, the materiality of objects, trauma, psychosis and death, 'the field of non-meaning' (Bristow 1997: 91). For Lacan, gendered identities, indeed identity at all, exist only in the intersubjectivity of language – the realm of the symbolic. This is where we bring ourselves into existence as subjects through identifying ourselves with the meanings of language which pre-exist us and which will continue to define the world after we are gone. 'The form in which language is expressed itself defines subjectivity.' For Lacan there is no subjectivity outside language, only the narcissistic, self-reflecting identities of what he calls the realm of the imaginary in which we constitute ourselves narcissistically through our identifications with self-reflecting images. The imaginary is based on what he calls the 'mirror stage'. This is the moment when the baby first joyously sees its image in the mirror or in the mother's mirroring look and misrecognizes itself as something apparently separate and distinct with edges, something with an apparently, separate, integrated identity. This illusion of an identity happens when its actual identity is still merged with the mother's and it still feels uncoordinated and 'all over the place'. (For related but somewhat different uses of the concept of the imaginary see chapter 7.)

Since the meanings of language or the symbolic have no direct links with the external world they describe, Lacan argues that all identities in language and all the knowledge they produce are also shifting and precarious. Lacan emphasizes that the apparent power of the phallus and language is never justified because it has been symbolically castrated by submission to the law of the father. Lacan sees all identity as created by our identification with the conventions of rational language. What distinguishes between imaginary identities based on narcissistic identifications or the emotional investments we make with objects or things (such as consumer goods, holidays, film and pop stars), as we first did with our mother, and our subjectivity in language, is that the first is rooted in the private, bodily world of the family and idea of bliss and completion with the mother, whereas the second is anchored in the public domain of the social and culture. So Lacan shifts all meaningful life into language, which both constrains our phantasies and empowers us. But in this symbolic realm we cannot become a subject without becoming a sexed subject. To become a subject at all requires us to place ourselves in relation to the primary signifier, which for Lacan is the phallus. This is supposed to give us access to autonomy and rational thought. However, because of the disjunction between the real and the symbolic and therefore the lack of identity between the penis and the phallus, even masculine identity remains phantasized (that is idealized). Its appearence of success disguises the repression of the original pleasures found in the mother's body. Yet, these remain in the unconscious as potentially disruptive of a supposedly unified and stable identity.

Women enter culture in a different way, as an absence or lack, those who do not have the phallus and are therefore without an autonomous position as a subject. Lacan describes this as women 'being' as opposed to 'having' the phallus. 'Being' and 'having' the phallus represent two complementary sexual positions. The woman, lacking a phallus, can gain subjectivity only through 'being' the phallus, that is, confirming the status of the phallus through her desire for men. (This harks back to Freud's idea of penis envy.) So, parodoxically, she confers on to the man a phallus which she herself does not possess, although her desire is constructed in relation to the phallic term. But she can only gain from the man a penis in the realm of phantasy – because the phallus he and she think he is in fact is idealized and therefore bogus. Judith Butler illuminatingly interprets Lacan's description of women 'being' as opposed to 'having' as follows:

> 'Being' the Phallus and 'having' the Phallus denote divergent sexual positions, or non-positions (impossible positions really) within language. To 'be' the phallus, is to be the 'signifier' of the desire of the Other. . . . For women to 'be' the Phallus means, then, to reflect the power of the Phallus . . . to signify the phallus through 'being' its Other . . . its lack, the dialectical confirmation of its identity. . . . Hence 'being' the Phallus is always a 'being for' a masculine subject who seeks to confirm and augment his identity through the recognition of that 'being for'. (Butler 1990a: 44)

Lacan sees relationships between embodied men and women as sterile where the object of our love can never be more than an empty substitute for the lost mother. For Lacan the heterosexual relation is an imaginary farce based on reflections of sameness rather than difference. Here, each partner offers the other that which neither possesses because the man's phallus is symbolically castrated and the phallus which the woman offers to the man is only her desire to be the phallus vicariously through the man. So Lacan, with considerable theoretical panache, paints a gloomy picture of a patriarchal 'reality' in which we are all imprisoned. Those who ally themselves with phallic rationality (mainly men) are offered cultural power, but this form of 'masculinity' is always fragile and precarious because it is rooted in loss of the mother and symbolic castration (by the father, as represented by language and culture). Women, on the other hand, seem to be irretrievably locked in absence and lack within language, caught up in what Lacan calls a female 'masquerade' which supports and confirms male power but which denies what they really are.

Women do not only feature in Lacan's theory as the lack, for, pre-symbolically, the possession of the mother's body is the source of '*jouissance*'. This is the form of sexual bliss which Lacan insists exceeds anything associated with heterosexual love. This becomes inaccessible to us after our entry into culture, but the satisfaction of the desires we can consciously articulate is doomed to failure because, Lacan argues, their 'official' objects never correspond to the objects of our unconscious phantasy. We cannot, however, use the position of the pre-Oedipal mother to articulate an autonomous position as a subject, for women. This, Lacan argues, can only leave women in the unsig-nified world of the real, in the clutches of hysteria and psychosis.

Lacan always argues that we have no choice about identifying our-selves with the conscious meanings of culture, at some level, because it is only through our entry into the constraining, pre-existing meanings of language that we can become coping human subjects at all. He there-fore paints a picture of a totalizing and suffocatingly enclosed patri-archal culture which we can escape from only at the risk of psychosis.

French Feminist Developments of Lacan

Lacan's decentring of all identity presumed previously to be stable and relatively unified has been a powerful component in what has been termed the postmodern enterprise. The 'feminine' as repressed unconscious desire, permanently ensconced in language, always has the potential to disturb the settled, surface meanings of any text. By equating the unconscious and the disruption of meaning exclusively with the 'feminine', Lacan's work has played a major part in the influential work of French feminist writers such as Julia Kristeva (1977, 1982, 1984), Luce Irigaray (1985a, 1985b) and Hélène Cixous (1976). These writers are critical of what they see as Lacan's phallo-centrism which views all identity, meaning and culture as constructed in relation to the phallus. Irigaray, in particular, argues that Lacan's theory, in making men synonymous with language and the symbolic and representing women as the lack of meaning, results from a blind refusal to recognize sexual difference; women are regarded as defective versions of men rather than themselves. She argues that what Lacan calls subjectivity in the symbolic is simply the representation of male desire in the male imaginary which denies symbolic castration. She suggests that Lacan's notion of woman as the lack is based on an unconscious projection of man's symbolic castration – that is the lack and loss as well as power unconsciously associated with the meaning of the phallus which patriarchal men fear and cannot consciously acknowledge in themselves. This means that women carry the feared and despised unconscious of men so they are seen as the same rather than different. Irigaray thinks that it is because patriarchal men still unconsciously identify with the mother and the 'feminine' that male culture is governed by men's love of the same (other men) rather than difference (women). In what she describes as a culture of the same, woman, instead of being able to represent difference – what she calls 'the other of the other' – can only represent reflections of men, what she describes as 'the other of the same'. This means, she argues, that women are effectively buried in culture and confined to a cultural wilderness. To the extent that for men the castration complex is about fear of loss of identity, women threaten men with potential disintegration and must therefore be rigorously controlled.

However, despite their criticism of Lacan, Irigaray, Kristeva and Cixous, each in her own distinctive way, use his ideas to build new theories emphasizing difference, fluidity and multiplicity of identity and sexuality. Building on Lacan's idea that the unconscious and desire can be located only in language, they reposition Lacan's negative view of 'femininity' as the lack or absence of meaning into a positive force for change. What they see as the bogus certainties of patriarchal rationality can be subverted and challenged only by using what has been repressed in language, the lack, a 'feminine' space capable of creating a revolution in language.

Cixous (a creative writer and literary theorist), Kristeva (a professor of linguistics and later practising psychoanalyst) and Irigaray (a philosopher and later practising psychoanalyst) argue, from significantly different perspectives, that culture stands in need of a new kind of discourse which reflects the little girl's phantasies around the mother, the female imaginary currently repressed in language. They reject Freud's view that she is simply 'a little man'. Cixous and Irigaray emphasize the need to undermine and eventually supersede current language based on male phantasies in the imaginary. They argue that the latter is characterized by false, excluding binary distinctions in which woman always occupies the inferior, negative term and by a desire for sameness rather than difference which effectively denies the meaning of embodied women and the origin of men in women's bodies. They want a new discourse, what Cixous calls '*écriture féminine*', in which the erotic mother–daughter relationship is symbolized and thus incorporated and, as Irigaray puts it, given symbolic 'shelter' in culture. This, for Irigaray, is a creative and utopian project to create a discourse in which 'woman' is not simply 'the other of the same'.

Kristeva, however, concerned to avoid any hint of a feminine essence, argues that culture requires a double discourse which symbolizes not only the meaning of the father and the need for law and boundaries on phantasy but also the subversive meaning of the mother and unconscious desire. Emphasizing the castration implicit in all identity and therefore the existence of the 'other' or 'stranger' within us all, she warns feminists against the dangers of idealizing 'woman' as the absolute 'Truth' and denigrating 'man', thus perpetuating the destructive projection implicit in the false idealization of power based on the phallus and the denigration of women. We shall be returning particularly to the work of Irigaray in chapter 8.

The Rejection of Experience: Lacan and Object-Relations Theory

Lacan makes it clear that he is not trying to justify the rule of the phallus in culture but rather trying to unravel how its power is derived. Rather than celebrating its power, he exposes the fragility and vulnerability of 'masculine' identity, knowledge and culture but at the same time argues that we cannot do without it. We cannot live in a sea of unconstrained longing for our mother, even though the meaning of the father who impedes us seems to evaporate before our eyes. Lacan insists that all identity and experience outside language is delusory. The neat connections Lacan makes between the social and the psychoanalytic, culture and sexuality, consciousness and the unconscious are theoretically enticing but, from a more eclectic psychoanalytic standpoint, it has been argued that his theory leaves out all the existential ways of being and knowing based on the intuitive, empathic experience which often occurs outside conscious knowledge or language.

The object-relations work of Klein (1931), Winnicott (1964), Bion (1967) and Bollas (1992) suggests that the way we 'learn from experience' is emotional and intuitive and that those who cannot 'learn' from experience suffer from an emotional disturbance. Focusing on the early relationship with the mother as the basis for identity, rather than the father, object-relations theory suggests that there can be a vital dimension of our identity that emerges intuitively and empathically within the emotional containment which characterizes our earliest pre-verbal relationship with what Winnicott calls the 'good enough' mother who can adapt to her baby rather than compelling its adaptation to her. This part of our identity is not delusory, although it may take place within the same space as narcissism. This experience prepares the child not only for its entry into the meaningful creativity offered by the symbolic but also into the intuitive dimensions of relationships which form a crucial component in the capacity for emotional intimacy in relationships and creative living. This is another level of thinking or knowing which may not be 'thought' in language and which goes beyond desire. Object-relations theory suggests that creativity and sexuality are about living in relationships with people as well as in texts. Individuals communicate intuitively and empathically as well as through signs. From a psychoanalytic perspective, Lacan's theory suggests a splitting off or defence against the painful emotional, pre-verbal dimensions of existence it leaves out. We shall explore object-relations theory through the influential and suggestive work of the American feminist Nancy Chodorow.

Nancy Chodorow

In her book *The Reproduction of Mothering*, which first appeared in 1978 at the height of the emergence of what has been called second-wave feminism, Chodorow argues that mothering, which is largely undertaken by women, produces different experiences of object relations for both sexes and therefore different psychical outcomes in men and women. This in turn, she insists, leads to a male-dominated culture. Her solution to this problem is that parenting should be fully shared between men and women. Subsequently, Chodorow has distanced herself from this early work (significantly, since writing the book she trained as a psychotherapist) because it fails to acknowledge the idea that 'masculinity' and 'femininity' exists in both men and women. However, it has appealed widely to women, who feel that what it describes resonates strikingly with their experience in two-parent families. Finally, in this chapter, let us look at some of her most important ideas.

Chodorow's analysis, drawing on the object-relations work of Winnicott rather than Freudian theory, emphasizes relationships and issues of intimacy and separation rather than sexuality. Firmly linking the role of mothering to the patriarchal perception of women as socially inferior, she asked why – in modern societies where mothering roles, as opposed to childbirth, could be shared much more equally in two-parent families – did most women continue to be primarily responsible for mothering in the family. Why, she went on to ask, did women seem, at one level, to want the mothering role, despite its emotional and social price. Chodorow rejects biological theories and approaches which suggest that women can consciously choose their gender roles and argues that the desire to be a mother is constructed in girls unconsciously, long before they become women. Chodorow argues that, although mothers are the first love-objects for children of both sexes, the intimacy and love associated with this relationship have to be resolved in different ways for girls and boys. This, she maintains, results in an entirely different psychical structure in men and women. As a consequence of being mothered by a woman, women are more likely than men to seek to be mothers; that is to relocate themselves in a primary mother–child relationship, to get enjoyment and fulfilment from the mothering relationship and to have the psychological and relational capacities for mothering. Chodorow, following Freud, argues that in early childhood girls, unlike boys, have to take both parents as love-objects. However, although the girl's erotic needs are eventually transferred to the father, Chodorow takes the view that her primary emotional rather than sexual interest remains with the mother. She argues that this means that the girl oscillates emotionally within a rich, triangular, relational experience which makes the girl's object world much more complex and developed than that of the boy, who must repress his emotional attachment to the mother in the Oedipal crisis. He is not, therefore, involved in the same emotional breadth of experience as the girl, who henceforth defines herself through her relationships.

Although Chodorow is heavily influenced by Freud's later emphasis on the importance of the pre-Oedipal mother–daughter relationship, it is striking that the girl's active desire for the mother in Freud's theory of the Oedipal crisis is subtly converted in Chodorow's version into an emotional, not sexual, 'turning back' towards the mother. For Chodorow gender development is determined largely around the issues of emotional intimacy and separation rather than difference and bisexual desire. Boys achieve their 'masculinity' only by separating themselves from the mother and denying the emotional, intimate world she represents. They have to deny their earliest experiences of helplessness and emotional need in relation to the mother and live an alienated existence which rejects feeling in favour of work. Chodorow argues that, because the relationship between mothers and sons is more sexually charged than that with girls, the development of social contempt for women helps the boy define himself in opposition to the 'femininity' his mother represents. This denial of their relational capacities, for Chodorow, explains men's difficulty in dealing with emotional matters because they see the acknowledgement of their emotions, and in particular feelings of vulnerability, as potentially 'feminizing' and threatening to their status as 'real' men. This means that many men are unable to relate adequately to their partners' emotional needs because they feel compelled to maintain a distance from the relational inner world they have denied.

The situation for the girl, Chodorow argues, is very different. Since society condones a continuation of the intense bond of relatedness with her mother, she is never required to make a complete break with her mother in order to achieve her sexual identity. The girl's relationship with her mother is one of prolonged symbiosis or narcissistic over-identification. She can express her heterosexual desires with her father but she need not put all her eggs into one basket. She does not need him for emotional sustenance (which, in Chodorow's view, he is unlikely to be able to give her anyway) because she still has an intense emotional bond with her mother. In fact, Chodorow argues that girls who want to be loved erotically by their fathers (as mothers might have erotic attachments to their male children) cope with the fact that (in her view) their fathers are normally not emotionally available to their daughters, by idealizing them. This means that they are unconsciously prevented from noticing what they are actually like. Chodorow argues that adult women who want heterosexual relationships with men also tend to protect themselves from men's emotional shortcomings through idealization. They can maintain their denial of their partner's limitations as long as they feel loved. (However, in some cases, idealization prevails even in the face of repeated disappointment.)

However, for Chodorow, the girl's long, intense, self-continuous relationship with her mother is not without its problems, despite its emotional advantages. Her continuing attachment to her mother gives the girl a stronger, more resilient sense of self than the boy, but it also explains why girls may suffer unconsciously from greater dependency needs. Since they do not need to separate completely from their mothers, they may never achieve an identity entirely distinct from her. A part of them remains in a state of merger or fusion which makes it difficult for them to distinguish their own feelings from those of their mother. This Oedipal love for the mother contains threats to the self because of the perpetual promise of unity it offers which the love for the father never contains. All this, Chodorow argues, creates a situation where women, much more than men, will be open to, and preoccupied with, those very relational issues that go with mothering – feelings of primary identification, lack of separateness or differentiation and problems with ego boundaries. This, Chodorow suggests, explains why women frequently long for more relatedness with their male partners – more openness and support, less separation and distance. It also explains why they rarely achieve it. Men, having been compelled to reject their identification with their mothers and their emotions, tend to individuate and separate more successfully than women but at the cost of the denial and repression of their earliest emotional experience. They may become contemptuous of those people, women, who can express emotional needs, as a way of denying their own. Fostering impersonal relationships in the public world and needing to keep their emotional visors up among other men, they then try to recoup their primary sense of identity in their heterosexual relationships with women.

Chodorow argues that shared parenting would produce a new situation where the role, meaning and status of mothering would be shared equally by men and women so that gender division could no longer be based on the perceived female inferiority which follows from the association of mothering only with women. In her new scenario, the role available to girls would be no different from that of boys, and boys would grow up no longer needing to deny their emotional life because this would be associated as much with men as with women. Men might then be better able to satisfy the emotional needs of their partners and both fathers and mothers would be 'good enough' to ensure the successful emotional nurturing of their children.

Chodorow's work has been criticized for failing to recognize the fluidity of gendered identity and the variation which exists in the nurturing capacities of both men and women. Chodorow has also been criticized for being over-optimistic about the possibility of radical psychical changes in many men. It has also been suggested that her work is less relevant in the more recent context of a massive increase in unconventional households no longer based on the nuclear family. In presenting the tragic dimension of men's psychical need to reject the 'feminine' in order to become 'masculine' men which has recently been taken up in men's studies (see chapter 6), it has been argued that Chodorow neglects the ways in which most men benefit from existing social arrangements and ignores many men's active agency in violence against women which can be seen, in the context of Chodorow's work, simply as the process of men dissociating from their 'femininity'. Despite these criticisms, Chodorow's work is highly suggestive and appears to resonate with the experiences of many women and men who share the cultural positioning to which she pays attention.

Conclusions

Psychoanalytic theory, particularly that of Freud and Lacan, suggests that our gendered subjectivity is always potentially precarious and un-stable because it is always vulnerable to the subversions of unconscious desire. It also sees our gender as fluid, crossing the boundaries of the body and determined largely by the kind of unconscious identifications we are able to make with both our parents. Freud's theory, whatever its omissions in the light of later theoretical developments, is valuable because by suggesting that gendered identity is determined by what we may unconsciously make of our bodies within the emotionally charged identifications within the family (whether single- or dual-parent, heterosexual or homosexual) it does justice to the complexities of the genders and sexualities we see around us. He suggests that even though our unconscious phantasies and earliest emotional experiences are unavailable to consciousness they none the less powerfully inform our subjectivities.

Freud's claim that his theory was universally applicable is a problem in an intellectual climate which emphasizes the role of history, language and culture in the construction of subjectivity and challenges the 'truth' or universality of 'grand narratives'. However, in certain respects his theory can be seen as dazzlingly suggestive, in particular his suggestion that gender is a matter of what we unconsciously make of bodily difference as a consequence of emotional factors deriving from our history of intimate and familial relationships. Overall, read eclectically but still rigorously, psychoanalytic perspectives suggest that the complexity of the qualities that add up to our gendered subjectivity make it always at some level precarious and likely to be determined by no single factor. Despite reservations about psychoanalytic accounts of gender construction by feminists and other gender theorists, psychoanalysis remains central to contemporary work on gender. One of the reasons for this is to bring the issue of subjectivity into the debate. Psychoanalysis directly addresses how we become constituted as gendered subjects, a process in which we attach considerable significance to bodily difference. In both Freud and object-relations theory this process of subject formation is anchored in our early personal histories and emotional entanglements which generate the desires we have in later life. The reworking of Freud found in Lacan has been particularly influential in what has been termed the 'turn to language' within contemporary gender theory (see chapter 3). The concentration on language and the symbolic in the formation of subjectivity which we find in Lacan offers a means of integrating the public world of culture with (as others see it) the private world of the individual psyche.

The psychoanalytic framework has been strongly criticized, in particular the central role assigned to the phallus. However, as Juliette Mitchell remarks, 'psychoanalysis is not a recommendation for a patriarchal society, but an analysis of one' (Mitchell 1974: xiii). The totalizing, closed and apparently deterministic nature of the symbolic order, as it features in the world of Lacan, has also been widely challenged. Resistance to both determination and closure comes from the work of the French feminist thinkers discussed here, and from the post-structuralist writers we shall be considering in the following chapters.

The Social Construction of Gender

Sex, Gender and Social Roles

Psychoanalysis is concerned with the question of what we make, in the formation of our subjectivities, of bodily difference. The conscious and unconscious emotional salience which becomes attached to differently shaped bodies is a consequence, on these accounts, of emotional attachments in the family and initiation into culture, including language. Different theorists put different degrees of emphasis on these two aspects. What emerges is a sense of ourselves as women or men and a sense of other bodies as appropriate or inappropriate objects of desire. Such gendered and sexual identities are, however, precarious. They are liable to disruption from an unconscious realm into which has been repressed those aspects of ourselves which cannot be fitted into our official identities. Such psychoanalytic accounts make use of a particular myth, that of Oedipus, to articulate the way in which our bodies gain the emotional salience they have. The universal applicability of this myth has been challenged. It was, after all, initially utilized to make sense of the experiences of middle- and upper-class Europeans, living in patriarchal family structures, at the end of the nineteenth century. Another feature which has been found problematic is the foundational role which is given within psychoanalysis to sexual difference as an aspect of our identity. (We return to this in chapter 8.) None the less key features of psychoanalysis remain central to attempts to make sense of gendered subjectivities. The emphasis on what we make, subjectively, of bodily difference and the recognition of the central roles both of early relationships and culture in the development of this, are themes which we will return to in chapter 7.

In psychoanalysis we find elements of both biological and social explanations. Although a purely biological account of Freud seems a misreading, he does accept something like basic drives, which are directed in certain ways via social factors. In Lacan, through his account of the formation of the imaginary and the symbolic, social structures, in particular language, have come to play the major role. In this chapter we want to turn our attention directly to social accounts of the process of gender formation. Theories stressing the social construction of gender can be (crudely) divided into two main types. First are broadly materialist theories that stress the structural features of the social world which ensure that women and men are fitted into distinct pathways within the society, and emphasize the concrete social relations, of work, the family, sexuality, etc. Second are what have been termed discursive theories. These place emphasis on the *meanings* which are attached to being male or female within society, emphasizing the role of language and of culture. The move from one kind of theory to the other is sometimes described as 'the shift from things to words' (Barrett 1992). Of course it is possible to claim that both types of social features are required in the process of gender formation. Indeed we shall be arguing that the often posed opposition between the material and the discursive is misplaced.

Either type of theory can be essentialist or non-essentialist. In chapter 1 we considered primarily biological essentialism, the assumption that a binary division into men and women is required by biology, and that each kind has essential biological features which then explain pychological and behavioural communalities. Essences do not have to be biological essences, however. Social essentialists would accept that all women, for example, share characteristics as a consequence of adopting the same social role, being placed within the same kind of social structures or being subject to the same symbolic order. Such essentialism will be subject to critique in this chapter. It is, moreover, the case that many social constructionist accounts rely on a residual biological essentialism. Accounts of gender which focus on the ways in which men and women learn to be masculine or feminine assume *a priori* that the human species is unproblematically divided biologically into men and women. Thus, while such approaches stress that what constitutes masculinity and femininity is socially constructed, they do not question the binary division of people into two sexes. Nicholson uses the analogy of a coat-hanger to describe this process. She suggests that it is useful to think of there being two coat-hangers: while the two coat-hangers remain constantly male and female, the 'clothes' hung on the hangers can vary (Nicholson 1995). This approach echoed the important early move within feminist thought, distinguishing between sex and gender, which we owe particularly to Ann Oakley. Oakley, in her work *Sex, Gender and Society*, argued that gender was distinct from sex, that gender referred to the social characteristics, masculinity and femininity, and were variable, whereas sex related to biological sex and was more fixed. 'The constancy of sex must be admitted, but so too must the variability of gender' (Oakley 1985b: 16). This division, about which we have already raised certain questions in chapter 1, formed the framework for much of the early work on the social construction of gender.

Social role theory, one such early form of social constructionism, was often employed to make sense of the processes by which gender was acquired. According to social role theory (also known as sex role theory), men and women become masculine and feminine through social conditioning, and we learn the gender role that relates to our biological sex through our interaction with social structures, such as the family, schools, the media and so on. There are a number of key problems with this approach. Its account of masculinity and femininity does not adequately explain the different forms of femininity or masculinity that exist. Furthermore, it does not show how we can explain changes within the lives of individual men and women or changes over a longer historical time frame. Nor does it adequately explain why resistance occurs and movements such as feminism emerge (Stacey 1993: 66). Why do some people learn, accept and follow certain roles and others reject them? Moreover, social role theory does not adequately describe how gender roles are taken on board – the processes by which we acquire a specific gender identity (Connell 1987, 1995). While social role theory marked an important shift away from biological explanations of masculinity and feminin- ity, in that it did not regard masculine and feminine behaviour as rooted in biology, it does not question the underlying assumption that there are two sexes. Delphy observes that the conventional sex– gender distinction, while seeking to show the social construction of

gender, was anchored in a form of biological essentialism in that it
took for granted the division into two sexes:

> We have continued to think of gender in terms of sex: to see it as a
> social dichotomy determined by a natural dichotomy. *The* context
> may vary . . . but the *container is* assumed to be invariable because it is
> part of nature and 'nature does not change'. Moreover, part of the
> nature of sex is seen to be its *tendency to* have a social content/to vary
> culturally. (1993: 3)

Much contemporary writing, however, recognizes that not only
gender characteristics but also the biological division into two sexes
are socially mediated: 'in the sense that the hierarchical division of
humanity into two transforms an anatomical difference (which is
itself devoid of social implication) into a relevant distinction for social
practice' (Delphy, cited Jackson 1996a: 121). We therefore need to be
attentive, in this chapter, to social constructionist accounts, not only
of gender, but also of sex. The materialist theories discussed in the
earlier part of the chapter are variable in this regard. Marxist work
mostly operated within the residual essentialism signalled above.
However, the French materialist writers, such as Delphy and Wittig,
argued that without social divisions the biological differences would
be without significance.

Materialist Feminism

The study of the social construction of gender helps us to understand
how gender is shaped and given meaning by the social structure of a
society. For materialists these structures are the systems of power
and control which give rise to sets of social relations. According
to feminist analysis the social relations of gender are ones in which
women are treated as inferior and subordinate to men, and thus gender divisions are exploitative and oppressive. For most of the 1970s
and 1980s the debates on this issue were addressed from a materialist
standpoint of which there are two feminist versions. The first attempts
to utilize an explicitly *Marxist framework* for analysing the structure
of social relations. The second makes central use of the concept of
patriarchy, which, although borrowing much from a Marxist method,
does not necessarily accept the Marxist analysis of the organization of

social relations, with priority given to the economic. Materialists see gender differences as rooted in social relations which give rise to social practices that produce and reproduce gender inequalities. People are made into social men and women by the particular positions which they are allocated in the social order. To understand what it is to be a man or woman in a given society is to grasp the social relations involved. There is a material reality to gender categories which, though socially constructed, constrains and forms people. For example, Gayle Rubin in 'The traffic in women' (1975), paraphrasing Marx, wrote:

> What is a domesticated woman? A female of the species. The one explanation is as good as the other. A woman is a woman. She only becomes a domestic, a wife, a chattel, a playboy bunny, a prostitute, or a human dictaphone in certain relations. Torn from these relationships, she is no more the helpmate of man than gold in itself is money. What then are these relationships by which a female becomes an oppressed woman? (Rubin 1975: 158)

Here Rubin explicitly adopts a social constructionist position in opposition to the inflexibility of Lacanian psychoanalytic accounts. If women and men become women and men by their social relationships, by changing these relations we can also modify gender identities and their current inequalities.

The work of Marx and Engels became the starting point for this type of analysis. The following selection from Engels's *The Origins of the Family, Private Property and the State* (1884) is a useful summary of the materialist method.

> According to the materialist conception, the determining factor in history is, in the last resort, the production and reproduction of immediate life. But this itself is of a twofold character. On the one hand: the production of the means of subsistence, of food, clothing and shelter and the tools requisite thereto; on the other, the production of human beings themselves, the propagation of the species. The social institutions under which men of a definite historical epoch and a definite country live are determined by both kinds of production; by the stage of development of labour, on the one hand, and of the family, on the other. (Engels 1972: 71–2)

Marxism represents both a method and an analysis. The division between feminist materialists derives from this. For example, the

French feminist theorist Christine Delphy states that she is using the method as a starting point for her analysis and Marxist feminists use both the method and the analysis. The *method* is summed up in the quotation from Engels and this provides a way of looking at and understanding the world, as it is organized not only now but also historically. The Marxist *analysis* of capitalism provides an explana- tion of how the system operates and offers a theory of how it can be overcome. In this analysis priority is given to the organization of productive work and the relations in which people stand to the pro- duction of capital. Other features of social organization are viewed as secondary to the divisions into classes dictated by the organization of paid labour. The classes which are economically dominant are also those whose interests are promoted by other aspects of social and political life and by the ideologies by means of which the members of a society come to make sense of the social order. Within this analysis Marxist feminists attempt to make sense of male dominance and women's subordination (Tong 1989; A. M. Jaggar 1983). How- ever, although it is clear that capitalism incorporates gender divisions, in terms for example of job segregation and low pay, it is less clear that the Marxist analysis provides adequate explanations of this. Gen- der divisions seem to pre-date and postdate capitalist forms of social organization, and themselves seem to play a role in determining the particular form which was given to the organization of production (Barrett 1980). This has led to Marxist feminists attempting to link such an analysis to one offered in terms of patriarchy.

Patriarchy

The concept of patriarchy dominated much of feminist theory and practice during the 1970s and 1980s from its appearance in the work of Kate Millett's *Sexual Politics* (1970). During this period the con- cept was used as an analytical tool which explained asymmetrical gender relations not only in the present day, in the capitalist mode of production, but also historically, across differing epochs and through various social formations. As Beechey (1979) points out, patriarchy is neither a single nor a simple concept but has been attributed a wide variety of different meanings. Her analysis demonstrates how vary- ing conceptions of patriarchy, within feminist theory, correspond to the different political tendencies within feminism.

Within radical and revolutionary feminist thought patriarchy emphasizes that women as a group are subordinated and oppressed by men. Radical feminist accounts look in particular to men's control over women's bodies, in terms of their fertility and sexuality and in their exercise of control over them through violence, both domestic and sexual (Daly 1978; Rich 1993; MacKinnon 1983). This is not to say that radical feminists are united in what they see as the fundamental basis of patriarchy. While some emphasize rape, others centre their analysis on control over reproduction. There is, however, a shared perception that Weedon summarizes: 'In radical feminist analysis patriarchy is founded on a fundamental polarization between men and women in which men exploit women for their own interests' (1999: 26–7). Part of the radical feminist project is to rework our understanding of women's bodies, to revalue and celebrate women's difference and to liberate ourselves from patriarchal understandings of womanhood, for example, in reclaiming derogatory terminology for women's bodies and giving it positive meaning, challenging male-dominated knowledge and practice in medicine. It is also centrally concerned with removing women practically away from violent and controlling men, by setting up women's refuges and establishing women-only spaces.

In Marxist and socialist feminist thought the status attributed to patriarchy in explaining women's position in society, and their standing *vis-à-vis* men is also varied. Beechey (1979) points to the different conceptions of patriarchy which can be traced within the works of feminists who would define themselves as either socialist feminists or Marxist feminists. Patriarchy is defined in one instance as a structure which can be traced to kinship systems in which men exchange women (Mitchell 1975). In another instance, patriarchy is defined as male power over women (Hartmann 1981). In another example, patriarchy is defined as the existence of a structure of hierarchical relations between the sexes (Z. R. Eisenstein 1979). The final illustration Beechey uses is the characterization of patriarchy as male control of women's reproductive capacity. Marxist and socialist feminists also remain divided in their analysis of patriarchy's relationship to capitalism and the weight both forces should be given in explaining women's position socially. Crudely speaking, Marxist feminists tend to give great explanatory status to capitalism in their analyses whereas socialist feminists look more to developing a synthesis of capitalism and patriarchy in their accounts, often known as dual-systems theories

(Hartmann 1981). For dual-systems theories there are two identifiable structures, capitalism and patriarchy, and the position of individual men and women is fixed by the intersection of these two systems. All of these positions, however, require an account to be given of specific social and material structures which constitute patriarchal modes of organization. The Marxist materialist method is retained but the analysis exclusively foregrounding economic relations is often rejected by socialist feminists.

One of the most influential and interesting attempts comes from France, in the work of Christine Delphy (1977, 1984). In her essay *The Main Enemy* (1977) Delphy develops a theory of gender which locates women and men in opposing classes. For Delphy it is this, as opposed to biology, which makes them men and women. She puts forward a model of capitalist society in which there exist two distinct modes of production: first, an industrial mode which is the arena of capitalist exploitation and, secondly, a family, domestic mode of production where women provide domestic services and where childbearing occurs. It is this second mode of production which she explores as the site of patriarchal exploitation. Delphy argues that by virtue of marriage women share a common class position. Since the majority of women marry, she suggests, all women are likely or destined to participate in these family relations of production. As a group which is subjected to these relations of production and to the ideologies which reinforce and perpetuate gender inequalities they therefore constitute a class. Essentially her argument is that the 'appropriation and exploitation of their labour within marriage constitutes the oppression common to all women' (Delphy 1977: 16). Thus women are oppressed and exploited by the two systems of patriarchy and capitalism.

The attractiveness of Delphy's hypothesis lay in her attempt to construct a theoretical analysis from which to address the material basis for the oppression of women rather than to attempt to integrate women into an already existing theoretical model. Thus the focus of Delphy's work is similar to that of Marxist and socialist feminists, but without an adherence to Marx's analysis of capitalism. This made her the focus for criticism. According to Stevi Jackson's account of Delphy's work: 'Many of these keepers of the faith focus on Delphy's deviations from established marxist dogma rather than the utility of her arguments for understanding women's subordinate position within families. Central to these charges of heresy is Delphy's claim that there are two modes of production coexisting in our society' (1996a: 72). Michele Barrett and Mary McIntosh (1979), for example, subjected Delphy's ideas to a critical review, centring on Delphy's use and application of the concept of 'mode of production'. They suggest that she employs the concept rather loosely and does not follow through the logic of the term, which, they point out, would entail a detailed analysis of the mechanisms of the patriarchal mode showing the interrelationships and interconnectedness with the capitalist mode of production. Thus they argue that: 'She is not interested in the relations between capitalism and patriarchy, since that would necessarily lead to a discussion of the extent to which women's oppression is related to other features of the capitalist mode of production' (1979: 102).

What was happening was that the concept of patriarchy was being theorized by Marxist and socialist feminists in one of two ways. The first method viewed patriarchy as an ideological and psychological structure. That is, women's position was a consequence of the ideas that were current about women and men, and actual men's and women's internalization of these ideas. (We return to the role of ideology below.) This formulation led Marxist feminists to seek to show the way in which these ideological factors related to other structures in society, primarily its capitalist organization. The second formulation, of which Delphy's work was an example, viewed patriarchy as generating its own set of material social relations. Here the theoretical task was to uncover these relations and show how they interacted with the social relations of production. French materialist feminist Monique Wittig, following Delphy, looks to heterosexuality and the marriage contract in particular as the basis of women's oppression. She suggests that 'The category of sex is the product of heterosexual society in which men appropriate for themselves the reproduction and production of women and also their physical persons by means of the marriage contract' (Wittig 1992: 6). Controversially, Wittig argues that *lesbians are not women* because they remove themselves from heterosexual and marriage relations. In Wittig's analysis there is therefore no biological core to woman (or to man); instead woman is constructed through and within such social relations. Those who do not take part in the social relations which make us men and women are thereby *not men and women*. Her work has come under criticism for its narrow analysis of patriarchy (Jackson 1999b: 131–2). 'This does not mean, as Wittig 1992 would have it, that lesbians are not women. We are all defined by our gender and there is no escaping the patriarchal hierarchy within which we are positioned as women.' Here, however, Jackson is drawing attention to Wittig's too restrictive accounts of patriarchal relations; she is not dissenting from her approach which sees such patriarchal relations as the means by which we are socially constructed as men and women. (We return to a discussion of Wittig in chapter 4).

Although patriarchy occupied centre stage in the feminist debates of the 1970s, it has since fallen from favour. In Britain Veronica Beechey (1979) and Sheila Rowbotham (1982) have been highly critical of the utility of the concept within feminist analysis. Rowbotham, for example, argued in an article for the *New Statesman* in 1979 that '"Patriarchy" implies a structure which is fixed, rather than the kaleidoscope of forms within which women and men have encountered one another. It does not carry any notion of how women might act to transform their situation as a sex. Nor does it even convey a sense of how women have resolutely manoeuvred for a better position within the general context of subordination' (1982: 74). Additionally the lack of consensus between the Marxist and socialist feminist perspective about the definition of patriarchy resulted in considerable confusion. While Rowbotham identified problems in the conceptualization of patriarchy, other theorists argue that the difficulties recognized are surmountable. Sylvia Walby, for example, defends the use of the term. She recognizes that certain theories of patriarchy are problematic but maintains that 'the problems in many theories of patriarchy are due to a contingent, not necessary feature in the analyses' (Walby, in Barrett and Phillips 1992: 36). In *Theorising Patriarchy* (1989) Walby rejects uni-causal models of patriarchy and instead puts forward a multi-causal analysis, thus divorcing the concept of patriarchy from a fixed, ahistoric and universalist understanding of 'women's oppression'. Walby identifies six key structures that determine patriarchal relations – paid work, housework, sexuality, culture, violence and the state. According to her analysis, the *different* articulation of the six structures produces *different* forms of patriarchy. She argues that her framework is therefore able to accommodate and explain variations in gender inequalities over time and between different social and cultural contexts.

Walby's analysis, however, despite attempting to show how patriarchy can vary in its manifestation, still relies at its core on an acceptance of men and women as clearly defined and distinct categories.

Indeed, the whole point of employing the concept 'patriarchy' is to show how hierarchical relations between men and women, conceived of as coherent and distinct groups, are constructed. The underlying premise of patriarchy is that women as a group are subordinated in relation to men as a group. Moves to illustrate difference among women, to explore the diversity of the category 'woman', and by implication 'man' (see the next section), undermined patriarchy as an explanatory concept. Moreover, once the the categories 'man' and 'woman' come into question, then the basis for analyses in terms of patriarchal structures are problematized.

Although the use of the term patriarchy has generally fallen from favour, however, the materialist standpoint which motivated much of the work done in its name has not. The central assumption that men and women are socially constructed by the operation of material and social structures, even if they are not neatly systematizable into the two systems of *capitalism* and *patriarchy*, has remained firmly in play. We return to this point in the final section of this chapter.

Debates about Difference

In the late 1970s and early 1980s there was an outpouring of feminist writing on the oppression of women historically, cross-culturally and contemporarily, much of which centred on the three areas of reproduction, sexuality and socialization. This outpouring of writing was, however, read in different ways. For those who accepted that 'the secondary status of women in society is one of the true universals, a pan-cultural fact' (Ortner 1974: 67) all of these writings were read as making manifest the structures of patriarchy. This is evident, for example, in the introduction to Robin Morgan's book *Sisterhood is Global* (Morgan 1984). This book gives an audit of the world, country by country, showing in Morgan's eyes that there is 'a common condition, which, despite variations in degree, is experienced by all human beings who are born female' (1984: 4). This common condition is a result not of biology but of common social structures, highlighted as the institutions of marriage, control of reproductive freedom, the war on women's sexuality, pornography, prostitution and sex tourism. Recognition of such a common condition will, Morgan argues, lead to a 'totally new way of viewing international affairs. For example, cross-cultural opposition . . . to war . . . healthy skepticism of certain technological advances . . . two instances of a common world view' (1984: 4).

Morgan's account is contrasted, in an article by Chandra Talpade Mohanty (1992), with writings by Bernice Johnson Reagon (1983). Morgan sees, for example, the workings of imperialism as a manifestation of the workings of patriarchy, and hence as something for which women have no responsibility. Her treatment of differences between women views them as a reflection of cultural pluralism, which marks variation on a theme. Johnson Reagon, however, signals the implicatedness of many women within imperialist structures, the benefits and power they gain from them and their role in keeping them in place. White women from colonial powers have both in the past and currently benefited from the imperialist project and the economic structures of globalization which followed it. This undermines claims of a 'common sisterhood'. At the extremes this inequality is manifested in the relations of the white madam and black maid epitomized, for example, in South Africa and the southern states of America. But the inequalities also pervade everyday practices in which privileged women construct their femininity with clothes manufactured in sweatshops around the world. Johnson Reagon also highlights differences in terms of experiences of racism. Racism is something which some women but not others experience. 'What concerns her is not the sameness which allows us to identify with each other as women, but the exclusions particular normative definitions of "women" enforce. What is required is a calling into question of the term "woman" as a basis for unity' (Mohanty 1992: 85).

Johnson Reagon's analysis here reflected that of many black and post-colonial women of that time and since who were challenging the apparent essentialism and universalism of prominent materialist analyses, particularly those which made central use of the concept of patriarchy. Such theorists were arguing against the idea that the material structures of society were operating in the same way for all women to produce a common condition of 'being a woman'. Also challenged, but with rather less attention, was the idea that such structures also worked to produce a single condition of 'being a man'. Ann Phoenix, for example, draws attention to the way the process of gender development is qualitatively different for black children than for white children. They grow up aware that black and white people occupy different structural positions in society and intimately acquainted with the workings of racism. Consequently they relate differently in a society governed by a negative 'white-ness'. Black women's participation in the labour market means black women grow up accepting that women can be employed. Also the prevalence of alternatives to the nuclear family ensures that the links between family structures and gender inequalities take a different form. The exclusion of many black men from the labour market also ensures that relations of power are inflected in a different way. Heidi Mirza also draws attention to the way that 'living submerged in whiteness, physical difference becomes a defining issue, a signifier, a mark of whether or not you belong' (Mirza 1997: 3). The gender of both white and black people is therefore calculated under the mask of such signifiers.

Some of the arguments that were being made here had elements in common with traditional Marxist arguments insisting on the priority of class differences, as a consequence of which it had been suggested that the differences in power between middle-class and working-class women ruled out their making common cause. To this, these writings added dimensions of colonial and postcolonial histories, ex-periences of racism, geographical locations, cultural traditions. What was argued was that different locations in respect of these features resulted in crucial differences attached to gendered positionality. The common opposition to violence remarked by Morgan was not shared by women fighting apartheid, or defending the Sandinistas in Nicaragua. The institution of marriage was positioning women in a different way when, for example, Palestinian families were scattered without travel documents, the men removed from the women and children and shipped out from Lebanon. The family, which was viewed as the structure for exploiting women's labour and sexuality on men's behalf, constitutes its subjects differently when it is the site for organizing resistance to racism. The control of women by rape and the threat of rape gains a quite different inflection when accusa-tions of rape justify widespread lynchings and hangings, while rape by colonizers of 'native' bodies is a routine part of the operation of colonial control (Davies 1981). The fight for abortion rights and safe birth control has a different meaning placed within the context of compulsory family planning and involuntary sterilization, which form the context of reproductive issues for black women in the North and the South of the world (James and Busia 1993: 141–60).

The insistence on difference was also noted in the writings of gay and lesbian writers for whom oppression of their sexuality as deviant led to a prioritizing of resistance to structures of normative hetero-sexuality. In this project women and men worked together, in a way that required that the insistence that both were being constituted by the structures of patriarchy at least required substantial modification (see chapter 5).

The recognition of the very different ways in which gender be-comes constructed is also manifest in the writings which come from people with disabilities. These writers make clear the extent to which norms of masculinity and feminity are not only 'submerged in white-ness', but also operate within a conception of what counts as a 'normal body'. As Jenny Morris points out, the association of disability with dependency and lack of autonomy has the consequent implication that 'to be a man in a wheelchair is to be impotent, unable to be a (hetero-) sexual being, and therefore not a "complete" man. As such it tells us little about the actual experience of being a disabled man, but a lot about the non-disabled society's definitions of both mas-culinity and disability' (Morris 1996: 87). 'Both work and leisure activities are linked with physical ability . . . and both these areas of life . . . [are] characterised by the social meaning of masculinity' (1996: 89–90). To be a disabled man on this account is not to be a proper man at all.

Parallel points can be made in relation to women with disabilities and norms of femininity. Visual disabilities often lead to the pre-sumption that women are asexual people for whom reproduction is inappropriate. These voices are therefore excluded from debates on reproduction and mothering. In place of the gaze of sexual objecti-fication, visibly disabled people often suffer not 'the appropriating gaze' but 'the stare'.

> If the male gaze informs the normative female self as a sexual spectacle, then the stare sculpts the disabled subject as a grotesque spectacle. The stare is the gaze intensified, framing her body as an icon of deviance . . . as every person with a visual disability knows intimately, manag-ing, deflecting, resisting, or renouncing that stare is the daily business of life. (Garland Thomson 1997: 285)

In the debates on abortion and reproductive technologies, writing from people with disability has also manifested a distinctive voice challenging 'the prejudicial assumption that "defective" foetuses destined to become disabled people should be eliminated' (Garland Thomson 1997: 286). Interconnectedly disabled people have resisted pressure to be sterilized and restrict reproduction because of the risk of producing disabled children.

In the earlier debates between Marxism and other forms of materialist feminism the recognition of the dual dimensions of class and gender had led to a development of theories which recognized these two axes of social formation, where individuals were constituted into social groupings in terms of their position on both axes. The recognition of the range of determinants of location indicated above, however, does not lend itself to this kind of resolution. We do not have here the interaction of two distinct and identifiable structures in the formation of social identity. There is rather a tangle of factors in relation. Moreover, it is not possible to identify a common factor throughout the tangle of 'being a woman' or 'being a man', to which we can then add further features of identity according to other aspects of positionality. What such additive models miss is 'the qualitative difference' in *gendered* experience when gender is instantiated simultaneously with other aspects of positionality (James and Busia 1993: 20). Different women and different men consequently reveal a patchwork of overlapping similarities and differences, which cannot be systematized in terms of discrete structures of social organization. The writings which we have been discussing here have therefore 'reformulated a monologic notion of gender identity as a dynamic matrix of interrelated, often contradictory, experiences, strategies, styles and attributions mediated by cultures and one's specific history, forming a network that cannot be separated meaningfully into discrete entities or ordered into a hierarchy' (Garland Thomson 1997: 284).

Such an approach also serves as a corrective against an overhomogenized conception of difference itself. As Carol Thomas (1999) and many other writers emphasize, all that united people as 'disabled' is a judgement that their bodies deviate in some way from a norm. This covers an enormous variety of different kinds of experience. These points are also emphasized in the collection by Heidi Safia Mirza (1997), who argues that black feminism undermines its own position by 'essentialist definitions of blackness' (1997: 15) which fail to recognize 'ethnic, religious, political and class differences among women' (p. 11) and excludes the experiences of those who are 'neither black or white' (p. 15). In the same volume Bibi Bakare Yusuf warns against 'over-emphasis' on black communities: 'Points of connection, disconnection, cross-connections among black people get subsumed under the limited code of "race" which impedes critical discussions'

(p. 82). Given this kind of a picture Johnson Reagon argues that what is required is not political organization, based on shared experiences, but coalitions across differences for shared political objectives. (This is an issue we shall return to in chapter 10.)

The Shift from Things to Words

The widespread attention to difference was one of the spurs to the shift from social theorizing of gender differences away from materialist accounts of patriarchal structures, 'things', and towards a concern with 'words' (Barrett 1992) (but for some reservations see below). 'Things' here refer to women's position in the labour market, women's position in the household, women's education, male control of sexuality and the pervasiveness of rape (Barrett 1992: 201). 'Words' refers to the turn to ideology or 'discursive constructions'. Increasingly, Marxist and socialist feminist analyses began to examine the role of ideology in defining the processes of the social construction of gender. Attention began to shift to an evaluation of the *meaning* of gender for individuals. In addition to the challenges posed by the writers insisting on differences within the categories 'woman' and 'man', one of the main reasons for this shift was a recognition that the materialist accounts of gender construction, through focusing on practices generating social divisions, had failed to accommodate gender *as an aspect of subjectivity*. What had not been explained was how gender as an aspect of self-understanding was produced or how this subjective understanding intersected with the structural gender divisions which the materialist feminists had accentuated. The debate motivating the shift from things to words is linked to the way gender as a category is conceptualized. There are those who use gender as simply a sociological variable, like other categories of stratification. Here there is a tendency to formulate gender as a stable and fixed category framed by the specific historical context. A shift to recognizing gender as a structure of subjectivity, which can vary greatly in different social locations, means that gendering can be seen as a *process* rather than as a 'role'. To this process of gendering the role of culture and language is central. The emphasis on process shifts attention to exploration of how meaning is constantly being reproduced and negotiated, and can have unexpected and contradictory effects. This provides a framework for understanding social change and the way in which individuals, through this process of negotiation with meaning, are constituting their world.

As we mentioned above the concern with the domain of gendered meanings can be addressed by use of the Marxist category of ideology. Ideologies are sets of ideas which reflect the interests of those members of society who are dominant economically. They are then adopted by other groups to form a framework of meanings guiding their actions, though this framework of meaning is often in conflict with their *own* interests. Such a use of the concept of ideology was, however, found problematic on several counts. Although it gave an account of the conditions under which certain ideas became dominant socially, linking them to the operation of social power (an important point we will return to below), the dominant ideology thesis suggested that ideologies formed much too coherent and systematic a set of ideas, which were then simply imposed on society as whole. This made it difficult to explain shifts and changes in ideologies. How, for instance, can the notion of an ideology of masculinity explain many different masculinities rather than masculinity in the singular? This difficulty is linked to another. The theory of ideology requires that dominant ideas be linked to economic structures in a way that seems difficult to achieve, and which all the difficulties attending Marxist feminism highlighted.

Things are much messier than such a picture would suggest. Many conflicting and contradictory ways of understanding the world are current at any one time, even within one person. Moreover the theory conceives of ideologies acting on people rather than people acting on ideologies. The human subject is passive rather than active in this framework. The use of the term ideology did not account for the ways in which ideas served to constitute people's subjectivity, their own understanding of themselves. It rather positioned them as passive dupes, internalizing conceptualizations which did not make proper sense of their worlds or serve their interests. To avoid these problems it was necessary to make use of the concept of discourse, the most influential version of which has derived from the work of Michel Foucault.[1]

Subjectivity and Subjectification

The writings of disabled writers, black and postcolonial feminists and writers from sexual minorities provokes a crisis in the understanding of the categories 'woman' and 'man'. What it means to be a 'woman' or a 'man' varies according to other differentiating features of positionality, historical time, class, ethnicity and bodily abilities. This crisis has led many feminist theorists to see the importance of what has been termed *postmodernist* forms of theorizing. Although it is impossible to generalize across very different thinkers, there are some common elements within postmodernist thought which have come to be of crucial importance here (Nicholson 1990; Weedon 1987). One of these is the insistence on the mediated nature of our relation to the world. Our understanding of the world is mediated through the ideas, concepts, etc., by means of which we make sense of it. 'Man' and 'woman' are not just labels for kinds of things already ordered independently of us. What counts as a man or woman will depend on the meanings we give to these terms. This recognition is linked to another, namely that the meanings we give are never fixed and closed. They can vary according to context and over time. They are open to contest and debate. As we noted in the Introduction to this book, the categories 'man' and 'woman' can be seen as both empty of and overflowing with meaning (Scott 1988).

The recognition of differences within the categories 'woman' and 'man' also echoes complexities and contradictions within individual subjects. Many narratives of women's lives make evident the complexities and contradictions and changes which individual subjects undergo, as well as the multiple strands which interweave to make up individual identities. This finds echoes in postmodernist theories which are rejecting notions of a coherent unified self, capable of rational reflection and agency, in favour of a model of a self which is fragmented, constantly in a process of formation, constituting itself out of its own self-understandings. The theorizing of gender in response to these strands of thought comes to emphasize the process whereby subjects *become gendered* as a process in which subjectivities form in relation to the meanings that people have available to them. This process is an open one, susceptible to change and development, never without contradictions. In this the process of becoming gendered cannot be separated from other aspects of becoming.

For Foucault discourses are anything which can carry meaning. Language, images, stories, scientific narratives and cultural products are all discourses. But discourses are also things we do. Social practices like segregating work, giving away the bride in marriage, and so on, also carry meaning. Crucially for Foucault discourses are not reflections of an already ordered reality; instead they are that with which reality becomes ordered. They are the means by which differences, for example between people, become produced. Discourses present themselves as *knowledges of an independent reality*, but are rather productive of the way that reality becomes viewed by us. To use one of his most famous examples, it is through our discourses of sexuality that the distinction between heterosexual and homosexual people is made. Foucault suggests that the category 'homosexual' did not emerge as a category of person until about the seventeenth century. There were at different times a variety of sexual practices but practising them did not mark categories of people. A merchant, for example, might sleep with his wife and his boy apprentice, in exercising both his power and his status, but neither act giving him a sexual identity. Once the category 'homosexual' is available, however, it provides a discourse in terms of which people can constitute their subjectivity. For Foucault discourses are *normative*. They carry with them norms for behaviour, standards of what counts as desirable and undesirable, proper and improper. With the categories 'homosexual' and 'heterosexual' come the standards of what counts as normal sexuality, and what is deviant. These are linked to other discourses concerning what constitutes a family, the position of men and women within it and the appropriate sexual behaviour for men and women.

Within this account the emergence of subjectivity is a process of subjectification. The subjectification concerned is the making of ourselves by becoming subject to the norms which are implicit in the discourses which provide our self-understandings. We mould our bodies and bend our behaviour in accordance with the 'men', 'women', 'gay' or 'straight', 'Irish' or 'Jamaican', 'able' or 'disabled', people we take ourselves to be – but are, in fact, turning ourselves into.

There are two crucial aspects of discourses for Foucault. One is that they are historically variable. Much of his work is concerned with providing *genealogies* of particular discourses, in other words looking at the historical circumstances in which they emerge. So, for example, in *The History of Sexuality* (Foucault 1978), he looks at the variety of discourses of sexuality which there have been in the West. In volume 1 he pays particular attention to the nineteenth-century discourses ('knowledges') surrounding sexuality, which led to an apparent 'natural' link between sexuality and reproduction. The discourses he draws particular attention to are: the 'hysterization of women's bodies', whereby women's bodies became viewed as thoroughly sexualized, and if not used for reproduction liable to lapse into hysterical symptoms; the 'pedagogization of children's sex', whereby children's masturbation was regarded as 'unnatural' and to be stopped; the socialization of the heterosexual couple as the appropriate reproductive unit; and 'the psychiatrization of perverse pleasures', where the failure to channel the 'natural' sex instinct into reproductive channels was seen to lead to psychiatric disturbance. This example also illustrates the second crucial feature of his account: the link between discourses and power. Discourses are tied up with power and serve to reinforce or undermine relations of power between people. The emergence of certain kinds of discourses of sexuality is interdependent with the social power exercised by medical, judicial and religious communities. Those who are labelled hysterical, perverse or insane are having power exercised over them. Power over sexuality is exercised through the complex discourses in terms of which people come to think about it. The primary task of Foucault's genealogies is to uncover the operation of power within the discursive practices to which he pays attention.

It is important to draw a distinction here, however, between Foucault's concept of power and that of the materialist writers we have been considering above. Foucault is not concerned with the power exercised by large social structures such as capitalism or patriarchy. Rather the power to which he pays attention, micro-power, is pervasive and operates through all relations in society. It is manifested in our everyday interactions and practices. When a woman asks a man to reverse her car into a difficult parking space she is participating in a discourse in which men are constructed as more technical and powerful than women. Although Foucault sees the relations of power among the most powerful groups in society as being constituted through discourses, discourses are none the less not monolithic. First, there are always many and contradictory discourses about different subject matters, which are linked with power in different ways. Alongside discourses of women as passive and technophobic are emerging images of women as assertive, competent and in control of technology. (Attention to advertisements will reveal these conflicting discourses of femininity and many more.) For Foucault, wherever power is exercised, a resistant discourse emerges which is empowering for different groups of people. Moreover, discourses can vary in meaning according to the context and can even be used in reverse ways in different situations. In Foucault's words, 'discourse transmits and produces power; it reinforces it, but also undermines and exposes it, renders it fragile and makes it possible to thwart it' (1978: 101). So, as Lois McNay points out, in the nineteenth century 'the massive proliferation of discourses on "deviant" sexualities served to reinforce . . . a notion of "normal" heterosexuality. Yet . . . this very multiplicity . . . created a "reverse discourse". . . used by those labelled deviant to establish their own identity' (McNay 1992: 39).

There are clearly similarities in the way in which Foucault used the notion of discourse and the way in which Marxist and other materialist writers used the notion of ideology (see the discussion above). In both cases there is an attempt to link aspects of subjectivity to the operation of power. Ideologies are internalized and become part of the means whereby subordinate groups articulate their own subjectivity. There are, however, important differences in the uses of the terms. First, within many uses of the concept of ideology which owe a debt to Marxism, ideologies are viewed as distortions, imposed on the society as a whole by dominant groups who thereby maintain their control. The ideologies work by becoming internalized by the oppressed groups. ('I'm unemployed because there is something wrong with me.') The role of revolutionary movements is, then, to reveal these distortions and produce a better, truer, picture of the social order. This then provides a means of dismantling the structures which were legitimated by the ideologies concerned. In this picture ideologies are a consequence of the structural (capitalist or patriarchal) ordering of the society which they also help to maintain. For Foucault, however, the implicit contrast between ideologies and truths which this account requires is not one which can be maintained. All we have access to are discourses which are tied up with power. We can oppose a discourse only with another discourse which is linked to power in a different way. We cannot adjudicate on questions of truth outside the norms of particular ways of thinking. Secondly, for Foucault, discourses are not imposed from outside already formed subjects and then internalized. Rather subjects become formed out of the discourses in terms of which they come to understand themselves. This is not a voluntary process, for we are not formed by making choices of what to be. But it is not determined either. There is a multiplicity of discourses and an openness in the process of subject formation which makes the outcomes in many ways unpredictable. This explains why we are not, in materialist terms, simply dupes to ideology.

Foucault and Feminism

Despite the fact that Foucault, in his writings, paid little attention to the construction of gendered subjectivities, many feminists engaged in that task have adopted much of his account of the discursive construction of the self. There is much to find attractive in such an account. It gives a role to subjects in the making of themselves as gendered, via the appropriation of discourse. This making is not that of a voluntary choice, but neither is it completely determined. There is a multiplicity of discourses at issue and a contingency of outcome. Moreover the making is a continual process and susceptible to modification and change. The discourses of femininity in which we might currently constitute ourselves as female may be different from those of our early teens which preceded awareness of feminism. 'In this view of the self, the relationship between the individual and society is not pictured as one of social determination– complete socialization. Socialization, rather, emerges as a project that is never fully realized in practice' (Sawicki 1988: 184). The discursive account consequently rejects an origin for gender differences in nature, and thereby refuses to view them as a given which cannot be modified. It also, in contrast to psychoanalytic accounts, does not see our identities as fixed by events in early infancy, but rather as processes which are constantly being renegotiated and changed. There are clearly some similarities between Foucault and the writings of Lacan and ensuing sexual difference theorists, which we discussed in chapter 2 and shall return to in chapter 8. For Lacan we become gendered selves through entry into the symbolic order which serves to define what it is to be a male or female subject. For Lacan, however, the symbolic order appears to have an irretrievably binary structure, with the only female position articulated in terms of lack. For Foucault there are a multiplicity of discourses. His framework therefore enables us to make sense of the varieties of masculinities and femininities which we can find articulated even within a single culture: hysterical woman, woman governed by hormones, superwoman, mother, whore, feminist woman, butch dyke, strong black woman, rational man, repressed man, violent and dominating bully, gentle father, caring son, new man, queen, real gentleman. Each of these formulations is tied up with norms and thereby power in different ways.

The discursive account also allows a recognition that gender becomes inter-articulated with other aspects of our subjectivities: Irish
woman, disabled man, working-class grammar school girl, Asian
wife, professional man, anti-racist activist. In the negotiation of these
complex discourses no special privilege will be given to gender identity, and the different aspects of subjectivity become constituted not
as a series of additions, but each in relation to the other. As a consequence gender loses the foundational place which psychoanalytic
theory gave it. Gender is part of an identity woven from a complex
and specific social whole, and requiring very specific and local readings. Anne McClintock (1995) makes the point in the following way:
'race, gender and class are not distinct realms of experience, existing
in splendid isolation from each other, nor can they be yoked together
retrospectively like armatures of Lego. Rather they come into existence *in and through* relation to each other – if in contradictory and
conflictual ways. In this sense, gender, race and class can be called
articulated categories' (pp. 4–5). The example which McClintock
uses is the way in which, in the latter half of the nineteenth century,
'the analogy between race and gender degeneration' was put to the
service of justifying empire, legitimating patriarchal marriage and
bourgeois control of capital. 'In the metropolis . . . the militant working class, Irish, Jews, feminist groups, gays and lesbians, prostitutes
. . . were collectively figured as racial deviants, atavistic throwbacks
to a primitive moment in human prehistory. . . . In the colonies,
black people were figured . . . as gender deviants, the embodiment
of . . . promiscuity and excess, "feminised" by their lack of history
and lack of reason' (pp. 43–4).

Attention to the workings of discourse also reveals how differences between women were constructed and put to the service of
imperialist projects. In the Victorian period white women were the
symbol of the higher moral and civil standards of Western civilization, justifying colonial expansion (Ware 1992). Eastern women of
the period are presented as exotic, promising excessive sexual delights;
or as victims of uncivilized practices (such as sati) from which they
need rescuing by their white colonizers, male and female. Writers
such as Chandra Mohanty have argued that the response of many
contemporary Western feminists to the question of difference has
resulted in parallel processes of construction. The emergence of the
concept of 'Third World women' has the effect of constructing a
homogenized 'other' to the subject position of Western women. The

representation of such women as 'ignorant, poor, uneducated, tradition bound, domesticated and victimized' allows a contrasting conception of Western women as 'educated, modern, having control
over their bodies and sexualities and the freedom to make their own
decisions' (Mohanty 1988: 200). This is a point which Spivak reinforces in her remark: 'when a cultural identity is thrust upon one
because the centre wants an identifiable margin, claims for marginal-
ity assure validation from the centre' (Spivak 1993: 55).

Many writers welcomed not just the shift from biological and
psychological determinisms and universalisms which Foucault's framework seemed to offer. They also welcomed the possibility of understanding gender difference outside the apparent determinism of the
economic or patriarchal structures to which we paid attention earlier
in the chapter. Here there is appreciation of the contribution made by
Foucault's concept of power to understanding the diffuse and specific
operations of masculinist power and the arenas in which it required
resistance. So Biddy Martin:

> What is crucial is the capacity to shift the terms of the struggle. . . .
> What Leftists have criticised in the women's movement as fragmenta-
> tion, lack of organisation, absence of a coherent and encompassing
> theory . . . may well represent fundamentally more radical and effective
> responses to the deployment of power in our society than the cent-
> ralization and abstraction that continues to plague Leftist thinking.
> (Martin 1988: 10)

Here what is being welcomed is a different conception of the sites of
political agency and resistance, outside the model of revolutionary
organizations taking on large-scale institutional structures of power.

Feminists also found theoretically illuminating the *disciplinary*
aspects of Foucault's accounts. To become a subject is, for Foucault,
to become subjected to certain norms, and such subjectification is a
process by which subjects make themselves by disciplining their body
and behaviour in accordance with the norms implicit in the discourses
in terms of which their subjectivity is constituted (see chapter 7). This
has been used to make sense particularly of women's and increasingly
men's attempts and failures to produce their bodies; in accordance
with the local norms of desirable masculinity and femininity. While
such uses take up the repressive aspects of Foucault's account, others
have emphasized the, often interrelated, *productive* aspects of discourse.
Discourses are productive of pleasures. In coming to view ourselves

as girls or boys we also become initiated into certain kinds of pleasure; combing the hair of our Little Ponies, watching football on television, enjoying exchanging insults with our friends.

None the less there have been a number of reservations expressed by other feminist writers about adopting a Foucauldian framework as the basis for a social constructionist account of gender. Some of these objections simply highlight Foucault's own lack of attention to gender, together with a lack of attention to imperialism and constructions of race. For other writers the problems with Foucault's account lay in its neglect of just those material factors discussed earlier on in our chapter.

Materialist Returns

Although it is often suggested (see above), it is misleading to set up a polarity between discursive accounts of gender formation and the explicitly materialist ones on the grounds that the latter are concerned with 'things' and the former only with 'words'. Foucault's discourses were not only words, but concrete practices by means of which people produced themselves and their bodies. Moreover he conceived of discourses as present in society, having effects on how people acted, what kinds of behaviours and structures became conceivable and were therefore able to be produced. His genealogies, anchoring the emergence of discourses in specific historical circumstances, also appear to recognize, not only that how we conceptualize affects the shape of the social, but also that the shape of the social affects how we conceptualize. For some contemporary materialist feminists, however, who want to make use of the insights of discursive accounts of subjectivity, we need a more robust materialism to withstand some of the dangers which such an account leads us towards.

Rosemary Hennessy, for example, argues for a position which she terms resistance postmodernism (Hennessy 1993). The aim of this is to adopt many of the insights which the discursive account of the production of subjectivities offers us, but to add to them further materialist elements which she sees as essential if we are to be able to develop effective political agency. Here Hennessy takes issue with Foucault's account of power purely as micro-power, which becomes evident in the unpacking of discourses in specific and local settings.

This account of power, she argues, makes it impossible to view power as exploitation. Hennessy claims that Foucault's exclusive attention to micro-power renders invisible 'systemic hierarchies', in relation to which it is possible to see, both within and across societies, that, for example, disabled people, the working class, or women or sexual minorities or black people are oppressed. These systemic or structural hierarchies are the same systems to which earlier materialist feminists were paying such detailed attention. This point links with another: that Foucault fails to pay attention to global connections. Hennessy argues that the economic and imperialist links between different parts of the globe are directly linked to the local and regional social features which form the background of Foucault's genealogies:

> a global social logic makes . . . sense of the ways capitalist imperialism binds the very different patriarchal oppression of 'first' and 'third' world women in exploitative relations of consumption and production . . . conceptualising the social in terms of a systemic logic rather than a local or contingent one implies that transformative change cannot happen within a single institution or social formation. (1993: 31)

The insistence on looking at a 'global social logic' to explain the way in which relations of both gender and race are constructed is reiterated in the writing of many black writers. Patricia Williams urges us to pay attention to 'the realities of a world in which national boundaries figure less in our fortunes than do the configurations of multinational corporations' (James and Busia 1993: 118). M. Jacqui Alexander and Chandra Mohanty point out that the international division of labour is central to the production of people, including the production of people as gendered subjects, differently in different parts of the world (1997: 5). Heidi Safia Mirza also insists on attention to materiality at the local as well as the global level: 'Black women remain preoccupied with their struggle against low pay, ill health and incarceration, and for access to care, welfare and education' (1997: 14). Many writers on disability also emphasize the centrality of material factors in constituting what counts as a disabled body. For these writers disability is constituted by a 'lack of fit' between body and environment in a way that inhibits agency.

The material relations which feature in these accounts are, however, mediated by discourses. These discourses differentially construct the gendered subjects linked, for example, by economic exchange. Sarah Ahmed discusses Body Shop advertisements which serve both to anchor African women in nature and tradition and to construct Western female consumers as saviours of their sisters in the Third World (2000: 169). Hennessy argues that we need to view such discourses as ideologies. She sees a crucial part of political activism to be to critique discourses which support structural inequalities and to argue for the legitimacy of those which promote political transformation. By accepting that ideologies are tied up with power, she recognizes that what is at issue is competing ideologies. However, in this contest we must argue for those which are tied to emancipatory goals. Here she wishes to reject many of the commitments which the term ideology has carried, to give up any suggestion that ideologies are *merely* superstructural, merely the effect of fundamental economic structures on the arena of consciousness and ideas.

For her, arguing that discourses are ideologies enables us to examine the way that they are both determined and determining. Discourses themselves have *material effects* in the world. They have an influence on actions, social structures, and political and judicial decisions. Discourses are also *a product* of particular economic and political conditions. Effective intervention requires us to pay attention to the two-way causal link between discourses and non-discursive social structures. This necessitates uncovering the social conditions of possibility of certain discourses which themselves make possible certain forms of subjectivity. We need to explain 'the relation between economic forces – like the formation of new markets through colonization, shifting centres of production, or the development of new technologies – and the reformation of subjectivities' (Hennessy 1993: 25). It is such changes which she thinks make possible the discourses of Western femininity in contrast to the 'otherness' of non-Western women which emerged in times of colonial expansion. These changes are also linked to the dominant discourses of heterosexuality and the reproductive family which Foucault described as emerging in the nineteenth century. Others (Jackson 1995) have pointed to links between changing discourses of women and domesticity as the labour needs of the capitalist market change. It is also the case that the causal links go the other way. The discourses make possible colonial expansion and economic changes. In unpacking these entanglements of discursive and non-discursive factors, Hennessy argues that without attention to such causality we 'cannot explain the relationship between events like acts of violence against women, the feminization of poverty and denigrating representations of femininity' (1993: 25). The need for such attention is highlighted, for her, in the claim that discourses are ideologies.

Hennessy argues that Foucault cannot pay attention to such links because of his refusal of notions of causality and insistence on the *logic of contingency*. What this means is that, for Foucault, we cannot make general causal claims. The outcome of particular sets of factors remains unpredictable. Despite his genealogical method which explicitly pays attention to the historical conditions surrounding the emergence of particular discourses, he refuses claims of direct causation. The conditions he signals are local and moreover the relations between the discursive and non-discursive remain contingent and not determining. But without knowledge of causal links, Hennessy argues, we could not plan for effective agency and intervention. Hennessy relates this point to the difficulty in Foucault's account of explaining the emergence of resistance discourses. Wherever there is power there is resistance, Foucault claims. But he does not explain where resistance comes from and in what conditions it emerges. But it is just this, Hennessy implies, that we need to theorize if we are to seek transformations in relations of power.

There clearly are critical differences here between Foucault and Hennessy (and other materialist feminists who make similar arguments: Jackson 1995; Ebert 1996). How far are we required to make choices between them? On the issue of power there are indications that Foucault recognized structural power but it was simply not power of this sort that he was analysing. He also signalled a recognition of the links between the global and the local, although again this is something that was not the focus of his attention.

> I believe that the manner in which the phenomena, the techniques and procedures of power enter into play at the most basic levels must be analysed . . . but above all what must be shown is the manner in which they are invested and annexed by more global phenomena and the subtle fashion in which more general powers or economic interests are able to engage with these technologies. (Gordon 1980: 99)

The difference over attention paid to systematic power relations is linked to another in relation to political agency. As we noted above, Biddy Martin has welcomed the recognition, which use of Foucault's

work enabled, that masculinist power works in diffuse ways and
thereby requires reverse discourses in a number of quite heterogeneous situations. This led to a reconceptualization of the domains and
arenas for political agency. Hennessy seems to be returning us to
models of collective political agency where large-scale political groupings aim to tackle global structural inequalities. The debates between
these two models of political agency is one to which we shall return
in chapter 10.

For the kind of agency which Hennessy commends we need
general and overarching theories of the workings of patriarchy or capitalism. The insistence on the local and the regional found in Foucault
does not rule out the tracing of *particular* connections, for example
between the bunches of flowers with which we nurture our relationships and the life of the Colombian woman producing them. What
he does throw into doubt are general causal theories of how this
works. This connects to the whole issue of the tracing of causal links
between the discursive and the non-discursive, which for Hennessy
is essential. Foucault does not think all reality is discursive, though
of course any attempt we make to understand it is in discourse.
Moreover his genealogies, as we noted above, point to the anchorage
of discourses in particular social arrangements. What he resists,
however, is the two-way determinism which Hennessy's picture
suggests. Instead what emerges is a sense of the contingency of the
process. For Foucault there is no strict causality in either direction
here. The emergence of discourses takes place in specific complex
circumstances. We can never attribute them to single sources which
could be repeated in other circumstances. Similarly the consequences
of any discourse are unpredictable: they can vary in different situations.
It can be interpreted and read differently. It cannot be systematized
under general regularities. Hence Foucault's insistence on the contingent and the local. Consequently the kind of links which for
Hennessy it is urgent to have, linking, for example, denigrating images
of women to violence, poverty, and so on, are not ones which we
should, in Foucault's terms, expect to have. We cannot generalize
about the meanings or effects of images. The reading of these images
will be different, as will their use, in different circumstances. This
explains the controversies within feminism over pornography, and
the difficulties of attempting to address concerns by means of legislation (A. M. Jaggar 1995). To be able to legislate we need to be able
to generalize about both meanings and effects. However, Foucault's

refusal to make causal claims leads to frustration for those who wish to plan for large-scale social change. We shall return to these issues in chapter 4, when we turn to the work of Judith Butler, and again in chapter 10.

Summary

In this chapter we have provided an overview of social constructionist accounts of gender. We have discussed two main accounts. The first lays emphasis on gender and other aspects of our identity as constructed by our positioning within social institutions and structures: paid work, marriage and family, the legal system, international capitalism. The second account pays attention to gender as produced by our subjection to discourses. Despite the tensions between them, both aspects seem required if we are to explain gendered positionality as an aspect both of social organization and, interconnectedly, of individual subjectivities.

What has become clear from attention to difference is not a privileging of discursive or material accounts but the necessary interweaving of both. What becomes problematic, however, are any universal theories of the workings of patriarchy or capitalism. Rather we need to trace the interwoven material and discursive elements in particular contexts.

Judith Butler:
'The Queen of Queer'

In contemporary gender theory the work of Judith Butler has come to occupy a central position. Butler developed what has been termed a performative theory of gender, forming the limit of social constructionist accounts. This became widely discussed with the publication of *Gender Trouble* in 1990 and has been developed in her work since (Butler 1993, 1997a, 1997b). Here we will be primarily considering the account put forward in *Gender Trouble*. Later works will be discussed in chapters 7 and 8. On the cover of *Gender Trouble* is an old photograph of two children dressed in fancy frocks, dating from the beginning of the century. We are immediately troubled because despite the frocks we cannot decide whether the children are boys or girls. The face and hair of one of them in particular looks like a young Robert Redford. Turning to the back cover for the acknowledgement we learn that they both have girls' names, and our trouble begins to subside. Here before we start reading we get an insight into Butler's strategy. She wishes to destabilize and denaturalize our binary gender categories. She rejects any view that gender differences have an origin in our biological or psychic natures, arguing instead that they are effects of contingent social practices. This opens up the possibility that they could be remade in different ways. (For earlier work imagining a world without strict gender boundaries see Haraway 1991b: 150.)

Queering

The year 1990, when *Gender Trouble* was published, was the year that Queer Nation came particularly to public attention in the United States. Groups like Queer Nation and Act Up (the Aids Coalition to Unleash Power) engaged in a public and theatrical challenge to gender norms. Such groups were dissatisfied with the kind of identity politics associated with the gay, and feminist movements. Queer Nation embraced many communities of sexual dissidents and those refusing to identify themselves by any of the available labels. They reappropriated the term 'queer' as the banner under which such *dishomogeneity* and *differences* could be claimed.

The term 'queer' was/is a hate word in everyday speech. It was/is used as a derogatory term for homosexual people. Its contemporary use within political activism and consequently academic theory is therefore a conscious reclaiming and resignification of the term to put it to use in a positive and productive way. Within the norms which govern our everyday notions of femininity and masculinity, heterosexuality occupies pride of place (see chapter 6). So, first, the public visibility of gay and lesbian desire serves to undermine the supposed naturalness of heterosexual gender. For those activists that reappropriated the concept 'queer', however, more was required than to make visible same-sex desire. There were strands of thinking about sexuality and identity within parts of the gay and lesbian movement which were themselves problematic. One such strand (compare LeVay in chapter 1) was to suggest that homosexuality was itself a natural category, given with biology and therefore deserving of the political recognition and respect attaching to heterosexuality. Another problematic strand of thinking was found in parts of the lesbian community, who in response to a psychoanalytic tendency to identify lesbians as mannish women, were insisting on women loving women as a key manifestation of feminism, a celebration of what it was to be a woman. However, such a view could often render invisible experiences within other parts of the lesbian community, for example of those who adopted butch/femme identifications and roles within erotic encounters. This was an invisibility which was also marked in class and race terms, political lesbianism being predominantly white and middle class (see the discussion in chapter 5). For those activists who have reappropriated the term 'queer', both naturalizing accounts of homosexuality and overtly feminist identifications within the lesbian movement excluded the experiences of large numbers of people who equally failed to fit within the dominant norms of heterosexuality. They therefore argue for the breaking down of both sexual and gender categories, the maintenance of which creates boundaries which need to be policed. The debates within the women's movement concerning whether transsexual women were really women (see chapter 9) and within gay and lesbian conferences concerning whether bisexual people were gay or straight were examples of such policing in operation. Queer politics therefore works to visibly challenge norms, to show their lack of naturalness and inevitability and to celebrate transgressions from them. This can take the form of ostentatious displays of same-sex desire, or juxtapositions of supposedly distinct masculine and feminine characteristics (macho men in tutus). The goal is to open up possibilities which our dominant discourses on sex and gender foreclose and which have also been missing from a gay and lesbian movement concerned to delimit its boundaries.

In exploring the academic theory which such queer activism has spawned it is important to maintain the link to anti-homophobic analysis, insisting on the variability of desire, such that there is no necessary line-up between bodily shape gender identification, and sexual desires and practices. A link to anti-homophobic practice enables us to recognize the central place that is played within our current gender binaries of what Butler and others call the 'heterosexual matrix', in which 'proper' men and 'proper' women are heterosexual. Butler has been termed the *queen of queer* theory for providing an account of the construction of gendered subjectivities and gendered social practices which places heterosexism at its centre but, crucially, refuses determinism. Our subjectivities are constructed out of social practices but are not reducible to them. There is always room for change and modification. Butler thereby provides the theoretical space for the emergence of queer desire and just the kind of destabilizing and resignifying of our categories which queer activists have been pursuing.

Sex and Gender in Butler

Butler comments on the radical potential in Simone de Beauvoir's suggestion that 'one is not born a woman, but, rather becomes one.'

If we accept that such a becoming is a social process, which is not dictated by bodily sex, then there is nothing to guarantee that the body of the one who becomes woman will necessarily be what is normally conceived of as a female body. Butler's goal here is to show as illusory the apparent essential unity of biological sex, gender identification and heterosexuality. This is a unity which some have seen as dictated by nature (see chapter 1). If we can show that such a unity is illusory, what she often calls phantasmatic, then the path is cleared for reconfigurations of each of the terms.

In refusing to accept that gender or sexuality is dictated by biological sex, however, Butler is not simply helping herself to the pervasive sex/gender distinction. She no more accepts sex as a natural category than gender itself (see our discussion in chapter 1). 'There is no recourse to a body that has not already been interpreted by cultural meanings, hence sex could not qualify as a prediscursive anatomical facticity' (1990a: 8). Our understanding of material, anatomical differences is mediated through our cultural frame of meaning. Rather than gender following from biology, for Butler, our gender norms are seen as structuring biology. We view biological factors as requiring a binary division into two sexes, male and female, because of a socially constructed gender to which *heterosexuality* is central. Heterosexuality, of course, requires a binary difference into male and female. For Butler, then, it is the 'epistemic regime of presumptive heterosexuality' (1990a: viii) which drives our division into male and female, and which itself structures our understanding of biology.

Performance and Performativity

Butler's first task is to explain how gender is socially constructed such that it takes on the appearance of being something natural, something given with our anatomy. Drawing on the work of Monique Wittig (see chapter 3), Butler accepts that a binary restriction on sex serves the reproductive aims of a system of compulsory heterosexuality. Wittig, as we saw earlier, places emphasis on the material institutions within a social order, which serve to construct gender differences by institutionalizing heterosexuality and the patriarchal family. She suggests that practices such as lesbianism which contest these institutions are a way of stepping outside the markers 'male' and 'female'. Butler, although contesting Wittig's positioning of the 'lesbian' as a new concept 'beyond the categories of sex' (Wittig 1981: 53), sees the heterosexual material pratices to which Wittig draws our attention as *productive of the meaning* of what it is to be gendered within cultures which adopt them. She therefore pays attention to such productivity of meaning rather than their concrete material consequences.

Butler takes from Foucault the notion that discourses are productive of the identities which they appear to be merely representing. When a baby is born and the midwife says 'It's a girl', she is not reporting an already determinate state of affairs but taking part in a practice which itself constitutes that state of affairs. It is by a repetition of numerous acts of this kind that what it is to be male or female in our society is formed. Butler's notion of gender as performative echoes discussions in the philosophy of language which argue that the making of promises, or saying 'I will' in the marriage ceremony, are actions in which the uttering of the words is itself a deed which constitutes the phenomenon. The deeds or performances which serve to consti- tute our identities as gendered subjects, however, go beyond simply the utterances of words. They range across the whole gamut of beha- viours, decisions, desires and 'corporeal styles' which we associate with being male or female (playing with dolls, curling up in bed with cuddly toys, reading pony books, immersion in car magazines, cooking meals, going to the pub with the lads). Here is an example of someone performing both gender and class. A smartly dressed woman emerging out of a university council meeting gets into an expensive car and drops her earring beside the gear-stick. She calls to one of the porters (male) who are in attendance, to come to her assistance. He manoeuvres the gear lever until he can reach the earring and returns it to her. Butler's claim here would be that our class and gender categories both make possible such acts and are constituted by them.

What counts as a performance of masculinity or femininity is highly contextual and varies according to social context over time, cross- culturally, and for one person throughout the course of their lives. The performance of gender is interdependent with the performance of other aspects of our identity, as the above example makes clear. Making ourselves as a good Irish Catholic mother would require something different from making ourselves as a successful and sexu- ally desirable TV presenter. Our gendered identities are formed from the performances of ourselves and others towards us. The effect of the range of gendered performance is to make it appear that there are two distinct natures, male and female. What we take to be 'nature' is therefore an effect rather than a cause of our gendered acts.

The notion of a performance here can suggest an actor on a stage, but Butler's notion is crucially different from this. Talking about gender as a performance can suggest an agent or subject who is formed prior to the acts and who then engages in them, maybe choosing which acts to perform. Butler is at pains to resist such a construal. There is, she argues, no doer behind the deed. The doer becomes formed from the doing. Her account, as is Foucault's, is an account of the formation of subjectivity. We become subjects from our performances and the performances of others towards us. The gendered performances in which we engage are performances in accordance with a *script*. Here Butler can be seen to be engaging with the ideas of Lacan, for the script which we attempt to enact is very like the Law which forms the contours of Lacan's symbolic order. It provides us with ideals of masculinity and femininity which render certain behaviour appropriate and others not. As with Lacan these ideals are phantasmatic, unachievable, but they are, none the less, the reference point in relation to which we act. Unlike Lacan and like Foucault, however, Butler argues that the scripts can be variable and can change over time. In this she shares Foucault's position, seeing the construction of subjectivity as a process of submitting ourselves to socially constituted norms and practices.

For Butler, gendered performances are tied up with relations of power. They embody norms of behaviour which subjects aspire to even if they remain an ideal which is not achieved. Butler shares with Foucault a conception of power which is all-pervasive, present in our everyday interactions as well as in institutional frameworks. Although there are a variety of ways in which gender can be performed, there remain certain *dominant* ideals which reinforce the power of certain groups, e.g. men, heterosexuals, over others. These others are treated socially as outsiders, 'the abject', and subject to social punishments. There are, however, crucial differences between Butler and Lacan in the way in which they see the 'Law', meaning the symbolic order, or domain of meaning, working. For Lacan the Law, which is patriarchal, provides us with the only means of intelligibility. What is outside becomes repressed, operative only at the unconscious level, available only symptomatically when it erupts to interrupt the coherence of our ego formation (see chapter 2). To attempt to think outside the Law is to return to the unintelligible, the disordered and the psychotic. For Butler the Law is not totalizing but hegemonic or dominant. What for Lacan is 'unthinkable' is for Butler unthinkable within dominant culture. The patriarchal and thereby heterosexist ways of understanding the world which are dominant, for Butler, requires possibilities which are constructed as marginal or outside – possibilities which are socially forbidden. But in forbidding these alternatives the Law none the less makes them thinkable, so that our conceptual structure includes more than the Lacanian structure suggests. It is from these marginal positions that disruption and destabilization of the dominant norms becomes possible. The examples which Butler draws on here reflect those of Foucault. The nineteenth-century discourses on sexuality, insisting on the deviancy of a range of sexual practices, brought these practices into view, made them thinkable. The debates over Section 28 in Britain have had a similar outcome. In banning the promotion of homosexual families Section 28 makes thinkable and visible the possibility of such family forms. For Butler the compulsory order of heterosexuality requires the exclusion of homosexuality, a possibility which it none the less requires to make its own directive intelligible:

> the bisexuality that is said to be 'outside' the Symbolic and that serves as the locus of subversion, is, in fact, a construction within the terms of that constitutive discourse . . . a concrete cultural possibility that is refused and redescribed as impossible. . . . Not to have social recognition as an effective heterosexual is to lose one possible social identity and possibly to gain one that is radically less sanctioned. The 'unthinkable' is thus fully within culture but excluded from *dominant* culture. (1990a: 77)

Failure to conform to the Law in the Lacanian picture is to become psychotic, to become unthinkable. In Butler's view such failure instead invokes social rather than intellectual sanctions, social punishments and exclusions.

The Performativity of Desire

Butler shares with Foucault the view that power is not only prohibitive but also enabling. Without such performativity we would have no way of becoming subjects, no way of exercising agency, no way of finding some activities desirable and others not. For desire itself is not prior, something moving us to act and choose our identities. As with Foucault, for Butler, our desires are also performatively constituted:

> pleasures are said to reside in the penis, the vagina and the breasts . . . but . . . some parts of the body become conceivable foci of pleasure precisely because they correspond to a normative ideal of a gender specific body. . . . Which pleasures shall live and which shall die is often a matter of which serve the legitimating practices of identity formation that take place within the matrix of gender norms. (1990a: 70)

Here, of course, the socially dominant performances are those of heterosexual desire.

We saw in the work of Lacan that a link had been made between the supposedly private inner identity of the subject and the public world of culture. On the Lacanian model, subject formation requires an internalization of this public order and a repression of what fails to conform to it. Butler takes this process further, rejecting the notion of repression:

> words, acts, gestures and desire produce the effect of an inner core or substance, but produce this on the surface of the body. . . . if . . . reality is fabricated as an interior essence that very interiority is an effect and function of a decidedly public and social discourse. . . . In other words acts, gestures articulated and enacted desires create the illusion of an interior and organizing gender core. (1990a: 136)

There is no inner realm of experience prior to the social, providing us with desires and moulding our identities. Our 'inner' life becomes constituted from the way we mould our bodies to social norms.

Real Genders

The actor on the stage requires us to make a distinction between what is performed and what is real. For Butler there is no such distinction. The performance constitutes the real: 'Gender is a kind of persistent impersonation that passes as the real' (1990a: viii). This discussion of the 'realness' of gender is taken further in her study of Jenny Livingston's film *Paris is Burning* (Livingston 1990). This film was a documentary about drag balls in New York City, attended by primarily Latino and some African American 'men'.

> the balls are contests in which the contestants compete under a variety of categories. The categories include a variety of social norms, many of which are established in white culture as signs of class, like the 'executive' and the Ivy League student; some of which are marked as feminine, ranging from high drag to butch queen; and some of them, like that of the 'bangie', are taken from straight black masculine street culture. (Butler 1993: 129)

In each category the winner is the person who is most real in their class: 'realness is the ability to compel belief, to produce the naturalized effect. This effect is itself the result of an embodiment of norms, an impersonation of a racial and class norm, . . . an . . . ideal that remains the standard which regulates the performance, but which no performance fully approximates' (1993: 129).

The 'realness' of the performances in these contests are, for Butler, not in contrast to the realness of everyday gender. It is rather the fact that the realness of everyday gender is also constituted out of just the same ability to compel belief, as a result of the embodiment of norms. There is nothing more to it than that. The contests involve an attempt to reach realness, but actually serve to show that such realness is itself only a phantasmatic ideal. The only difference between the gender of those at the balls and others is that in some cases the contestants fail to embody the norm which requires a certain alignment between anatomical shape and gendered performance. This failure is one which, in Butler's account, is punished particularly severely. During the making of the film Venus Xtravaganza, who could pass as a light-skinned woman and was working as a prostitute to pay for an operation to change her body, is murdered. For Butler 'her life is taken presumably by a client who, upon the discovery of her "little secret", mutilates her for having seduced him' (1993: 128).

Attention to the contests and categories within the film *Paris is Burning* also serves to highlight an important strength in Butler's account. The categories which inform the contest are not simply gendered categories. In each case gender is inter-articulated with race and class. The different categories therefore provide quite different performances of gender. Moreover Venus aspires to be 'a rich white girl'. Here the desire for a certain gender is a desire to be rescued from poverty, racism and homophobia. In this we cannot identify gender as in any way more fundamental than the whiteness and the richness to which gender is hoped to provide the route.

The Importance of Iterability

To complete the exposition of Butler's account we need another strand of theory, that derived from post-structuralists such as Derrida. Within the structuralist account of meaning, utilized by Lacan, the meaning of a term is fixed by its position in a system or structure. This meaning is then simply invoked when the term is used. Within post-structuralist accounts, however, such fixity of meaning is challenged. Central to this is the view that meaning has a temporal dimension. The meaning of a word is dependent on a temporal history of usages. Whenever we use a term, according to Derrida, we are engaged in an act of citation. We are repeating a term, echoing its previous usages. This repeatability, termed *iterability*, does not always produce stability of meaning. For although we can repeat the term we do so in different contexts and circumstances and these affect the meaning which is to be derived from it, rendering it indeterminate and not always predictable.

Butler exploits this post-structuralist account of language in describing the operation of gender norms: 'the action of gender requires a performance that is repeated. This repetition is at once a reenactment and reexperiencing of a set of meanings already socially established' (Butler 1990a: 140). They are repetitions constrained by the regulatory norms which we deviate from at our peril. But these repetitions are never completely stable: 'let us remember that reiterations are never simply replicas of the same' (Butler 1993: 226). In different contexts and times a repetition can take on a different meaning, undermining or subverting the dominant norms. This openness of terms is central to Butler's understanding of gender and to the politics which accompanies her account. We have already seen that, unlike Lacan, she allows alternatives to dominant ways of thinking to be thinkable, conceptualizable, even if socially excluded. These alternatives, such as homosexuality, can then provide the base for resistance to norms, as they do in Foucault's work. Butler, however, wants space for something further. She wants our ways of thinking to be susceptible to change, so that, for example, the distinction between homosexuality and heterosexuality, or masculinity and femininity, as distinct categories can be undermined. This space is given in her theory by her acceptance of the account of iterability. If we repeat performances in different contexts then different meanings can emerge which can undermine and subvert dominant ones.

Butler uses two central examples of such a process in *Gender Trouble*. One is her discussion of the operation of butch/femme roles within the context of lesbian sexual practice. These roles she argues cannot be understood as simple repetitions of heterosexual stereotypes. Rather the repetition and playful use of such roles within the framework of gay sexuality serves to highlight the constructed nature of the heterosexual original: 'lesbian femmes may recall the heterosexual scene, as it were, but also displace it at the same time. In both butch and femme identities, the very notion of an original or natural identity is put into question' (1990a: 123). This employment of categorization to effect a denaturalization of it is also found for Butler in the operation of drag, viewed as a parodic or exaggerated form of gender enactment in which originary or authentic gender identity is exposed as itself an effect of performance. In the performance of drag the apparent coherence of a unified package of gender/sex/sexuality is pulled apart. The audience, aware that they are watching a body sexed in a certain way, watch as a gendered identity is produced which is, according to regulatory gender norms, at variance with it. Butler returns to this discussion of drag when considering the film *Paris is Burning*, discussed above. Here she recognizes the ambivalence of the performances that drag involves. While we are aware of the dissonance between the performance and the anatomical body, the performance serves to *denaturalize* our views of gender. None the less many drag performances also involve a process of 'reidealizing' the norms and reconsolidating them. The process of denaturalization is not necessarily a process of liberation from the dominant norms.

In her discussion of this film, however, Butler also draws attention to the notions of 'home' and 'kinship' which are reconfigured within it, and serve as examples of the kind of shifts which the theory of iterability is highlighting. Contestants in the balls belong to houses. Here the term house has echoes both of conventional homes and of fashion houses. The 'mothers' of the house are those who achieve most realness in their chosen roles. But they also look after and advise other members of their houses, both personally and in relation to performance at the balls. 'These men "mother" one another, "house" one another.' Here what is emerging is a resignification of kinship relations 'in the face of dislocation, poverty and homelessness'. The result is the creation of a discursive and social space for a community. The instability of meaning and the space created for new meanings to emerge transforms restrictive and exclusory norms of the family and turns us towards 'a more enabling future'. Butler contrasts the possibility for an enabling resignification of conceptions of the 'natural family' here with what she regards as simply a reinforcement of the heterosexual family norm in the writings of Nancy Chodorow (see chapter 2).

For Butler, no more than Lacan, is it possible simply to step outside our signifying practices and devise new conceptual schemes. However, she differs from Lacan in seeing the regulatory norms of discourses as not fully determining. 'If the rules governing significa-tion not only restrict, but enable the assertion of alternative domains of cultural possibility, i.e. new possibilities for gender, that contest the rigid codes of hierarchical binarisms, then it is only within the practices of repetitive signifying that a subversion of identity becomes possible' (1990a: 145). The possibility of undermining the dominant norms is helped by the fact that gender discourses are themselves multiple and they also interact with a number of other discourses serving to construct our identity. The result is a multiplicity of demands which cannot all be obeyed coherently but which can be 'reconfigured and redeployed' (1990a: p. 145). To make such moves allows us to explore the possibilities when we reject the false stabilities of normative gender and explore 'the gender discontinuities that run rampant within heterosexual, bisexual and gay and lesbian contexts in which gender does not necessarily follow from sex, and desire, or sexuality generally, does not seem to follow from gender – indeed where none of these dimensions of significant corporeality express or reflect one another' (1990a: pp. 135–6).

Political Strategies and Problematics

The critique of identity

One consequence of Butler's theoretical position is that political action is to be directed at destabilizing the binary gendered and sexual categories of 'man' and 'woman', 'gay' and 'straight'. The goal of such destabilization is to make visible the performativity of gender, to render it evident that neither gender nor sex is a natural category – indeed, that the very idea of a 'natural' category is simply an effect of discourse. But the effect of such destabilization is often seen as being the rejection of such categories altogether. Such a conception of politics puts queer theory in tension with the political strategies of many activists both within feminism, gay and lesbian movements and within anti-racist groups. Such activism is based on a sense of collectivity, of shared interests and objectives, but not only that. Often it has as part of its goals a rearticulation of a shared identity, reversing negative stereotypes to instil a sense of pride in being a woman or being gay or being black. In the course of this, 'hate' language is sometimes reclaimed to be put to affirmative purposes (see below). Reference is sometimes made to shared experiences, bodily and social, which can serve as the basis of the rearticulated identity.

Without completely rejecting the place for such political moves Butler sees them as being fraught with dangers. First, any reference to bodily or psychological experiences, outside of discourse, providing a foundation for identities within it, is rejected for assuming that we could have unmediated access to an extra-discursive realm which could serve as a justificatory base for our classificatory practices. Secondly, all such categorization, for Butler, works by creating the illusion of a unified and coherent group. It works, for her, on the basis of exclusions, marking the boundaries of those who fail to fit into the group. This denies 'the internal complexity and indeterminacy of the term and constitutes itself only through the exclusion of some part of the constituency that it simultaneously seeks to represent' (Butler 1990a: 14). She concludes that there is no 'ontology of gender' on which we can construct a politics, for any such ontology would fix and constrain the subjects it is attempting to liberate, failing to free itself from the dominant norms in which the categories have their origin.

Although Butler makes room in this way for a lack of homogeneity within our identity categories, and recognizes the very different ways in which one can be a woman or man, her apparent rejection of identity categories is not always enthusiastically embraced by those writers who most brought the issue of difference to the fore. bell hooks, for example (1990: 23–33), reflecting on the relevance of postmodernist ideas to black studies, welcomes the anti-essentialism which such ideas make central. Such anti-essentialism forces the recognition that there are many black experiences, and, in the American context, problematizes a notion of authentic blackness which privileges the rural south. 'Such a critique allows us to affirm multiple black identities, varied black experience. It also challenges colonial imperialist paradigms of black identity which represent blackness one-dimensionally in ways that reinforce and sustain white supremacy' (1990: 28). None the less hooks is less happy with the refusal of blackness as a category of identity. She sees the need to identify as black both to accommodate the specific subjectivities of black people and to form a basis for political activity. Moreover the very fragmentation of identity categories which for Butler is a cause of celebration is viewed by hooks as yielding 'displacement, profound alienation and despair' (1990: 26).

The anxieties which hooks expresses here find echoes in reflections of Biddy Martin on the politics of queering (Martin 1994a). Welcoming Butler's account of performativity as enabling gender norms to be less controlling, Martin none the less expresses reservations. The goal of transgression and destabilization can lead to a view that gender categories are purely negative, traps to ensnare us. To retain one's identification as a woman or man, or, as Martin discusses at length, as 'femme', is apparently to be a victim of prohibitive norms. The implication is that to continue to use such terms is to be locked into the fixity dictated by the dominant norms governing it. Although Butler, like Foucault, recognizes the enabling as well as disciplinary use of discourse, in her discussion of categories of gender and sexualities it is the disciplinary effect which is foregrounded. Martin's writings, however, suggest that without the use of such categories 'language with which to conceive of one's sexual specificities, or to conceive of them positively' is lost (1994a: 110). She quotes MacCowan, who argues that the problems are not gender itself but the 'correlations between biological sex, gender identity, gender or sex roles, sexual object choice, sexual identity. . . . It is this system and the denial of any other construction of gender' which is problematic (Martin 1994a: 112). In addition to the need for gender and sexual categories to make sense of specificity, Martin also suggests that we need to utilize gender categories if we are to be able to articulate, for example, misogyny. Discussing Butler's account of the death of Venus Xtravaganza, Martin points out that Butler assumes the death was for failing to conform to gender norms. Martin points out that Venus's death could equally have been a result of her successfully passing as a woman, and suffering the death that many other women face (1994a: 112).

Butler, in her later work (1997b: 16), emphasizes the role of linguistic categories in making possible the process of becoming subjects. It is a condition of the possibility of our being subjects at all that we are socially recognized. None the less the process is still conceived of, as in Foucault, as a process of *subjectification* to social norms. This itself forecloses possibilities and is still regarded primarily in negative terms. Lois McNay challenges 'the persistence of the negative paradigm of subjectification in Butler's works' (2000: 45). She accuses Butler of implying a false dualism between 'normal' and 'excluded' identities and 'dominant' (and thereby compliant) and 'resistant' responses to subjectification. Resistant responses are assumed, McNay claims, to originate from those in the position of the 'abject' in relation to dominant culture. For McNay this belies the complexity of ways in which people inhabit their identity categories which makes such dualisms inappropriate. There are, however, points where Butler herself recognizes the falsity of the dualisms suggested here, and points to the degendering that can go on within apparently routine heterosexual relations. She seems less able to contemplate any positive gains from our inhabiting the categories which are on offer.

We return in chapter 9 to the question of the need for gender categories to capture the specificities of people's subjectivities and in chapter 10 to the question of the need for identity politics of the kind which Butler appears to be challenging.

The question of political agency

One of the concerns which has been expressed in relation to Butler's work is the extent to which she leaves space for personal and political agency. When *Gender Trouble* was first being read she was accused of seeing gender as in some sense voluntary – something which people could choose to put on or change, rather like clothes. This, however, was clearly a misreading. As was clear in *Gender Trouble* and in her texts since, there is no question of choice here, for it is only through performative practices that we are subjects at all. This can, however, provoke the opposite anxiety, namely that the social norms are so constraining that change at both the personal and political level becomes impossible. Butler is also keen to avoid such determinism. In ways which become increasingly highlighted in later work (1997a,

1997b), she insists that we need to avoid both positing a subject which exists pre-socially and can make choices about identity and political agency; and assuming a position in which the process of subjectification is a determining one. The subject always *exceeds* the norms in relation to which it is constituted. For Butler the psychic 'operation of the norm' (1997b: 21) is neither mechanical nor predictable. Moreover, because of iterability, the meanings of the categories become open to resignification and reversal: 'the analysis of subjection is always double, tracing the conditions of subject formation and tracing the turn against those conditions, for the subject, "to emerge"' (1997b: 29).

The political possibilities of iterability are explored further in *Excitable Speech* (Butler 1997a). In a discussion of 'hate speech' she argues: 'hate speech is an act that recalls prior acts, requiring a future repetition to endure. Is there a repetition that might disjoin the speech act from its supporting conventions such that its repetition confounds rather than consolidates its injurious efficacy?' (1997a: 20). (We might note that it is just such a process that has resulted in the resignifications of the term 'queer'.) Butler recommends the exploration of such responses to hate speech in place of the juridical interventions such as MacKinnon propounds in relation, for example, to pornography (MacKinnon 1993). Juridical interventions require stability of meaning. For Butler it is the very absence of this which can be used to effect change.

Lois McNay argues, however, that the theoretical space which Butler provides is insufficient to allow for effective political agency (2000: 57). She claims we are given no insight into the conditions under which subversive identities might be adopted. Equally we have no account of the conditions under which destabilization of identity may occur. Moreover, when such destabilization does occur we have no way of predicting whether it will undermine or reinscribe current power relations. The public visibility of gay relationships has, for example, been appropriated by a consumerism anxious to cash in on the 'pink pound'. Butler herself recognized this process in her discussion of the balls in *Paris is Burning*. The conditions in which destabilization can effect shifts in relations of power remain unpredictable. McNay also points out that the fact that individuals do not straight forwardly reproduce categories does not necessarily make the differences resistant or subversive ones. What we need, McNay suggests, is a connection between symbolic constructions and the material relations in terms of which these constructions take place. This would require attention to historical and social specificity which would provide us with 'a logic of practice', enabling us to distinguish cases where an act is likely to be politically effective. For McNay the unpredictability of meaning which is central to Butler's account is inadequate for political action.

The differences between Butler and McNay here parallel those between Foucault and Hennessy in the previous chapter. The kind of generalities which McNay is seeking would be ones which, for Butler, it would be difficult to give. For her the consequences of repetition in variable circumstances are both unpredictable and also in any concrete case capable of differing interpretations. Butler's own discussion of *Paris is Burning* sees the balls as displaying the 'unstable coexistence of insurrection and resubordination' (1993: 128). She regarded the remaking of themselves that was available to the contestants as some kind of agency, although it would be inappropriate to give a voluntarist construal of it. None the less in many instances the performances reidealized gender norms. Following Foucault and Derrida, Butler views the difference made by particular contexts as yielding both a contingency and a lack of predictability to both social processes and the production of meaning. These rule out the possibility of producing a 'logic of practice' of the kind which McNay seeks.

Merely cultural

Some writers have pointed out the fact that outside the context of the balls the participants remained constrained by institutional power. They remained poor and subject to racist and homophobic discrimination. When the film was a success, they wished, for example, to cash in financially on that success. All had, however, signed releases which meant that they could not pursue those claims legally (Martin 1994a). McNay criticizes Butler for reducing questions of gender hierarchies to questions about the construction of sexed identities, and thereby failing to attend sufficiently to material and social factors which are structuring peoples lives along gendered lines. These arguments are echoed in other writers. Stevi Jackson suggests that performative accounts of gender 'ignore those material social relations which underpin the category of sex' (1995: 17). Butler is accused of failing to recognize the way in which heterosexuality operates not only as a norm governing the construction of our subjective identities but also as a concrete social structure which involves 'the appropriation of women's bodies and labour' (p. 18). The institution of marriage gives men access to women's bodies; the inequalities in the labour market restrict women's financial independence and leave them playing an additional role as carers and homemakers. Legal and economic structures are therefore playing a key role in the enforcement of heterosexuality (compare again Hennessy's discussion of Foucault in chapter 3). McClintock makes a similar point with relation to colonial discourses. It is important 'not to read the contradictions of colonial discourse as a matter of textuality alone . . . [discourse was] backed up by the planned institutional violence of armies and law courts, prisons and state machinary. The power of guns, whips and shackles . . . is not reducible to the "violence of the letter"' (1995: 16).

The apparent dichotomy which is being drawn here between performative identity as, in some sense, 'merely cultural' and the sphere of the legal and economic is one which Butler would herself reject (1998). The reproduction of ourselves as heterosexual gendered beings was recognized by early Marxist feminists as being central to the realm of the economic. Here the sexual division of labour within the household and outside both required the production of gendered selves and formed practices which were part of that production. The performances whereby gender is produced do not simply carry meanings about what it is to be male and female; they are themselves material practices which serve to constitute the economic and legal frame. Here is an acute example demonstrating the materiality of gender norms. In northern Nigeria there is a practice whereby older men marry very young girls who are just reaching puberty. This practice is part of an institution of polygamy and also part of a system of economic exchange in which daughters are often given to business partners (Wahid 2000). As a consequence of this practice, early pregnancies cause severe internal damage to these girls' bodies which leads to the leakage of urine and faeces. They become outcasts from husbands and family, and often resort to work as prostitutes, unable to afford even simple medical procedures which would alleviate their internal damage. Intervention in this situation requires legal, medical and economic changes to the structures which are conditioning these women's lives. What a performative account of gender draws our attention to is that these material practices are the means whereby such Nigerian men constitute themselves as male. Here virility is performed in relation to the bodies of young girls, a performance which structures and is structured by the legal and economic institutions. Changes therefore require the deconstruction of masculinity of that form, a destabilizing and denaturalizing of it to make conceivable other possibilities. In this instance the legal and economic moves are intertwined with 'cultural' ones, which clearly themselves have material effects.

Parallel points can be made in relation to McClintock's examples. She herself describes the use of 'guns, whips and shackles' as a 'violent excess of militarized masculinity' (McClintock 1995: 11). She could have added colonizing masculinity. To act differently these men needed to find alternative ways of performing both masculinity and their white identities, outside the framework of imperialism. What these examples show is that we cannot disentangle the material and the cultural in the way that some criticisms of Butler would seem to suggest.

The body and the psyche

Perhaps the most widespread unease felt with Butler's position is often expressed by the remark 'But what about the body?' Such a query is prompted by the apparent disregard within Butler's work for any constraints on gender performance which might be set by our biological bodies. Because she emphasizes the mobility of gender, and the possibilities of gender crossings, any significance attached to bodily form seems to get lost. It is simply a dominant norm that certain kinds of gendered performances attach themselves to certain anatomical shapes. Surely, people often claim, the facts of reproduction, childbirth, menstruation, the production or not of semen, play some role in our gendered identities, even if not a determining one. (Can we accept that any part of the body could have the sensitivity of the clitoris if it was suitably inscribed?)

Biddy Martin, while accepting that we can have no way of thinking about our bodies outside discourse, none the less suggests 'that the body constitutes more of a drag on signification, that we pay more respect to what is given, to limits, even as we open the future to what is now unthinkable or delegitimated' (1994a: 112). She argues for 'the body, the material [to be conceived of] as a drag or limit as well as a potential [although] the kind of drag it is cannot and should not be predetermined' (p. 119). The concerns she expresses here about the body also extend to the psyche. Though 'body and psyche can be said to be the effects of power, they are irreducible to it' (p. 119). In response to Butler's insistence that the appearance of an inner life is a consequence of social mouldings of the surface of the body, Martin insists that the lines of force run in both directions: 'though never constituted outside of given social/discursive relations, power also moves from bodies/psyches/minds outward' (p. 119). Martin's thoughts here have links with questions which others have asked regarding Butler's work, particularly with regard to the attachments people have to their gendered identities and the need to consider unconscious investments in masculinity and femininity. We return to a detailed discussion of the role of the body and the psyche in chapter 7, where we discuss more of Butler's later work.

Gender and Sexuality

This chapter examines how theorists have discussed the relationship between gender and sexuality. There will be no attempt here to summarize the literature on theories of sexuality *per se* (see Bristow (1997) for a clear introduction). The intention is to use a number of feminist writers as examples of the *relationship* between gender and sexuality. These range from writers who view gender as the frame which structures sexuality to those who see sexuality as structuring gender, and finally those who give sexuality a degree of autonomy from the gender system, viewing it as a separate system or as an arena for empowerment and pleasure.

The Intersection of Gender and Sexuality

One of the key concepts shaping discussions of sexuality is the existence of two sexes – men and women. Just as in the discussions on the naturalizing trick in relation to gender in previous chapters, the same effect occurs in discussions of sexuality. Thus, heterosexuality is usually conceived as a 'natural', given, drive or instinct. This notion that gender and sexuality are given by nature and biology, that the relationship between gender and sexuality is one of symmetry, is the gender and sexual orthodoxy adopted by the medical community and sexologists at the turn of the century in their explorations of homosexuality. Tamsin Wilton writes, 'This profoundly ideological notion of complementary gendered polarity – heteropolarity – has become the mystified and naturalised organising principle which saturates Western culture, structuring thought and social organisation around notions of binarism, complementarity, unidirectionality and polarity' (1996: 127).

The medical discourse from the mid-nineteenth century to the early part of this century offered a set of explanations for same-sex desire which was shaped by assumptions that 'normal' sexual relations are heterosexual. This sometimes produced a view of homosexuals as belonging to a *third sex*, as having a male body with a female brain or having a male brain and a female body. The terms used to describe homosexuality were 'sexual inversion', or 'contrary sexual feeling', and it was believed that same-sex desire was due to problems with the development of biological sex organs. Havelock Ellis wrote that 'the male invert is a person with an unusual proportion of female elements, the female invert a person with an unusual proportion of male elements' (1933: 197). These biological elements translated into corresponding gender roles, as gay men are labelled as 'effeminate' and lesbians characterized in terms of 'manliness'.

The interdependence between gender and sexuality, which such naturalizing accounts provided, was also found in the psychoanalytic accounts which we discussed in chapter 2. Within these accounts, to become properly gendered was to become heterosexual. The development of masculinity was discussed in terms of the development of sexual desire for women, initially the mother and then other women. The development of femininity was particularly problematic because it involved the transfer of desired object from mother to father and then to other men. It also, according to Freud, involved the transfer of areas of bodily pleasure from the clitoris to the vagina. On this story the failure to achieve heterosexuality was simultaneously a gendered failure, so that lesbian women and gay men were not proper women and men (see the discussion in chapter 2).

The shift from this biologically based account of the relationship between gender and sexuality to one of the socially constructed nature of gender and sexuality does not immediately signal a need to disengage the two concepts. The interweaving of gender and sexuality is central to social constructionist accounts of both a materialist and discursive kind. As we saw in chapter 3, early discussions of patriarchy, for example those deriving from French feminists such as Delphy and Wittig, saw gender as constituted out of positionality with regard to certain social practices and institutions. Central to these were the institutions of marriage and the family in which men appropriated not only women's labour but also access to their bodies. This was the very thing which for those writers served to constitute women as a class. This was what led Wittig to conclude that lesbians who removed themselves from such relations were not women (see the discussion in chapter 3). In this way the institutions which found heterosexuality are the very institutions which found gender relations and vice versa.

In the move to more discursive accounts of gender relations, gender and sexuality are also interwoven. Despite the fact that Foucault himself saw the discursive production and regulation of sexuality as forming a system somewhat autonomous of gender relations anchored in kinship (see below), for many feminists who make use of his ideas the two are produced and regulated interdependently. What such feminist work highlights is the way in which dominant discourses of femininity and masculinity are tied up with heterosexuality, for example that feminine women are attractive to men, and make good wives and mothers. Masculine men display not only strength but heterosexual prowess (see the discussion of masculinity and homophobia in chapter 6).

Stevi Jackson's work is an example of a materialist feminist analysis of gender and sexuality that attempts to deal with sexuality and incorporates insights from discursive accounts. Her writings on heterosexuality represent an attempt to update the radical materialist approach that traditionally has concerned itself with marriage rather than sexuality *per se* (see chapter 3's discussion of Delphy). Jackson's writings on sexuality span nearly three decades and as such provide a useful overview of some of the debates on feminism and sexuality. She writes from a feminist sociological perspective and identifies herself as a white, heterosexual, radical feminist, which places her at a useful vantage point to reflect on some of the contradictions and problems of feminist analysis of sexuality. Her account of gender and sexuality attempts to bring together some of the different levels of analysis which have been alluded to in relation to sexuality – for example, sexuality as discourse and as a social practice. Her articles on gender and sexuality use heterosexuality as a focus for these discussions. She argues that 'gender – as a socially constructed product of patriarchal hierarchies – is fundamental to an analysis of sexuality' (Jackson 1999b: 123). The theory is based on a form of radical feminism that is based on the work of, especially, Christine Delphy and

Monique Wittig. Jackson views heterosexuality and homosexuality (these are the only two sexualities referred to) as constructed through gender categories: 'the categories heterosexual and lesbian could not exist without our being able to define ourselves and others by gender. To desire the "other sex" or indeed to desire "the same sex" presupposes the prior existence of "men" and "women" as socially — and erotically – meaningful categories. Desire as currently socially constituted, whether lesbian or heterosexual, is inevitably gendered' (1996b: 176). Jackson views sexuality as just one aspect of women's oppression and gender inequality and as a set of social practices that has to be contextualized in relation to other gendered institutions and social processes. 'Sexuality per se is neither inherently oppressive to women nor inherently liberating. It has no intrinsic qualities – good or bad. Since it is a social phenomenon, it is particular, culturally and historically rooted, forms of sexuality which are oppressive' (1999b: 4).

The framework for understanding sexuality and gender provided by Jackson is one in which the variety of sexual practices, available cross-culturally, in differing historical conditions, are gendered. She defines sexuality as a combination of an identity, erotic activities, practices and desires. Sexuality is constructed at the level of social structure through institutions such as the law, the state, the media and the family. These constructions constitute the gendered nature of a heterosexuality that is deemed to be the 'normal sexuality' for women and men. This produces a discourse of sexuality that regulates and naturalizes heterosexuality as the norm and other sexualities as deviant or perverted. Ordinary women and men use these discourses to direct their practices and these are the scripts through which people make sense of their sexuality. These intersecting levels of the construction and meaning of sexuality are constantly in a process of negotiation, resistance, compliance and reconstruction of both gender and sexuality. None the less contemporary research into the sexuality of young people indicates that 'the underlying patterns of heterosexual relationships are striking in their resilience' (see Holland et al. (1998), and discussion in Jackson (1999b)). For Jackson, therefore, sexuality and gender, while they can be treated as analytically distinct, nevertheless are empirically connected (1999b: 6). Wilton argues that, in order to shift the dominance of the heterosexual assumption in discussions of gender and sexuality, feminists need to signal the sexuality of the women under discussion. By explicitly referring to the sexual identity and orientation of women, in, for example, discussions of domestic labour and childcare, the possibility of alternative living and working relationships is opened up. Feminists, she argues, need to adopt a specific tactic in making heterosexuality visible in discussions of gender, and not simply reserve its use for discussions of sexuality (Wilton 1996).

In the work of Judith Butler, which we discussed in chapter 4, the primacy which in the above accounts is given to gender in the structuring of sexuality is reversed. Instead the predominance of heterosexuality is used to found not only the binary between two genders but also the division of bodies into two biological sexes (see chapter 4 and chapter 1). Butler accepts, along with Wittig, that the 'binary restriction on sex serves the reproductive aims of a system of compulsory heterosexuality' (1990a: 19). Without the norm of heterosexuality these sexed and gendered binaries would prove unfounded. Consequently the exploration of alternative sexual practices is itself a way to undermine the gender binary.

In the rest of this chapter we wish to explore the suggested analytical interdependence of the categories of sexuality and gender, together with the proposal that they should, for different purposes, be prised apart.

Gender, Sexuality and Power

In second-wave feminist writings on sexuality, it was axiomatic to consider a relationship between gender and sexuality and view this relationship as not benign. Here the operation of heterosexuality was seen as one of the key mechanisms by which unequal gender relations were retained. The most famous example of such an account is Adrienne Rich's essay on 'Compulsory Heterosexuality', first published as a pamphlet in 1979. This article has a number of aims. The first was to challenge the neglect of lesbianism evidenced by the absence of academic feminist studies of lesbianism. The second was to encourage heterosexual feminists to question the normalization of compulsory heterosexuality and to view this sexual practice as a political institution constructed in the interests of men. The third was to suggest that the relationship of women to women operated either as a lesbian existence or on a lesbian continuum. Finally, she wanted to bridge the political divisions between feminists and lesbians.

With regard to compulsory heterosexuality, Rich argues, women are coerced into this sexual practice through routine socialization, the media, the family and the institution of motherhood. She writes:

> the assumption that 'most women are innately heterosexual' stands as a theoretical and political stumbling block for feminism. It remains a tenable assumption partly because lesbian existence has been written out of history or catalogued under disease, partly because it has been treated as exceptional rather than intrinsic, partly because to acknowledge that for women heterosexuality may not be a 'preference' at all, but has had to be imposed, managed, organized, propagandized, and maintained by force, is an immense step to take if you consider yourself freely and 'innately' heterosexual. (Rich 1993: 238–9)

One of the strongest arguments in the article is the suggestion that feminism up to the 1980s had adopted the orthodoxy promulgated by male sexologists and psychologists that viewed heterosexuality as the 'normal' preferred and assumed choice for most women.

In response to such compulsory heterosexuality Rich suggested the notion of a lesbian continuum. She calls for a distinction between lesbian existence and a lesbian continuum. By lesbian existence Rich is referring to women living together, not necessarily in a sexual relationship but rather in an environment of loving, sharing both emotional and political support. Lesbian continuum refers to 'a range – through each woman's life and throughout history – of woman-identified experience, not simply the fact that a woman has had or consciously desired genital sexual experience with another woman' (Rich 1993: 239). This continuum can include the giving and receiving of political and practical support, sharing problems and ideas, and creating a culture of sisterhood which supports women's resistance to male patriarchy and power. Lesbianism became conceptualized here as a sexuality which is not about unequal power relations, about violence or domination, but as a safe space for women. In this account therefore Rich reverses the relations between gender and sexuality suggested in, for example, both naturalizing and some psychoanalytic theories. In place of heterosexuality being necessarily intertwined with femininity, lesbianism becomes the marker of being authentically female: the mark of the woman-identified woman. In Rich's discussion, however, lesbianism becomes less about sexuality and more about a point of resistance for women against male patriarchy. In a similar way Sheila Jeffreys writes: 'The demolition of heterosexual desire is a necessary step on the route to women's liberation' (1990: 312). Cora Kaplan, however, argues that such a position amounts to 'naturalistic essentialism', stating that for Rich 'female hetero- sexuality is socially constructed and female homosexuality is natural. . . . Political lesbianism becomes more than a strategic position for feminism, it is a return to nature' (cited in Weeks 1987: 46). Further criticisms of Rich will be discussed below.

Another writer who explores the intersection of gender, sexuality and patriarchal power is Catherine MacKinnon. For this writer femin- ism is the discipline that is central to the study of sexuality. She sets out to provide not a feminist theory of sexuality and gender but an agenda for the construction of such a theory (1982). The starting point for this is that sexuality constructs gender. MacKinnon writes:

> Sexuality is that social process which creates, organizes, expresses, and directs desire, creating the social beings we know as women and men, as their relations create society. As work is to marxism, sexuality to feminism, socially constructed yet constructing, universal as activity yet historically specific, jointly comprised of matter and mind. . . . Heterosexuality is its structure, gender and family its congealed forms, sex roles its qualities generalized to social persona, reproduction a consequence, and control its issue. (1982: 516)

One of the central strategies in the articles is the attempt to compare a Marxist analysis of capitalism with a feminist analysis of sexuality and gender. The comparison here is between the bourgeoisie as a class that dominates and subjugates the proletariat and a system where men dominate and subjugate women. The emphasis is on the role of men who dominate women through compulsory heterosexuality. Women as a social group are defined and oppressed by men, not simply by capitalism. Here sexuality is viewed as the foundation of male power. This analysis is very explicit in not giving sexuality this foundational aspect through a reliance on psychoanalytic theory. Rather the analysis flows from the materiality of women's experi- ences of sexual oppression and male dominance through the institu- tions of heterosexuality. MacKinnon makes reference to empirical work by writers on a range of issues from restrictions on abortion and birth control to sexual harassment, rape, incest, pornography, prostitution and domestic abuse. These accounts are used to form a feminist theory of male power and control of women through heterosexuality. She argues that the feminist literature on gender socialization and sex roles demonstrates the centrality of sexuality to the formation of femininity and the social construction of what it means to be a woman: 'Gender socialization is the process through which women come to identify themselves as sexual beings, as beings that exist for men. It is that process through which women internalize (make their own) a male image of their sexuality as their identity as women' (1982: 531). The method that is used to subjugate women is the objectification of women in sexual terms. The male perspective on sexuality is the dominant one; thus female sexuality is constructed in relation to male sexuality but the relationship is founded on gender hierarchy in which men are dominant and women are subordinate, socially, economically, politically and sexually: 'Sex as gender and sex as sexuality are thus defined in terms of each other, but it is sexuality that determines gender, not the other way around' (1982: 531).

This perspective on sexuality and male power was very influential in feminist writings on sexuality and gender throughout the 1980s. It was the dominant perspective in establishing the theoretical basis for feminist activists on rape, pornography, prostitution, and domestic and sexual abuse. Not only was sexuality defined as the central focus for feminists but, as MacKinnon wrote, 'Radical feminism is feminism' (1983: 639). This perspective provided a very negative view of sexuality. Sexuality, especially heterosexuality, is by definition oppressive, as this sexual practice is constructed for male pleasure, subordinates women and oppresses other sexual practices such as lesbianism and homosexuality. Thus the privileging of heterosexuality is really about male power over women. The emphasis on male power, dominance and coercion, as well as on the violent and brutal forms of sexual abuse such as rape, negates sexual pleasure and stresses the dangers of sexual desire and curiosity for women (see discussion in Vance 1984).

Sexual Pleasures and Sexual Oppressions

Opposition to the view of sexuality put forward by both Rich and MacKinnon forms one of the main arguments for theorizing sexuality, at least partially, independently from gender. One of the key issues here was that in both Rich and MacKinnon sexuality had become separated from accounts of desire and pleasure. The distinctiveness of lesbianism as marked by specificity of desire and a variety of erotic practices thereby becomes obscured (Califia 1980). Gayle Rubin argues:

> By defining lesbianism entirely as something about supportive rela-
> tions between women rather than as something which has sexual
> content . . . essentially evacuated it . . . of any sexual content. . . . I did
> not like the way in which lesbians motivated by lust, or lesbians who
> were invested in butch/femme roles, were treated as inferior residents
> of the lesbian continuum, while some women who never had sexual
> desire for women were granted more elevated status. (Rubin with
> Butler 1994)

The Barnard Sexuality Conference in 1982 has come to epitomize the start of what was to become known as the 'sex wars' in the lesbian and feminist community. Here arguments erupted between what was subsequently named anti-sex feminists and libertarian feminists. Libertarian feminists argued against the limitation of 'vanilla sex' – 'that is, gentle, "touchy-feely", side-by-side (no one on the top or the bottom), altogether pretty sex' (Tong 1989: 121). Sexual libertarians were accused of supporting forms of 'patriarchal' sexuality such as sadomasochism and the use of erotica and pornography.

> On that day several hundred women gathered to attend the Feminist
> IX Conference held at Barnard College in New York City. The title
> of the conference sounded innocent enough – 'Towards a Politics of
> Sexuality' – but the night before, several members of Women against
> Pornography had called the college informing them of the unaccep-
> tability of several of the speakers. When I arrived at the campus that
> bright spring morning, I found a picket line walked by women wearing
> black t-shirts stating their position on certain sexual practices and
> handing out leaflets that named the unacceptable speakers and topics;
> butch–femme was included in the list. (Nestle 1992: 254)

The notion of a 'real' lesbian or 'sex radicals' emerged in the wake of the 1982 conference. Articles appeared which celebrated the sexual and erotic experiences of sadomasochism, 'butch/femme' role playing, fetishism and other sexual desires. Lesbianism was no longer considered to be synonymous with feminism and lesbian identity could not be easily equated with an anti-male stance.

The notion of a lesbian continuum was also criticized for its class bias. The lesbianism found in street bars and among working-class lesbians frequently involved the taking on of roles, while the lesbian continuum view was associated primarily with middle-class feminists. The debates on sexuality became divided between those who concentrated on rape, pornography and sexual harassment and those who attempted to examine the complexities of a variety of sexual practices enjoyed by women. A collection of essays edited by Carole Vance (1984), entitled *Pleasure and Danger: exploring female sexuality*, reflects the intensity of these debates and set the scene for the emergence of a feminist discourse on sexuality which differed markedly from the earlier debates.[1]

The rethinking of sexuality sparked by the so-called sex wars has also been fuelled from other sources. Women working in prostitution and pornography have demanded recognition as workers and campaigned for improved working conditions and protection of health and safety, and can no longer be theorized solely as victims. There has also been an outpouring of writing from gay male writers on issues of gay male sexual practice 'including cross dressing, gay public sex, gay male promiscuity, gay male masculinity, gay leather, gay fist fucking, gay cruising' (Rubin with Butler 1994), which cannot be accommodated, except purely negatively, in the kind of feminist work discussed in the previous section.

There has been an upsurge, particularly in the USA, of New Right thinking. This has led to the prosecution of sexual minorities of all kinds. This has gone hand in hand with the emergence of AIDS and a moral panic in the Western world over homosexual practices. All of which suggested that there was a political need for sexual minorities to form political groupings independent of feminist ones to fight oppression and discrimination on the grounds of sexuality.

These issues formed the context for Gayle Rubin's highly influential article 'Thinking Sex', which first appeared in 1984 (Vance 1984; reprinted in Rubin 1993). She begins with an outline of some of the political history of sexuality in relation to a variety of moral panics around sexual behaviour deemed to be offensive, such as masturbation, sodomy, homosexuality, pornography, contraception and abortion. These panics point to the need to develop a radical perspective on sexuality. There are a number of barriers to the development of such a theory. One of the significant barriers is the view that sexuality is a 'natural', pre-social instinct or drive and that this instinct can be destructive and dangerous if it is not controlled, repressed and regulated. As Rubin explains, sex is considered bad unless it can be excused by explanations of loving relationships or reproduction preferably in marriage. This view of sexuality as biology has shifted, at least in some academic circles, through the work of writers like Weeks (1981) and Foucault (1978). As Rubin observes:

> The new scholarship on sexual behaviour has given sex a history and created a constructivist alternative to sexual essentialism. Underlying this body of work is an assumption that sexuality is constituted in society and history, not biologically ordained. This does not mean the biological capacities are not prerequisites for human sexuality. It does mean that human sexuality is not comprehensible in purely biological terms. . . . the body, the brain, the genitalia, and the capacity for language are all necessary for human sexuality. But they do not determine its content, its experiences, or its institutional forms. (in Vance 1984: 276)

Rubin writes of a sexual erotic pyramid that has heterosexuality at the top and transsexuals, sadomasochists and other 'transgressors' at the bottom. She writes:

> Individuals whose behaviour stands high in this hierarchy are rewarded with certified mental health, respectability, legality, social and physical mobility, institutional support, and material benefits. As sexual behaviours or occupations fall lower on the scale, the individuals who practise them are subjected to a presumption of mental illness, disreputability, criminality, restricted social and physical mobility, loss of institutional support, and economic sanctions. (Rubin, in Vance 1984: 279)

The starting point for a radical theory of sexuality is a displacement of the negativity that surrounds some kinds of sexual activity. Rubin's analysis rests on a distinction between sex (as sexuality) and gender. She argues that the sex system 'is not reducible to, or understandable in terms of, class, race, ethnicity, or gender' (in Vance 1984: 293). She believes that 'feminism is the theory of gender oppression' (p. 307) and that there is a need to distinguish between the study of gender oppression and sexual oppression. Thus it is not possible to theorize sexuality within a gender analysis. This, as she explains, is a retreat from her earlier position on the sex/gender system in her article on 'The traffic in women' (1975), where the regulation of sexuality is viewed as integral to kinship practices trading on women's bodies. The dominant theoretical and methodological influence in 'Traffic in Women' was Marxism. It was a radical, critical Marxism that attempted to use the paradigm as a way of exploring the production and reproduction of unequal gender and sexual relations. Her intention was to transcend the weakness and limitations of Marxism in relation to gender and sexuality. In the later essay, 'Thinking Sex', Rubin is attempting to develop a complex understanding of sexuality outside the frame imposed by gender as a basis for developing theories of sexuality. For her, differences in sexuality cannot be thought about solely in terms of gender binaries. This is, for her, the primary focus of the piece. She did not intend to leave the debates on sexuality to the feminism of the anti-pornography movement. As she says, MacKinnon 'wanted to make feminism the privileged site for analysing sexuality and to subordinate sexual politics not only to feminism, but to a particular type of feminism. On the grand chessboard of life, I wanted to block this particular move' (Rubin with Butler 1994: 71). Rubin also wanted to intervene in the political differences in the feminist movement on transsexuality, and the apparent indifference of feminists to the re-emergence of gay hate crimes, a homophobia fuelled by AIDS, and the dismissal of gay male politics as masculinist behaviour and therefore not relevant. The New Right had a strong sexual agenda, and at certain points this agenda coincided with some feminist activities, such as the anti-pornography movement, feminist critiques of transsexuality, and condemnations of some kinds of sexual practices. Rubin points out some of these contradictions and, inspired by Foucault, she attempts to employ his analysis to the construction of a new theoretical approach. *Foucault's History of Sexuality* claims that at a certain point in history – he mentions the eighteenth century – a specific system of sexuality emerges which can be distinguished from a system of gender. The inspiration from Foucault centres on his outline of a new system of discourses that regulated sexuality but did not conflate sexuality with reproduction. Rubin argues: 'what he was saying helped me to think about the outlines of another system that had different dynamics, a different topography, and different lines of force' (Rubin with Butler 1994: 85). So she argued: 'Gender affects the operation of the sexual system, and the sexual system has had gender-specific manifestations. But although sex and gender are related, they are not the same thing, and they form the basis of two distinct arenas of social practice' (in Vance 1984: 308).

This position of Rubin's is endorsed and further developed by
Eve Kosofsky Sedgwick in the *Epistemology of the Closet* (1990).
Sedgwick argues that sexuality cannot be adequately theorized within
a gendered frame. Within that frame the most significant aspect of
sexuality becomes choice of desired object, same sex/opposite sex.
This then leads to a typography of sexual identities, homosexual/
heterosexual. Other aspects of sexual practice remain unattended
to (we don't have an identity as 'masturbator', for example). For
Sedgwick, while some people experience their sexuality 'deeply embedded in a matrix of gender meaning', others do not (1990: 26).
Within the gendered frame, moreover, we have two models of homosexuality. In the first, desire is fundamentally heterosexual, in lesbian
couples at least one of the pair must be mannish and in gay couples
one of the men effeminate. In the second model, instanced by Rich's
lesbian continuum and played out by aspects of the gay leather community, the most real women and men are gay. Desire is assimilated
with identification. Lesbian women are 'women-identified women',
more womanly than women of other kinds. Neither account, for
Sedgwick, is satisfactory. A third consideration for Sedgwick in
arguing for separation is that, for her, sexuality is more ambivalent,
more apt for destabilization and reconfiguration than gender. There
is a greater opportunity for fluidity and crossings. Our gender assign-
ments, for her, are viewed as having a greater fixity. Following from
these considerations Sedgwick suggests that, in relation to sexuality,
feminism should concern itself with 'the question of who is to have
control of women's (biologically) distinctive reproductive capacity'
(p. 28). Sexuality becomes the domain of 'anti-homophobic inquiry'
(p. 15).

Against Proper Objects

The autonomy which both Sedgwick and Rubin propose for studies
of sexuality has, however, been problematized by Judith Butler (1994).
Rubin's position has been taken by some to provide the basis for a
lesbian and gay studies whose proper object is the study of sexuality
in contrast to feminism, whose proper object is the study of gender.
Butler objects to such a separation on a number of grounds. First, even
in relation to Rubin, who argues that feminism should not be the
only framework for theorizing sexuality, the emphasis is on a variety

of sexualities, whereas lesbian and gay studies seems more restricted than this. Secondly, this separation ignores the radical theories of sex which have emerged from within feminism, many strands of which have challenged 'MacKinnon's structurally static account of gender, its pro-censorship position, and its falsifying cultural generalizations about the eternally victimized position of women' (Butler 1994).

Butler sees a fundamental interdependency in the social construction of gender and sexuality, focused on 'the ideological fiction of marriage and the family as the normalized and privileged domain of sexuality' (1994: 14). For her, as we have seen previously, the matrix of heterosexuality is fundamental to the sex and gender binary. Kinship relations, normalized in the heterosexual family, are thereby central to gender and sexuality: 'kinship survives psychically as the force of prohibition and guilt in sexual life' (p. 13). Thus Butler challenges whether 'the historical and analytic distinction between gender and sexuality is finally tenable' (p. 13).

Such an analysis of the contemporary construction of gender and sexuality is not, of course, a static or determinate one. We can, she argues, think of sexuality apart from reproduction, but reproduction is only one aspect of kinship relations, and thereby of gendered relations. Butler points to the transformative possibilities of thinking kinship 'as a site of redefinition which can move beyond patrilineality, compulsory heterosexuality, and the symbolic over-determination of biology. Examples of the convergence of queer and kinship concerns include the "buddy" system set up by Gay Men's Health crisis . . . laws legitimating lesbian and gay parenting and adoption . . . the rights to make medical decisions for incapacitated lovers' (Butler 1994: 14). Here we might also be reminded of her discussion of the 'houses' in the film *Paris is Burning* (see the discussion in chapter 4). The transformations which such arrangements signal, however, for Butler, are transformations of gender as well as and interdependently with sexuality.

What Butler wishes to draw attention to, in resisting the notion that different arenas can specify 'proper objects' of study, is the development of feminist frameworks in which gender is theorized alongside race, colonial positionality, able-bodiedness, sexuality, class. Within such frameworks gender is regarded as no more fundamental than other aspects of identity, and crucially any manifestations of race or class are gendered, and manifestations of sexuality are gendered and raced and dependent on assumptions of certain kinds of embodiment

(and so on). If we refuse proper objects and thereby distinct areas of
study then we will, for example, be able to detect the racial text in
certain representations of butch/femme encounters. Biddy Martin
(1994a) discusses the way racial difference operates as a marker of difference within lesbian texts and also markers 'to secure butch–femme
roles'. In her discussion of representations of butch/femme roles she
notes that black bodies are marked predominantly as butch (p. 114).
We will also be able to recognize, as Butler suggests, that destabilization of normative heterosexuality is simultaneously destabilization of
gender norms.

An interconnected strand of argument concerns the way in which
'playing with gender roles' is central to a range of sexual practices,
practices which themselves serve to undermine the 'naturalness' of
gender. Butler, for example, in *Gender Trouble* gives the example of
a femme who articulated the specificity of her desire as liking her
'girls to be boys' (1990a: 123), where the destabilization achieved by
such 'erotic interplay' is of masculinity, femininity and heterosexuality. Here the ambivalence, which for Sedgwick attaches to sexuality
but not to gender, is manifest in both. Crossing is a phenomenon of
interdependent sexuality and gender.

In her list of minority sexual practices which suffer social discrimination Rubin includes transsexuality. Given her suggestion that
sexuality and gender should be theorized separately, this is a surprising
inclusion. (We look at the phenomenon of transsexuality as instances
of gendered crossings in chapter 9.) Its inclusion by Rubin, however,
serves to highlight the connections on which Butler is insisting. There
are close connections between lesbian butch experiences, for example,
and female-to-male transsexual experiences (see Halberstam 1998). It
is not always possible clearly to place an identity as sexual or gendered.
Both transsexual men and lesbians claim the character Brandon
Teena, whose story was recently dramatized in the film *Boys Don't
Cry*. Moreover, Western anthropologists in, for example, Thailand
and the Philippines are often unable to characterize the identities they
encounter as exclusively sexual or gendered categories (Johnson 1997).

Notes for a Radical Future

Butler's arguments here should not be taken to imply a reduction
of sexuality to gender or gender to sexuality. They do not invalidate

Rubin's arguments that sexual oppression requires political group-ings on the grounds of sexuality or Rubin's and Sedgwick's that we need an exploration of sexuality as a domain of pleasure. What they do imply, however, is that a radical future for sexuality will also be a radical future for gender.

Theorizing Men and Masculinities

In a book on gender theory why look at men and masculinities in a separate chapter? Surely any exploration of the ways in which gender has been theorized needs to encompass the multiple aspects of gender and therefore masculinity as well as femininity throughout? Indeed the discussion so far has been based on this assumption. The examination of naturalizing discourses, psychoanalytic theories and social constructionist accounts in the previous chapters has focused its attention on the different ways in which we can make sense of *gender*, the multiple modes of theorizing masculinities *and* femininities. What then can a separate section on men and masculinities offer that is not already incorporated into the general analysis of gender?

Since the 1970s, and particularly in the past two decades, there has been an explosion of interest in issues relating specifically to men and masculinities. Within popular culture the media have pounced upon the perceived 'crisis of masculinity' in Western cultures – newspapers, documentaries and talk shows have increasingly pondered the changing meaning of manhood in our modern age. What should we make of girls outperforming boys in schools, of growing male unemployment, of falls in male fertility rates? Popular British films such as *The Full Monty* (1997) and *Brassed Off* (1996) have reflected this growing preoccupation with the changing meaning of masculinity, highlighting in particular the impact of shifting socio-economic circumstances on men's lives and the individual and collective strategies employed by men to cope with their changing environment. In parallel there has been a heightened interest in the particularity of men's lives within Western academia, giving rise to an eruption of texts, conferences and courses looking specifically at men and masculinities. This recent work on men and masculinities spans a variety of different disciplines and employs a wide and often conflicting range of theoretical resources. Likewise the focus of studies varies enormously, taking on a broad range of issues pertinent to masculinity – schooling (Mac an Ghaill 1994), fatherhood (Pleck 1987), race (Staples 1982), fascism (Theweleit 1987, 1989), to name just some examples. Some engage with theory, others are more empirical, descriptive or autobiographical in their approach. A separate section thus provides an opportunity to review the contribution such studies have made and can make to our understanding of gender, and makes possible the exploration of the kinds of theories that have been and may be appropriated, reworked or challenged through the study of men and masculinities. Importantly, this chapter on masculinities operates as a form of case study, to illustrate the ways in which various modes of theorizing employed to facilitate our understanding of gender can be and have been used in the analysis of masculinities.

Such has been the upsurge in interest and work on men and masculinities that 'men's studies' has become increasingly recognized as an academic field in its own right (Brod 1987). As Carrigan, Connell and Lee remark: 'Though there had been books about masculinity before the 1970s there has not been a *genre* debating the nature of masculinity and its social expression. There is such a genre now' (1985: 567). The label 'men's studies' relates to a body of work that encompasses certain key characteristics. Although the range of theories used within men's studies varies, this body of work has in common a belief that masculinity (like femininity) is a social construct. A further common theme is the desire to rework gender relations on a more equitable basis contingent upon the belief that the gender order oppresses and inhibits men as well as women. Furthermore the majority (although not all) of work falling under the umbrella term 'men's studies' is produced by men. Indeed the analysis *of men by men* could be seen as a defining feature of much of what is conventionally defined as the men's studies literature. At the very least the new men's studies is based on the assumption that men can contribute an additional perspective to the study of men and masculinities (Canaan and Griffin 1990). In addition to these factors the vast majority of the work under scrutiny tends to examine masculinity primarily in relation to biologically born men. The relation between masculinity and the male-sexed body is usually assumed within the analysis. In the same vein it tends to employ the distinction male/female unprob-lematically. Thus even critical studies of masculinity which draw on a social constructionist tradition often retain a residual essentialism in that a division between men and women and the assumption that masculinity belongs to men and femininity to women unquestion-ingly underpin analysis.

But while the term 'men's studies' is useful in identifying an emer-ging body of work within the field of gender analysis it does not exhaust the work pertinent to men and masculinities within academia (Canaan and Griffin 1990). If one is to employ the term 'men's studies' one should be aware of its possible limitations. For instance, do we include work by women on men and masculinities under the heading men's studies? Feminist writers such as Cynthia Cockburn (1983, 1985, 1991) have added much to our understanding of mascu-linity but would not necessarily self-label their work 'men's studies', nor would it be labelled as such by others. Indeed, it is vitally import-ant not to overlook the significant contribution feminist writers have made to the study of masculinities (Robinson 1996). In addition, the work by gay scholars on sexuality has been pioneering in the analysis of masculinity but has in the past been ignored or marginalized by many recognized men's studies writers (Carrigan, Connell and Lee 1985: 583). As Carrigan, Connell and Lee observe, 'Gay activists were the first contemporary group of men to address the problem of hegemonic masculinity outside of a clinical context' (1985: 583–4). The gay liberation movement and the research conducted by gay academics challenged society's norms governing masculinity (and sexuality), particularly 'the assumptions by which heterosexuality is taken for granted as the natural order of things' (p. 586). Studies of gay male sexuality highlighted the hierarchical power relationship between different modes of masculinity, signalling the heterosexism and homophobia at the heart of hegemonic masculinity. More re-cently, the impact of queer theory on gender studies adds another dimension to the debates on men and masculinity. By destabilizing the link between sex and gender, between the male body and the construct 'masculinity', queer analysis potentially explodes the very foundations upon which the 'new men's studies' is built. It chal-lenges the assumption that masculinity belongs exclusively to men and femininity to women. How can we confidently study men and masculinities if the very categories are unstable? Finally alongside men's studies is quite a different body of work on men and masculinity, often labelled masculinist studies. As stated above, authors identifying with the new men's studies produce work which defines gender as socially constructed. In parallel there has been a growth of masculinist studies of men and masculinity which stress the 'natural' divisions between men and women. While most (although by no means all) critical studies of men and masculinities declare an affinity with the aims of the feminist movement, 'masculinist studies' draw on naturalizing discourses and stand in opposition, either implicitly or explicitly, to basic feminist principles. While the former is firmly rooted in the academic camp the latter tends to traverse the boundaries between academic scholarship, popular culture and New Right political rhetoric. So while recognition of the growing body of literature – variously known as 'men's studies', 'the new men's studies', 'critical men's studies', 'pro-feminist men's studies' – is important in charting the development of ideas and research on men and masculinity within the field of gender studies, one must also be aware of the possible boundaries the use of such labels generates.

Given the mass of work on men and masculinities, both within and outside 'men's studies', and the scope of theories employed, it would be unfeasible to provide an exhaustive account of all theoretical ideas which have been developed (Hearn 1989: 671; McMahon 1993: 675). By consequence the following discussion of the literature is necessarily partial and incomplete. Instead of attempting a chronological account of developments the aim of this chapter is thus to outline some of the principal concepts developed within the contemporary literature on men and masculinities, using this body of literature as a case study to evaluate various approaches to and themes within gender theory. In short, what contribution does this work make to our understanding of gender?

Naturalizing Masculinity

As discussed above, there exists, in parallel to the men's studies literature which foregrounds the social production of gender, a vast body of work that regards masculinity as an essential quality. Like men's studies, '*masculinist*' literature also makes men and masculinity the focus of its study but instead emphasizes the natural differences between men and women.

Masculinist studies of men and masculinity share a belief in the essential nature of men and women. Drawing on a range of theoretical resources, spanning sociobiology, evolutionary psychology, religious teachings and mythical legend, masculinist writers propound the view that men and women are intrinsically different; that they have sex-specific personality traits and therefore are suited to occupying separate positions within society. As was illustrated in chapter 1, accounts which appeal to nature usually appeal to a certain kind of givenness, to a world which has order and structure independent of our actions and which conditions our lives and our agency. Sociobiologists, for example, have pointed to a variety of biological markers – genes, hormones, size of brains – both to explain and to justify the social organization of men and women. Richard Dawkins's (1976) book *The Selfish Gene* famously argues that men's genetic make-up makes them programmed to philander in order to maximize their reproductive potential. Women, on the other hand, because of their greater investment in reproduction – encompassing gestation, childbirth, breastfeeding and the nurturing of children – are likely to be much more selective in their choice of partner, preferring quality rather than quantity of sexual partner (see chapter 1 for a fuller account of sex difference research).

While masculinist writers offer naturalizing accounts of gender, alluding to a universal male nature which transcends time and space, a common theme within the writings is that modern society is alienating men from their true nature and thus perverting natural masculinity and with it the natural order. To maintain the natural order, it is argued, requires the restoration of men's control of the public sphere and for women to confine themselves to the roles of reproducers. Ben Greenstein in his work *The Fragile Male* draws on sociobiology to argue that men and women are genetically programmed to follow different paths. Men, he argues, are victims of their biological make-up – 'the human male's thoughts, wills and actions are driven by forces outside his control' (Greenstein 1993: 202). In his analysis men have evolved biologically to take a superior place in society. The challenge to male superiority in contemporary society brought about by women's increased role in the public sphere, he warns, may end in violent conflict.

Women may not know it, but they have started something big. They are taking over the human male's last hunting grounds. For the human male is and always has been a hunter. He started out hunting large animals, other men and women, and went on to hunt money, other men and women. Now women have started hunting as well, and men are going to lose their two most important prey, money and women, and they aren't allowed to hunt other men. Women are making the male redundant except as a stud and the consequences are impossible to predict. Men don't understand women and never have. They have never found it easy to cope with women when they were cooped up in the home, let alone rampant in the market place. And when the male runs into something he can't cope with, he fights. (1993: 6–7)

Whereas writers such as Greenstein use sociobiology to support their account of masculinity, other writers in the masculinist tradition take a different approach, preferring instead to make use of Roman and Greek mythology and ancient ritual in their analysis of masculinity. Robert Bly, author of *Iron John* (1990), a seminal text within masculinist studies, argues that modern men have lost touch with their true male essence, their 'Zeus' energy (Coltrane 1994; Hondagneu-Soleto and Messner 1994; Kimmel and Kaufmann 1994; Messner 1997). He advocates men's involvement in all-male retreats and the use of traditional rituals to revive the 'wildman' within (Kimmel and Kaufmann 1994), to help men reassert 'the masculine voice' and to reconnect with their inner manhood. Although Bly is careful in the wording of his argument and 'manages to convey a false symmetry between the feminist movement and his men's movement' (Hondagneu-Soleto and Messner 1994: 203), his account is representative of work in this area in that it is anti-feminist in its approach. Bly, assuming that feminism relies on the notion of a feminine essence, implies that just as feminism has allowed women to assert their female voice men need to be able to assert their own masculine values (Messner 1997). At the heart of Bly's work is the idea that modern society is either feminizing men or forcing them into hypermasculinity, both of which are harmful to the natural order. The 'new man' image, in particular, is castigated as an affront to man's natural essence.

Masculinist studies lack critical scrutiny of the power relations in which gender is constructed. Not only are men and women defined as naturally different, but also the natural order depends upon a hierarchy between the sexes in which men are dominant. In modern Western society, it is argued, this natural order is threatened, primarily by women's increased involvement in the public sphere and the resulting emasculation of men. Messner (1997) argues that there is a distinct anti-intellectualism within much of the work, which manifests itself most visibly in a resistance to take on board or engage with social scientific research on men and masculinities. But while Bly's work, for example, has been slated within the academic community for its 'inaccurate reading of human history and its profound misuse of biological and anthropological evidence' (Coltrane 1994: 46) (add to that a clear misunderstanding of and unfamiliarity with feminism), the ideas he puts forward have struck a chord within the public imaginary. *Iron John* has sold widely, topping the best-seller list in the USA for more than six months after it was published (Kimmel and Kaufmann 1994: 259). The associated 'wildman retreats' have also been hugely popular in the US, albeit primarily with white, middle-class, middle-aged men. The popularity of *Iron John* exists because it (along with other works like it) echoes already widely held notions that men and women are naturally different. Moreover, it feeds upon men's anxiety about their changing role within society in the light of global socio-economic transformations, the shifting terrain of sexual politics and women's changing social status and offers a solution, which relies upon a return to the gender status quo it perceives to be natural.

From Masculinity to Masculinities

Masculinist studies adopt a singular unitary notion of manhood (see, for example, the extract from Greenstein above). The idea that there is a definitive inner masculine core to men is central to such accounts. Men's studies, on the other hand, see masculinity as varied, dynamic, changing; indeed the move from masculinity to masculinities underpins the men's studies' genre. Historical studies have been important in charting shifting patterns in ideals of masculinity and variation in men's social practices, and have made a vital contribution to the development of work on masculinity. Attention to historical specificity and historical change illustrates the social constructedness of masculinity, the multiplicity of ways in which masculinities can be enacted or lived and the existence and potential of change. Kimmel (1994), for example, notes the changing models of manhood in the USA as a result of the expansion of capitalist enterprise. In his account, the Genteel Patriarch and the Heroic Artisan, models of masculinity over the turn of the eighteenth century, gave way to Marketplace Manhood in the 1830s, a form of masculinity characterized by a lack of involvement in day-to-day family affairs and devoted to the male-dominated public world of business. Pleck (1987) examines how fatherhood in the US has changed over time, similarly noting the shifts in models of fatherhood through different historical epochs. Other writers have explored the construction of masculinity in times of war and conflict. Over two volumes Theweleit explores the construction of masculinity in the German *Freikorps*, looking at over 200 *Freikorps* novels and memoirs. The study of the *Freikorps*, set up as it was in Germany after the First World War, allows an intriguing analysis of the political culture in which Nazism developed and the constructions of masculinity upon which this was dependent (Theweleit 1987, 1989).

The mode of theorizing variation and plurality within such accounts varies. However, in early social science perspectives on masculinity there was a tendency to draw on sex role theory to theorize men's position within society (Kimmel 1987: 12). As detailed in chapter 3, sex role theory is inherently limited, providing a static, overly uniform picture of gender socialization. Carrigan, Connell and Lee's seminal article 'Toward a new sociology of masculinity' (1985) provides an extensive critique of studies of men using sex role theory, clearly outlining the limitations of this theoretical approach. In their analysis they conclude:

> The role framework, then, is neither conceptually stable nor a practically and empirically adequate basis for the analysis of masculinity. Let us be blunt about it. The 'male sex role' does not exist. It is impossible to isolate a 'role' that constructs masculinity (or another that constructs femininity). Because there is no area of social life that is not the arena of sexual differentiation and gender relations, the notion of a sex role necessarily simplifies and abstracts to an impossible degree. (1985: 581)

Sex role theory did acknowledge the potential diversity of male roles. Both historical and ethnographical accounts employing sex role theory point to the existence of different constructions of masculinity across time and between cultures (Connell 1995: 27–34). In particular, anthropological studies of non-Western cultures have been crucial in challenging the natural status of Western notions of masculinity, pointing to other norms of masculinity and male behaviour elsewhere. However, any accounts from a sex role perspective tend simply to note that in other societies there are other scripts, other ways to be male just as there are other ways to be female. Thus the plurality of masculine roles has been explained in terms of difference between cultures and not upon difference within cultures (Conway-Long 1994: 61) nor in terms of diversity and contradiction at the level of the individual. Within this framework men and women who fail to conform to the prescribed (expected) pattern of gender behaviour appropriate to their sex within any specific context are instead written off as deviant and anomalous (Brittan 1989: 22).

As Connell argues elsewhere, 'The conceptualization of gender through role theory . . . reifies expectations and self-descriptions, exaggerates consensus, marginalizes questions of power, and cannot analyze historical change' (1992: 735–6). In *Gender and Power* (1987) Connell provides a critique of current theoretical frameworks, which are used to make sense of gender, focusing here in part on the problems of sex role theory. Drawing on both sociological and psychoanalytic analysis, Connell develops through this critique an approach intended to help make sense of the complexities of gender, to provide what he calls 'a serviceable understanding of current history'. Importantly, for this analysis of men's studies literature the theoretical framework he elaborates in this text underpins his specific studies of masculinity elsewhere (see, for example, Connell 1995). In *Gender and Power* Connell argues that each institution or organization has its own gender regime: 'Gender relations are present in *all* types of institutions. They may not be the most important structure in a particular case, but they are certainly a major structure of most' (1987: 120). He identifies three key structures – labour, power and cathexis – through which one can usefully explore the gender composition – the gender regime – of institutions and organizations. By looking at labour Connell takes into account not only the allocation of jobs between men and women but also the nature and organization of work (1987: 102). His analysis of power as a social structure is concerned with authority, control and the construction of hierarchies in between institutions and organizations and over and amongst people. Cathexis, which is perhaps a less familiar term, is concerned with structures of emotional relations.

It has to do with the patterning of object-choice, desire and desirability; with the production of heterosexuality and homosexuality and the relationship between them; with the socially structured antagonisms of gender (woman-hating, man-hating and self-hatred); with trust and distrust, jealousy and solidarity in marriages and other relationships; and with the emotional relationships involved in rearing children. (1987: 97)

A principal criticism of Connell's approach is that by separating labour, power and cathexis it may miss the interconnections between the three, thus oversimplifying the complexities of gender relations. As Segal points out, 'power and desire appear to be aspects and dimensions of all structures' (1990: 102). But, as Connell argues, 'none of the three structures is or can be independent of the others' (1987: 116) but they are instead interwoven. Moreover, he recognizes that the three structures that he identifies are not the only structures that may exist. They are, in his words, 'empirically the major structures of the field of gender relations', while he does not presume 'that they are the only discoverable structures, that they exhaust the field' (1987: 97).

What Connell's approach allows is a means for mapping gender regimes and for exploring the ways in which they contradict each other, change or consolidate. Additionally, by fusing a social structural account with psychoanalysis, Connell attempts to address a key problem with sex role theory (and many materialist accounts of gender) – the inability to illustrate adequately how gender is internalized, 'how structures of gender relations enter into personal life and shape personality' (1987: 219). For Connell, individual personality is not something that is or should be considered as separate from the structural conditions of social life. He writes:

So a personal life is a path through a field of practices which are following a range of collective logics, and are responding to a range of structural conditions which routinely intersect and often contradict each other. It is no wonder that theories of personal life which reify 'the individual' and his or her features . . . give very little grip on reality. The structure of personality is not the structure of an object. It is a particular unification of diverse and often contradictory practices. (1987: 222)

The emphasis within Connell's work on the interconnections between social structure and individual personality has resonance with the materialist analyses of gender outlined in chapter 3 which seek to explore the causal connections between gender and other social structures. Moreover Connell points to the place of ideology 'in the constitution of social interests' (1987: 245) – he identifies as an example the ways in which sexual ideology naturalizes gender practices, portraying that which is socially constructed as biological, natural and unchangeable. Yet Connell's endeavour to theorize gender incorporates much more in that he attempts also to integrate elements of psychoanalysis with the insights of a materialist account, thereby acknowledging gender as a feature of subjectivity as well as social structure.

Hegemonic Masculinity

The concept 'hegemonic masculinity' has been developed and is used widely in critical studies of men and masculinity to explore power relations between men as well as to illustrate the disparities and interconnections between cultural norms of masculinities and the realities of men's lives. The work of Connell in particular has led the way here (Carrigan, Connell and Lee 1985; Connell 1987, 1992, 1995). Within a particular society or social context, he suggests, there is a culturally dominant construction of masculinity, a hegemonic discourse. Hegemonic masculinity is an ideal-type. It is not embodied by all men; it is not the only form of masculinity; in fact it is not regarded as the form of masculinity most common to men (Connell 1993; see also Donaldson 1993). Instead it is the type of masculinity performed by popular heroes, fantasy figures and role models (Donaldson 1993). As Connell indicates, 'Hegemony is a question of relations of cultural domination, not of head-counts' (Connell 1993: 610). The observation that many, indeed most men fail to live up to societal norms prescribing masculinity has become a prominent theme within men's studies literature and one which often draws either implicitly or explicitly on post-structuralist notions of discourse.

Erving Goffman suggests that there is only one unblushing American male. He is 'A young, married, white, urban, northern heterosexual, Protestant father of college education, fully employed, of good complexion, weight and height, and a recent record in sports. . . . Any male who fails to qualify in any one of these ways is likely to view himself . . . as unworthy, incomplete, and inferior' (cited in

Kimmel 1994: 125). Goffman's description of hegemonic masculinity, while pertaining to US society at a particular point in time, does, however, identify certain key aspects of masculinity seen as desirable and 'normal' across contemporary Western society. Hegemonic masculinity in Western society is recognized in most literature as hinging on heterosexuality, economic autonomy, being able to provide for one's family, being rational, being successful, keeping one's emotions in check, and above all not doing anything considered feminine. Yet what constitutes hegemonic masculinity is not fixed. Indeed, it is increasingly recognized within the literature on men and masculinities that hegemonic masculinity is a 'historically mobile relation' (Connell 1995: 77) and that the content of hegemonic masculinity is fluid over time and between cultural contexts. Moreover, within a particular society cultural ideals of masculinity can manifest differently according to social context (Ramazanoglu, cited in Lupton and Barclay 1997: 12). For example, traditionally dominant discourses of masculinity in relation to the family have tended to emphasize the importance of men providing for their family members while day-to-day nurturing has been regarded as a feminine activity and thus to be rejected by 'real men'. However, middle-class ideals of masculinity in the West increasingly stress the acceptability and desirability of men's greater involvement in childcare. This new father image is essentially a white, middle-class construction, formulated as a means of asserting a certain class- (and race-) specific performance of masculinity (Lupton and Barclay 1997: 15). As Brod remarks, 'the use of working-class male images to denote traditional sexism renders the sexism of middle- and upper-middle-class men less visible and therefore less challenged' (1994: 92). Interestingly, while dangerous or 'deadbeat' dads are usually portrayed as poor, working-class or non-white (Lupton and Barclay 1997: 15), research in the US suggests that Latino and black men actually do more domestic labour than their white counterparts (Messner 1997: 47).

While on the one hand working-class masculinity, black masculinity and gay masculinity are presented as subordinate or marginal masculinities, such sub-groups also generate their own cultural norms of masculinity. Nardi, for example, points to historical shifts in the conceptualization of hegemonic notions of gay masculinity in the United States, suggesting that hypermasculinity has displaced effeminacy and drag queens as 'the privileged image' (2000: 5). Westwood (1990) in her analysis of working-class, black masculinity in Britain argues that ideals of masculinity for young black men in working-class communities hinge on being streetwise, in part articulated via physical prowess but also through being cool, knowing and appearing in control of the local environment (see the sections on subordinated masculinities below).

The pursuit of 'the masculine ideal' is articulated in different ways according to the resources available to individual and groups of men (Kaufmann 1994). Kaufmann suggests that 'Each sub-group, based on race, class, sexual orientation, or whatever, defines manhood in ways that conform to the economic and social possibilities of that group' (1994: 145). For example, Western conceptions of masculinity generally emphasize the importance of being, and being seen as, successful as central to the attainment of manhood. If making your mark in the world through employment or educational success is unavailable to some men because of their position within the social structure, they may seek alternative ways to prove their worth and ability – crime being one such option. Alternatively, they may emphasize physical ability or sexual prowess. Likewise the norms of masculinity change over generations as well as from context to context. What was expected of men in our fathers' generation often differs from the expectations placed on men in our own. Changing economic circumstances, for example, have whittled away some of the clearly defined markers of movement, the rites of passage, from boyhood to manhood (Willis 1977).

In general the notion of hegemonic masculinity as represented within critical studies of men and masculinities encompasses two main features. First, that hegemonic masculinity is a cultural *ideal* and is as such an uninhabitable goal for the majority of men. Although neither Lacan nor Butler features widely in traditional men's studies literature the understanding of hegemonic masculinity as a cultural ideal is consonant with Butler's argument that the gender performances which we enact are performances in accordance with a script – a script which supplies us with ideals of both masculinity and femininity. As illustrated in chapter 4, Butler draws on Lacan's notion of a symbolic order. The ideals are unachievable yet they act as a reference point for all our actions. Secondly, while the content of hegemonic masculinity is fluid, common to dominant ideals of masculinity in Western society is a rejection of both femininity and homosexuality. As in Butler's account of gender the ideal of masculinity in our society is heterosexual.

To return to the depiction of ideal-type masculinity put forward by Goffman, the demands of hegemonic masculinity are clearly out of reach for most men. Masculinity is portrayed in the literature as something that is unresolved and therefore subject to eternal doubt (Kimmel 1994). Because of the unobtainability of the masculine ideal, it is argued, there is a constant need for men to prove that they are achieving the goals of masculinity and with it a permanent insecurity attached to manhood. Being able to display signs of hegemonic masculinity – for example, strength, sexual prowess with women, the ability to consume beer – becomes vital to demonstrate that one is a 'real man'. Masculinity is presented as a process which needs constantly reaffirming; one's status as a man is never secure but in perpetual need of validation by other men (again, although Butler is not explicitly used, such ideas are consistent with her notion of gender as performance, a repetition of acts and deeds). As Kimmel notes, 'We [men] are under the constant careful scrutiny of other men. Other men watch us, rank us, grant our acceptance into the realm of manhood. Manhood is demonstrated for other men's approval. It is other men who evaluate the performance' (1994: 128). As a result, it is suggested, men often feel inadequate and powerless even if they occupy positions of power within the public arena, for instance in employment, an issue to which we shall return in more depth below.

Masculinity and Homophobia

Hegemonic notions of masculinity demand that to be a 'real man' requires the rejection of all things feminine, in that masculinity is constructed in opposition to femininity. For men to conform to dominant ideas of manliness they must distance themselves from all traits and characteristics associated with femininity. Wearing pink, reading romantic fiction and caring for babies are cultural symbols of femininity in Anglo-Saxon culture and thus regarded as antithetical to the demands of masculinity. In addition, hegemonic masculinity, within contemporary Western society, is inextricably entwined with cultural constructions of hegemonic sexuality – to be a 'real man' is to be a heterosexual man. To prove one's masculinity a man needs therefore to display a coherent heterosexuality. This is achieved not only via active displays of desire for women – bragging about sexual conquests, putting up calendars of naked women – but also through men purposefully distancing themselves from homosexuality through homophobic behaviour. Homophobia amongst men is not so much to do with the sexuality of others but more a means to display one's own heterosexual masculinity.

As Kimmel writes, 'Homophobia is more than the irrational fear of gay men, more than the fear that we may be perceived as gay. . . . Homophobia is the fear that other men will unmask us, emasculate us, reveal to us and the world that we do not measure up, that we are not real men' (1994: 131). Boys who are subject to homophobic taunts are not exposed to taunting because of their sexuality but perhaps because they flouted other rules of masculinity, by not taking part in 'boyish' activities, having close friendships with girls, perhaps being perceived as a swot. Homosexuality becomes, as Connell acknowledges, 'the repository of whatever is symbolically expelled from hegemonic masculinity' (Connell 1995: 78). When in 1999 the British footballer Graeme Le Saux hit the headlines for lashing out against a fellow footballer who had subjected him to homophobic taunts during a match, it became apparent that Le Saux's sexuality had been questioned because of his fondness for art galleries, collecting antiques and reading broadsheet newspapers and his aversion to beery post-match celebrations, rather than any alleged sexual involvement with men. Indeed his status as a married father was irrelevant to his harasser. The case of Le Saux shows not only how dominant constructions of masculinity and sexuality are entwined – he broke the rules of masculinity and therefore his heterosexuality was attacked – but also the contextuality of hegemonic masculinity. Le Saux was demonstrating what could be perceived as a middle-class maleness in a context built around working-class values. In a different social milieu his behaviour would not necessarily have appeared out of sync with the demands of masculinity and would not have provoked such a backlash.

In theoretical terms the interrelationship between hegemonic masculinity, heterosexuality and homophobia is explored from a variety of different perspectives. While some authors focus on the material effects of homophobia or the discursive articulation of homophobic prejudice, others link homophobia to the development of the gendered psyche or consider its performative dimensions. Kimmel, for example, links the repudiation of the feminine directly with homophobia, drawing on Freudian ideas to explore their interconnectedness (see

chapter 2). Boys, he argues, as part of their masculine development
need to separate from the mother, the first object of identification,
and to identify instead with the father. As part of the process boys
come to despise the mother and by implication femininity as the
mother retains the power to expose his dependency upon her (Kimmel
1994: 126–7). Furthermore, in the pre-Oedipal stage the young boy,
while identifying with the mother, *'sees the world through his mother's
eyes'* (1994: 130). When he moves to identify with the father he has to
come to terms with having seen his father through his mother's eyes
and therefore as an object of desire. Desire for the father and therefore men generally is seen as feminine desire and therefore has to be
quelled. 'Homophobia', Kimmel argues, arises from 'the effort to
suppress this desire' (p. 130).

Nayak and Kehily (1996) instead look at the performative, ritualistic
nature of homophobia in their analysis of homophobic behaviour
amongst young boys at school. Taking Butler's idea that 'gender is
the repeated stylization of the body, a set of repeated acts . . . to
produce the appearance of substance, of a natural sort of being',
the authors point to the ways in which homophobia is verbally and
physically exhibited by the boys within the school environment.
Homophobic humour, language and insults, and exaggerated actions
(e.g. making a fuss about not going into men's toilets/not bending
over in the company of some men/making the sign of the crucifix
towards boys targeted as gay) were part of the everyday routine of
school life; acts displayed by the young boys to convince not only
others of their heterosexual masculine status but also themselves.
Nayak and Kehily (1996: 225) conclude that

> the performance style [of homophobia] says more about the ongoing
> construction of the self, than the sexual identities of Others. . . . In the
> constant struggle for coherence subjects engage in various forms of
> splitting, projection and displacement which are 'articulated' in the
> homophobic performance. These processes of self-production appear
> to go largely unacknowledged by the individuals concerned as they
> struggle to achieve the illusion of internal consistency. . . . Homophobic
> performances are part of the self-convincing rituals of masculinity
> young men engage in. The performance is as much for self as others,
> where heterosexual masculinities are constituted through action.
> These actions are not simply a momentary social performance for
> an external audience, but form a technique for styling masculine
> self-identity.

Subordinated Masculinities: Gay Men

Although the interrelationship between hegemonic masculinity, homophobia and heterosexism has become a key theme in 'men's studies' literature it is to the work of gay studies writers and gay activists that we must turn in order to explore fully the interconnections of gender and sexuality in the formulation of masculine identities. Gay studies theorists and commentators have highlighted the synonymy within our culture of heterosexuality and hegemonic masculinity, emphasizing the ways in which hegemonic notions of gender and sexuality are intermeshed within our cultural imaginary. Dennis Altman's groundbreaking text, *Homosexual: oppression and liberation*, first published in 1971, for example, explored not only the myriad of ways in which gay men and women were oppressed and the development of a resistant gay identity through the emergence of the gay liberation movement in the US, but also the cultural specificity of the homo/hetero divide. For Altman homosexual identity was constructed in resistance to the dominance of heterosexuality (see Weeks 2000 for a fuller discussion of Altman's text). The end of homosexual oppression entails the end of the homosexual and the heterosexual as distinct identities. Altman explains that 'the vision of liberation that I hold is one that would make the homo/hetero distinction irrelevant. For that to happen, however, we shall have to recognize our bisexual potential, and until that is done, homosexuality, like blackness, will remain a major category that defines our lives' (1971: 218).

Altman's work is representative of a key strand in gay studies literature which emphasizes the cultural and historical construction of 'the homosexual' as an identity category. Mary McIntosh's article, 'The homosexual role', which first appeared in 1968, has been hugely significant here (see Weeks 2000 for an analysis of McIntosh's contribution) and pre-dates the influence of Foucault (*The History of Sexuality*, vol. 1 (1978)), a key contributor to the debate. McIntosh, looking at the British context, argues that the category 'the homosexual' is not a historical constant but instead produced within the context of the eighteenth century. While same-sex behaviour has always existed, the identity 'gay man', she argues, has not. It was only in the eighteenth century, she claims, that sexual practice became a source of identity (Mackintosh 1981). The task of excavating the historical roots of homosexual identity, of historicizing sexuality, has been taken up by a number of other authors (see, for example, Foucault 1979; Weeks 1977, 1981, 2000; Plummer, 1981). Weeks, for example, argues against what he sees as fruitless attempts to uncover the causes of homosexual desire and instead for an exploration of the historical and social processes in which classification and categorization occur. In a similar vein to Altman, he argues that gay and lesbian identities are 'necessary fictions', required to negotiate and combat the discrimination and persecution that gay men and women encounter because of their sexual practices.

Analyses of homosexual identities bring into question the interconnections between gender and sexuality. Popular culture has traditionally conflated sexuality and gender, seeing gay men as feminine and lesbians as masculine. The binaries male/female, gay/straight become superimposed. To be a 'real man', we learn from dominant discourses, is to be a straight man. If you are not straight, then, the discourses suggest, you are lacking in masculinity, and if one is lacking in masculinity then one is feminine. Hence the ready association within our culture of male homosexuality with effeminacy (and lesbianism with masculine behavioural traits) (see chapter 1). But as Nardi observes there is in reality a plurality of ways in which gay men act out their masculinity:

> Gay men exhibit a multiplicity of ways of 'doing' masculinity that can best be described by the plural form 'masculinities'. Some enact the strongest of masculine stereotypes through bodybuilding and sexual prowess, whereas others express a less dominant form through spirituality or female impersonation. Many simply blend the 'traditional' instrumental masculinity with the more 'emotional' masculinity that comes merely by living their everyday lives when they are hanging out with their friends and lovers, working out at the gym, or dealing with the oppressions related to their class and ethnic identities. (Nardi 2000: 1–2)

Drawing on a wealth of gay studies literature (for example, Chauncey 1994; Katz 1983), Nardi outlines the historical variability and multiplicities of gay identities, pointing in particular to the divisions and tensions between effeminate and masculine gay men, both historically and contemporarily.

As Segal observes in her analysis of masculinities, 'homosexual subcultures have a tantalizing relationship with the masculine ideal – part challenge, part endorsement' (1990: 145). On the one hand the gay activism and academia have done much to subvert and undermine the norms of hegemonic masculinity, particularly to denaturalize the status of heterosexual manhood. 'Camp', although often interpreted as indicative of the effeminacy of gay men, can also be employed and interpreted as subversive parody. Similarly, the increasing macho-ization of gay culture from the late 1970s, characterized by the adoption of a hypermasculine style – bodybuilding/muscular physiques, leather biker look, 'bovver boy' clones, etc. – works, on one level, to undermine the dominant status of heterosexual masculinity. Leaving aside the erotic aspects of 'butch' (see Humphries 1985), the 'butch shift' has political (albeit contradictory) undertones. By appropriating the symbols of masculinity and exaggerating them macho/butch gay men are exposing the artificiality of normative heterosexual masculinity. Gay men, the look suggests, can be even more 'masculine' than their heterosexual counterparts, thus challenging claims that only heterosexual men are 'real men'.

At the same time, however, both camp and macho styles have come under criticism for reinforcing and buying into masculine/feminine stereotypes, thus validating the traditional gender order. Camp gay culture, it has been argued, depends upon and strengthens orthodox masculine/feminine roles. Likewise the machoization of gay culture can be seen as an endorsement of elements of hegemonic masculinity. As Messner suggests, 'despite the potential of gay liberation to strip off the masks of masculinity, it appears that the dominant tendency in gay culture eventually became an attempt to claim, eroticize, and display the dominant symbols of hegemonic masculinity' (1997: 83). D. Harris points to the prejudice that exists *within* gay communities against effeminate gay men: 'When we attempted to heal the pathology of the gay body by embarking on the costume dramas of the new machismo, we did not succeed in freeing ourselves from our belief in the heterosexual male's evolutionary superiority. . . . In fact, we . . . became our own worst enemies, harsh, homophobic critics of the campy demeanour of the typical queen' (cited in Nardi 2000: 5).

Blachford (1981) examines the masculinization of gay sub-culture and the reproduction of patterns of male dominance in gay communities. He suggests promiscuity amongst gay men and activities such as gay cruising and pick-ups can be read as both reinforcing traditional masculine values relating to sexuality as well as challenging dominant notions of sexual behaviour. On the one hand, casual sexual encounters appear to fit conventional male patterns of sexual detachment and objectification. At the same time, however, casual sexual encounters challenge notions that legitimate sex should only take place 'in the context of love and possible reproduction inside a long-term monogamous relationship' (1981: 198). Blachford continues:

> Gay casual sex can be seen as a rejection of this narrow definition of legitimate sex as it expands its range of possible meanings. It includes seeing sex as a form of recreation, simply a game or hobby, as fun. It is divested of all its moral and guilt overtones and is enjoyed as an end in itself. Perhaps the possibility has arisen for this wider and creative range of public meanings because the reproductive aspect of sex is impossible. (1981: 198)

Subordinated Masculinities: Black Masculinities

Male homosexuality, as argued above, can act as a challenge to dominant discourses which equate manhood with heterosexuality. Yet being gay does not preclude conformity to other facets of hegemonic maleness, nor does it mean that in certain contexts gay men may reap the rewards of being male. As Connell observes,

> In our culture, men who have sex with men are generally oppressed, but they are not definitively excluded from masculinity. Rather, they face *structurally-induced conflicts* about masculinity – conflicts between their sexuality and their social presence as men, about the meaning of their choice of sexual object, and in their constructions of relationships with women and with heterosexual men. (1992: 737)

Although homosexuality contravenes hegemonic, heterosexualized notions of manhood, this does not mean that gay men themselves do not draw on and reinforce conventional ideas of masculinity just as they may actively or inadvertently seek to undermine them. As argued above, the hypermasculine, butch image adopted by some gay men can be seen as both subversive and conformist. Gay men in a work situation may, for instance, benefit from and reinforce gender hierarchies in which women find themselves lacking power. Likewise white gay men, as with white men of any sexual orientation, benefit from white cultural dominance. The gay liberation movement is not immune to racist practices and stereotyping and has been criticized from both within and without as being overtly white in terms both of its membership and of its views on sexuality. Mercer and Julien (1988) provide a damning critique of the ways in which white racism has and can operate within gay culture. Not only are black gay men marginalized within the movement, they argue, but also racist stereotypes of black/oriental sexuality have remained unchallenged. Echoing many of the debates within the feminist movement around difference, black gay men point to the ethnocentric biases of gay politics. Calls by white gay men to dismantle the heterosexual nuclear family – seen as it is as a bastion of heterosexism and symbolic of heterosexual privilege – ignore, for example, the importance of family networks in providing support and resistance within a racist culture.

Within the literature on men and masculinities black masculinity is usually defined as a 'subordinate masculinity'. Hegemonic masculinity in Western culture, it is argued, is intrinsically white. The socioeconomic and material disadvantages experienced by many black men in Britain has been well-documented. Although we must be careful not to equate blackness with being socio-economically deprived, unemployment data and poverty statistics, for example, show clearly that ethnic minorities in Britain are more prone to long-term joblessness, poor health and bad housing than their white counterparts. Likewise research on the intersections of gender and race point to the ways in which racist, colonialist assumptions structure and produce dominant images of black masculinity within white Western culture. Men of Afro-Caribbean descent are stereotyped variously as absent fathers, lazy, violent, sexually and physically dominating; indeed cultural stereotypes of black masculinity often exhibit a fixation with the black male body. Dominant discourses equate whiteness with the mind and therefore rational action, blackness with the body and therefore irrationality. Asian men, on the other hand, are often feminized, seen as manipulative, untrustworthy and wily (Westwood 1990; Looby 1997; McDowell 1997). Looby (1997) points to the inconsistencies and contradictions at the heart of racist discourses. On the one hand black men of African descent are seen as lacking masculinity – portrayed as being childlike, lacking intelligence – on the other they are seen as having an excess of masculinity, producing, for example, an out-of-control sexual appetite.

Analyses of black masculinities can be used to illustrate the ways in which our conceptions of gender, sexuality and race are interwoven and are constituent of each other. As argued in previous chapters, gendered, sexed and sexualized categories are themselves raced. As Mercer and Julien note, 'Traditional notions of sexuality are deeply linked to race and racism because sex is regarded as that thing which *par excellence* is a threat to the moral order of Western civilisation. Hence, one is civilised at the expense of sexuality, and sexual at the expense of civilisation' (1988: 108). The various negative constructions of black and oriental masculinity are rooted, it has been argued, in the exploitation and violence of colonialism. Western constructions of sexuality formulated during the period of colonial expansion are inherently racist, equating sexual excess and a lack of civilization in their conceptualizations of the colonized. White, Western discourses traditionally define African men as having animal-like, uncontrollable sexual demands; oriental men (and women) as subservient, yet perversely malleable.

The negative constructions of the 'black man' are integral to white men's construction of self. The construction of a dominant white masculinity is dependent upon constructions of the black masculine 'other'. The over-sexualization of men of African descent, for example, is contrived not only from the sexual neuroses of the colonizer but also as an attempt to produce an untainted, healthful image of white heterosexual masculinity and a representation of white heterosexual femininity as under threat and in need of protection and surveillance by white men. As one commentator remarked, 'to be an American Negro male is also to be a kind of walking phallic symbol, which means one pays in one's own personality, for the sexual insecurity of others' (Baldwin, cited in McDowell 1997: 362–3). Just as the gay man becomes, as Connell noted, the repository for all things 'symbolically expelled from hegemonic masculinity' (1995: 78) the 'black man' becomes the repository for the sexual fantasies, deviancies (sexual and social), and so on, of the white heterosexual male. Fanon in his 1950s account of the psychosocial aspects of race and racism, *Black Skin, White Masks*, argues that 'The Negro is a phobogenic object, a stimulus to anxiety' (1968: 151). Similarly, McDowell points to 'culture's habitual tendency to use black men to focus the nation's attention on rape, sexual harassment, and wife battering' (1997: 376). Soap operas in Britain such as *Eastenders* have been castigated in the past for stereotyping Asian men as sexually dysfunctional. Reynolds (1997) notes the equation of absent fatherhood with Afro-Caribbean men in contemporary Britain. 'In no other culture', she argues, 'is the issue of male absenteeism given such dominant coverage. This makes male absenteeism appear to be culturally specific to black families of Caribbean descent, although it can be identified across different societies and cultures. The social and economic factors which determine black male absenteeism are rarely discussed' (Reynolds 1997: 104–5).

A central debate within the literature dealing with black masculinity is its relation to white hegemonic masculinity. Staples, for example, in his analysis of the socio-historical dimensions of black maleness argues that while black masculinity is 'in conflict with the normative definitions of masculinity' black men, in a bid to retrieve some of the power and authority denied to them within a white-dominated culture, look to other means of asserting authority. Dominant discourses of masculinity define maleness as being in control, having power over others and one's environment. Racism, colonialism and slavery have denied and continue to deny black men such authority; indeed the conditions of racism threaten to take away many of the staple dimensions of hegemonic masculinity. The hustler, streetwise role adopted by many of the young black men involved in Westwood's research project (see above) provided one such way for black men to reclaim authority (Westwood 1990). Recovering male power may also be sought via the subordination and devaluing of women or through homophobic discrimination.

Mac an Ghaill's study of young black men in an English school highlights the ways in which the men themselves are active in the formation of their masculine identities, simultaneously negotiating, resisting and adapting discourses on gender and 'race' (1994). The young men known as Rasta Heads in the study actively resisted Englishness through their asserted identification with Rastafarian culture.

> For large sectors of working-class young men, their experience of English society can be read in terms of a defensive culture of masculine survival against social marginalization. It is within this culture that they construct and live out images of what it means to be a man. A central component of the Rasta Heads' survival was their projection and amplification of a specific form of masculinity that overemphasized 'toughness'. In this process, they can be seen as active gender makers. (Mac an Ghaill 1994: 187)

Within their own cultural context the Rasta Heads were constructing a counter-hegemonic masculinity. Not only did it encompass physical strength, toughness and a proclaimed identification with black culture, it also involved the assertion of both heterosexist and homophobic attitudes. The black masculinity they were asserting in resistance to white authority also served to marginalize and distance other groups of black men as well as black women. As Mac an Ghaill noted, the group in question distanced themselves from another group of black male students within the school who were in the higher academic groups, subjecting them to homophobic insults.

Although the Rasta Heads were actively distancing themselves from white maleness, overlaps were clearly observable; and both hegemonic maleness and the masculinity the Rasta Heads were performing hinged on heterosexist, homophobic beliefs. 'There is a further contradiction,' Mercer and Julien note, 'another turn of the screw of oppression, which occurs when black men subjectively internalise and incorporate aspects of the dominant definitions of masculinity in order to contest the conditions of dependency and powerlessness which racism and racial oppression enforce' (1988: 112). The image of black males as sexually irrepressible is one such example; although based on racist/colonialist assumptions of black as dirty, animal, uncivilized, purely physical and lacking in the rational sensitivity of the white man it is an image drawn on and perpetuated by some black men.

The Rasta Heads articulated their resistance to white authority not just in terms of black people's rights but also in terms of their rights as black *men*. As one of the young men argued, 'You see a man he's supposed to have respect, right. Well the black man can't get respect in this society. So what are we supposed to do? We have to let them know that we exist, that we exist as a people' (Mac an Ghaill 1994: 189). The crisis of the black community is often interpreted from within and without the black community (by men) as the crisis of black masculinity, with black women becoming invisible within the discussions. The work of black feminists (as well as black gay writers) has done much to expose and deal with the contradictions at the heart of black masculinity. Writers such as bell hooks and Alice Walker point to the dilemmas black women face in their relationships with black men, at once wishing to retain solidarity as a means of resisting racism but also wanting to confront sexism and oppression where it occurs within the black community (see, for example, hooks 1990; Walker 1982; Angelou 1984), challenging with it the male bias of the black civil rights movement. hooks notes that:

Historically the language used to describe the way black men are victimized within racist society has been sexualized. When words like castration, emasculation, impotency are the commonly used terms to describe the nature of black male suffering, a discursive practice is established that links black male liberation with gaining the right to participate fully within patriarchy. Embedded within this assumption is the idea that black women who are not willing to assist black men in their efforts to become patriarchs are 'the enemy'. (1990: 76)

Wallace (1979) is particularly damning in her critique of black masculinity and in relation to black male activists argues that their misogyny disfigured the black rights movement. Challenges by black men to white oppression, it is argued, have been a gender struggle; a struggle for black men to reclaim the status and authority of manhood denied to them by a predominantly white, racist society (see, for example, the rhetoric of Malcolm X, and Eldridge Cleaver of the Black Panthers) involving often the subordination of women and gay men in the process. Contemporarily, McDowell notes that, within popular black culture, male rappers and cinematographers often assert their masculinity via an overtly sexualized degradation of women. They are, she argues, ' "shooting back" [not only] at the white establishment and its dominant cultural forms, but also at a society that they rightly perceive as denying them the rights and privileges of masculinity.' Central to this masculinity is the subordination of women and the elevation of male heterosexuality. 'That masculinity – almost always assumed to be heterosexual – includes the right to render women inessential, superfluous, on the one hand, and to dominate and degrade them on the other' (1997: 375).

At the same time, however, writers point to the ways in which black men have resisted white hegemonic maleness through forms of cultural expression, or have sought to subvert dominant images of black masculinity. Music with its roots in African American communities of the US, such as blues and soul, are, it has been noted, emotionally expressive forms of music – arenas in which black males have deliberated and challenged the confines of masculinity, thereby subverting the association of masculinity with 'emotional illiteracy' (Mercer and Julien 1988: 140). Within the arena of black cultural expression we can identify the multiplicity of black masculinities. Looking particularly at black African masculinity we can see in rap music the ways in which a hypermasculine, supremely macho black male identity is constructed. Alternatively, black male artists such as

Prince and Michael Jackson in their theatrical performances actively strive to subvert and undermine such dominant codes of masculinity. In British society, television comedy has often been used by black and Asian men as a context in which to play with images of black/ Asian masculinity – see, for example, the characters performed by Lenny Henry or the *Goodness Gracious Me* team. As Mercer and Julien note, 'by destabilising signs of race, gender and sexuality these artists draw critical attention to the cultural *constructedness*, the artifice, of the sexual roles and identities we inhabit' (1988: 141). Also we would add the constructedness, the artifices of race and gender.

Psychoanalytic Analyses

A common theme within the 'men's studies' literature is the contradictory position of men in relation to power. The norms of masculinity are, it is argued, impossible to live up to and as a result men are often left feeling insecure, powerless and afraid, even if they access material advantage, status and authority in public life or in family/ kinship networks.

> Whatever power might be associated with dominant masculinities, they can also be the source of enormous pain. Because the images are, ultimately, childhood pictures of omnipotence, they are impossible to obtain. Surface appearances aside, no man is able to completely live up to these ideals and images. For one thing we all continue to experience a range of needs and feelings that are deemed inconsistent with manhood. Such experiences become the source of enormous fear. (Kaufmann 1994: 148)

From a theoretical standpoint writers on men and masculinities have looked often to psychoanalytic thought to explore the ways in which the construction of the male psyche may inhibit men's well-being and generate such feelings of insecurity and anxiety. As Seidler notes, 'Psychoanalysis alerts us to the fragmentation of the person that relations of power and subordination bring about, and to the importance of emotions and feelings, which have their own inner logic, in grasping the damage to people' (1989: 10). Psychoanalysis provides the resources for exploring the various ways in which men internalize their gender identity, the ways in which the unconscious operates in the formation of the gendered psyche, and a means of understanding the emotional investment men may have in their identities and/or the pain and conflict that arises from them. Psycho-analysis thus offers us additional resources with which to compre-hend masculinities unavailable within discourse theory. 'One area which discourse theory has tended to overlook', argue Lupton and Barclay, 'is an understanding of the inner world of the subject and the importance of emotional states, mutuality and intimate relations between people' (1997: 21).

The strand of psychoanalytic thought which is used most per-vasively in men's studies accounts is object-relations theory (see chapter 2), although Freud is also drawn upon (see the section on 'Masculinity and Homophobia', pp. 143–5 above; Kimmel 1994). Within object-relations theory it is the work of Chodorow, particu-larly the text *The Reproduction of Mothering* (1978), which features primarily. Within this account masculinity represents an ongoing struggle to reject the feminine, as a result of the role the mother plays as primary carer and the boy's early identification with her. For boys to distance themselves from the mother, all characteristics associated with her have to be suppressed and denied. As a result traits that are identified as feminine, such as displays of 'softer' emotions, caring and nurturing, have to be destroyed or buried. In short, to be a man therefore involves the constant cancellation of what is thought to be the feminine within, leading, as argued above, not only to sexism and misogyny but also to homophobia. Summing up such a psycho-analytic approach to masculinity, Edley and Wetherell suggest, 'this perspective explains why masculinity is typically defined in popular culture and by men in defensive terms – against femininity – and why men often find it easier to say what masculinity is *not* rather than what it positively is' (1995: 51).

Object-relations theory has been appropriated within various men's studies texts to highlight and explain the vulnerability and insecurity many men experience, despite the general equation of men with power within our culture (see, for example, the collection edited by Metcalf and Humphries 1985). The comparatively high suicide rates among men, particularly among young men, are often cited, for example, as indication of the psychological pressures of masculine identity. Women may be less likely to occupy positions of power within the public sphere yet within this approach women are seen as potentially more secure with their gender identity. Men's studies theorists have used psychoanalysis to show that the power that men have is 'something *not worth having*' (Segal 1990: 80), the costs are too high. The need for the male to disassociate himself from all things female explains not only men's difficulties expressing emotions but also their perceived lack of involvement in the nurturing process. To reject the mother – the female within – all expressions of nurturing and caring need to be suppressed. Within this framework even male violence towards women can be attributed to the process of men disassociating from 'feminine' traits. Instead of the act of repudiating the feminine being an internalized process, 'men may turn more *actively* against women, abusing them sexually and/or physically as a way of denying their feelings of dependence' (Edley and Wetherell 1995: 100). A reconfiguration of masculinity, it is suggested, would be beneficial to men as well as to women. The emphasis within psychoanalytic thought on the impact of early infant care by the mother on the development of the male (and female) psyche has led many to pinpoint the need for men's greater involvement in the early care of children as a key step in this reconfiguration.

Such psychoanalytic accounts of masculinity have been criticized, however, for a lack of engagement with social hierarchies of power (McMahon 1993; Segal 1990). Segal points to both the potential and the limitations of a purely psychoanalytic approach when she comments:

> it is only with the insights of psychoanalysis that the intensities of men's paranoia over masculinity, their endemic violence towards women, and the cultural fear and hatred of women become comprehensible. But it is also by placing the psychology of men within the social context of those broader patterns of existence which maintain and disrupt male domination that we can understand the contemporary dilemmas of masculinity. (1990: 103)

McMahon (1993) takes this issue further in a detailed critique of the problematic appropriation of the object-relations school of psychoanalysis in some areas of men's studies. He argues that the literature on men and masculinities which draws on psychoanalysis has the tendency to overlook the material benefits men derive from current forms of gender relations and to deny men's agency in perpetuating male power. The appropriation of object-relations theory about gender identity formation, such as the early work of Chodorow,

enables theorists, he continues, to present an account of masculinity
that emphasizes the disadvantaged and tragic status of masculinity
when compared to femininity (McMahon 1993: 687–8). 'Reliance on
this approach', suggests McMahon, 'allows male writers to employ
rhetoric about men that is highly critical, and, at the same time,
to ground these criticisms in an analysis that directs attention away
from men's practices. Thus it is possible to speak in terms of male
power, domination, and advantage while proposing an explanation in terms of the agent-less reproduction of a social structure'
(1993: 687).

In addition, psychoanalysis has difficulties coping with the issue of
diversity among men. First, accounts such as that put forward by
Chodorow in *The Reproduction of Mothering* assume a certain type of
family form, a nuclear family with the mother as primary carer and
the father relatively detached from the nurturing process; a family
form which is by no means universal. Moreover, psychoanalysis
tends to overlook the potential significance of ethnic or class divisions.
As Edley and Wetherell observe, 'It is often unclear, for example,
whether psychoanalysts commenting on men and male experience
are referring exclusively to white, middle-class, heterosexual, able-
bodied men . . . or whether they assume that masculinity has a common genesis and shape and thus the experiences of black men in
different class positions can be incorporated into their models' (1995:
67). Chodorow in her later work acknowledges the limitations of
psychoanalytic feminism, her own work included (1989), particularly its inability to deal with diversity, change and the specific and
varied circumstances of family and social life. 'Like all theoretical
approaches within the feminist project,' she argues, 'psychoanalytic
feminism does specific things and not others. First, like the theory
from which it derives, it is not easily or often historically, socially,
or culturally specific. It tends towards universalism and can be read,
even if it avoids the essentialism of psychoanalysis itself, to imply
that there is a psychological commonality among all women and
among all men' (cited in Edley and Wetherell 1995: 68). But, as
Chodorow observes, psychoanalysis should not be abandoned because
of its limitations and failings: 'Until we have another theory which
can tell us about unconscious mental processes, conflict, and relations
of gender, sexuality, and self, we had best take psychoanalysis for
what it does include and can tell us rather than dismissing it out of
hand' (cited in Edley and Wetherell 1995: 69).

It is less clear why men's studies accounts have appropriated object-relations theory and paid less attention to other forms of psycho-analytic theory, particularly the work of Lacan. Within the Lacanian picture men enter into the symbolic order as inheritors of the phallus, and thereby as inheritors of power and privilege. It is women who have no determinate subject position, being articulated only as 'lack' – in other words, what is not male (this is particularly interesting given that much work in men's studies sees masculinity as defined in terms of that which is *not* feminine). The Lacanian framework is illuminating particularly for drawing attention to the unobtainable nature of the position 'inheritor of the phallus'. It is something men recognize that they are supposed to achieve, but is in fact a phantasmic ideal. For Freud also it was the construction of femininity that remained most fragile. Boys had to shift their object of desire from their mother to a mother substitute (another woman). Girls had to shift not only from the mother but across to the father and to a father substitute – a double transition, which for Freud was particularly unstable.

Queer-y-ing Masculinity: Female Masculinity

Within the new men's studies, despite variation and often ambiguity in the ways in which masculinity has been conceptualized, a common, underlying assumption in much of the literature is that masculinity exists only in relation to men; that masculinity and bodily maleness are inextricably linked. Accordingly, any discussion of female masculinity is excluded from the analysis of masculinity. What then emerges is 'a body of work on masculinity that evinces absolutely no interest in masculinity without men'. Masculinity becomes 'a synonym for men and maleness' (Halberstam 1998: 13). In this sense the new critical studies of men and masculinities tend to leave unquestioned the validity of the sex–gender distinction and the link between biological maleness and the cultural construct 'masculinity'. It often works unproblematically with the notion that gender, in this case masculinity, can be read from sex, here the male-sexed body (see, for example, Kaufmann 1994).

Halberstam's text *Female Masculinity* (1998) will be used here as context in which to explore further some of the theoretical issues that a consideration of female masculinity evokes, bearing in mind of course, that Halberstam's work does not exhaust the field of inquiry into female masculinity (see also Newton 1979; Munt 1998). In her analysis of female masculinity Halberstam uses Butler's notion of gender as performance to assert that masculinity (like femininity) is constituted by a set of culturally recognized acts that can be achieved by all individuals regardless of their sexed body. By removing the analysis of masculinity from the site of the male body the essential base of masculinity is revealed as a fabrication and the constructedness and artificiality of masculinity is exposed. Within this theoretical framework, having a penis, male hormones or XY chromosomes are not prerequisites of being masculine or performing masculinity, nor are they barriers to the performance of femininity.

Within this framework the male body loses significance. Halberstam, for example, responds at some length to the claims made by Smith that 'in terms of cultural and political *power*, it still makes a difference when masculinity coincides with biological maleness' (Smith 1996: 16). Her initial criticisms of Smith's work relate mainly to his primary focus on male power (the power derived from men's practices) rather than masculinity, which, she believes, elevates the status of white masculinity above other masculinities. As the power occupied by biologically born men varies according to race, class, sexual orientation and other factors, Halberstam argues that to begin an analysis of masculinity with a reference to male power (i.e. the power of men) is to perpetuate the marginalization of non-dominant/other masculinities (including female masculinity). Not only does she suggest that a straightforward equation of masculinity with men's power reinforces a hierarchy of masculinities with white masculinity at the pinnacle, but she also maintains that such an assertion assumes that the categories men/women and male/female are stable and unproblematic in the sense that one can talk of men exerting power over women without any reflection on the stability and validity of the categories man/woman.

Halberstam does, however, recognize the potential significance of the gendered performance in terms of cultural and political power. In her discussion of transsexuality Halberstam acknowledges that

> The recent visibility of female-to-male transsexuals has immensely complicated the discussions around transsexuality because gender transition from female to male allows biological women to access male privilege within their re-assigned genders. Although few commentators

would be so foolish as to ascribe FTM transition solely to the aspiration for mobility within a gender hierarchy, the fact is that gender reassignment for FTMs does have social and political consequences. (1998: 143)

What Halberstam is not saying here is that biologically born women who change their sexed body to become male and pass as male gain power and privilege because of the change in their biological/physical sex. She is careful not to provide a rigid definition of transsexuality and instead defines female-to-male transsexuals broadly to incorporate FTMs who 'live out their masculinity in deliberately ambiguous bodies' as well as those who 'desire complete transitions from female to male' (1998: 154). What Halberstam is acknowledging is the social significance of the gendered inscription of the body – that, for example, women who perform masculinity and pass, through dress, mannerisms and/or body change (hormones, surgical operations) can access status and power assigned to the masculine. However, she is not privileging sex but gender; it is not the possession of the male-sexed body *per se* that accrues status and power but the performance of masculine gender. At the same time she does acknowledge that ambiguous gender performance produced by female masculinity in its destabilizing effects can attract enormous hostility. She uses the example of public toilets to illustrate the ways in which women police the gender performance of others within public spaces.

One of the aims of queer theory is to destabilize the binary distinction male–female and to undermine the categories man/woman, replacing the fixed gender categories by gender fluidity. On one level Halberstam's analysis of female masculinity achieves this. By exploring masculinity as detached from the male body she undermines the categories man/woman; in doing so she undermines the basis of the new men's studies. However, while trying to escape the binary Halberstam also manages to reinforce it, not only in her use of the term 'female masculinity' to describe women who do not conform to established codes of femininity but also in her very fixed classification of what falls within the categories femininity and masculinity. Halberstam on the one hand argues that one reason why the binary distinction male–female is so durable is that the categories male/female are able to evolve to encompass new patterns of behaviour. 'Precisely because virtually nobody fits the definitions of male and female, the categories gain power and currency from their impossibility' (1998: 27). Yet she represents a very narrow and stereotypical depiction of femininity. Although she veers away from an exploration of what female femininity actually entails, her analysis of female masculinity suggests that female femininity is in fact very passive, quite 'girly'. In her discussion of the James Bond film *Goldeneye*, for example, she asserts that it is M (played by Judi Dench) who 'most convincingly performs masculinity' (1998: 3), not Bond. But why read the M character as masculine? She exhibits many of the characteristics traditionally associated with masculinity – she is assertive, commanding, in a position of power – but why not see these attributes as a variant of femininity?

Conclusions

The status of recent critical work on men and masculinities within gender studies as a whole is a contested one. Some male writers on masculinity have argued that while the work by men's studies theorists has begun to fill a gap in the literature on gender, feminism, they argue, has been concerned primarily with the position of women (Edwards 1990). Feminist commentators have, however, been quick to point to the wealth of work on masculinities produced within feminist academia (Robinson 1996). The analysis here, however, has not been to assess the relative contributions of feminist as opposed to men's studies theorists to the study of masculinity, but instead to focus primarily on the work of men's studies theorists and to explore the ways in which this body of work and these writers may contribute to our understanding of gender.

As stated at the beginning of this chapter, the new 'men's studies' literature has a varied relationship with gender theory. Where theory is engaged with there is a tendency for writers to draw on existing theory to enhance our understanding of masculinity rather than to develop new approaches. A key exception here is Connell (see, for example, Connell 1987). The appropriation of theory by men's studies tends to be concentrated in certain areas of gender theory (for example, object-relations theory) and sparse in others. Notably Butler and Lacan do not feature widely within men's studies literature despite the general acceptance of the notion of hegemonic masculinity and the common use of other strands of psychoanalysis.

The work on gender undertaken in men's studies literature still tends to take quite an insular approach. Although most pro-feminist work on masculinities, in response to criticism from feminist writers (Hamner 1990), does now acknowledge the existence of feminist work on gender and its contribution either implicitly or explicitly to the study of masculinity, it tends still to focus exclusively on masculinity without extending its observations or analysis to issues of femininity. It tends therefore to leave unaddressed the relational aspects of gender, in other words, what we can learn about masculinity by the study of femininity and vice versa. Importantly, some key questions arise from the masculinities literature in relation to femininity. For example, is homophobia really more central to the construction of hegemonic masculinity than hegemonic femininity, as much of the literature implies? Is masculinity a more fragile identity than femininity? Some of these issues have been taken up elsewhere. Gill Clarke's work on gender, sexuality and sport illustrates how women who contravene codes of acceptable femininity by participating in traditionally male sports such as rugby are often subject to homophobic taunts, suggesting that homophobia does play a part in the construction of femininity (Clarke 1998). Is it just men that have constantly to prove their masculinity through acts of bravado, economic success, and so on, or does the same process apply to women and femininity? While the tests of femininity may not be the same, it does not mean that the construction of femininity is any more secure or any less policed. The pressure on young women to achieve a certain body shape and to be attractive to the male (heterosexual) eye imposes tests of femininity. It is suggested within much of the critical men's studies literature that masculinity is defined more by what it is not than what it is – that masculinity is constructed in opposition and contrast to femininity. (As indicated above, this runs contrary to the Lacanian construction of gender difference in the symbolic order, which privileges the phallus and defines women as 'lack'.) While Western women may have in practice more scope to assimilate male characteristics and behaviour (dress, types of work, codes of behaviour) than men have to access feminine characteristics and behaviour, it does not mean that women have unbridled access to masculinity. As Halberstam aptly points out, while boyish behaviour is tolerated, sometimes even encouraged, among young girls, being a tomboy becomes unacceptable at puberty and beyond (1998). 'Masculine' behaviour among adult women has to be tempered by overt femininity. Hargreaves's work on women and sport (1994) indicates that while female body-builders, for example, flout conventions of femininity by acquiring a muscle-bound body type, the muscularity of their bodies is usually balanced with signs of traditional femininity – make-up, jewellery, bikinis, and so on (1994: 168–9). Only by adopting a more relational focus, for example asking the same questions of femininities as we do of masculinities, can we really understand both the symmetries and asymmetries of gender construction.

Bodily Imaginaries

Polarities

Discussions of the formation of gendered identities have often, as has been highlighted in previous chapters, polarized around the biological/ cultural divide. An opposition is set up between accounts which emphasize the sexed body as an origin of our gendered subjectivities and those which insist on social construction.

The view that our gendered identities can simply be the effect of our biological bodies has been criticized in chapter 1 for failing to accommodate differences in gender formation, but also for failing to recognize that our understanding of those biological bodies themselves is mediated through culture. Thus Anne Fausto-Sterling (1993) points out the great variance to be found within the biological markers of sex and the difficulties that are faced in forcing them to fit within a binary classification of male and female, which a cultural attachment to two genders demands.

The other side of the opposition is that of cultural or social construction. Here biological bodies are regarded rather as blank sheets which either via social practices of segregation or via the operation of layers of cultural meaning are turned into gendered subjects. Such social constructionism was discussed in chapters 3 and 4. Here the body is relevant to our gendered identities only in so far as it is given significance by the discourses which we have available to make sense of ourselves. Currently the most discussed version of social constructionism is the work of Judith Butler, who, through her performative account of gender, seems to have removed any necessary link between masculinity, femininity and what are commonly termed male and female bodies. As we made clear in the discussion in chapter 4 above, her account in *Gender Trouble*, like Foucault's, is an account of the formation of subjectivity which resists any account of the origin or source of our gendered characteristics in either biological or psychic structures. For some theorists, however, this is to give no standing to our biological bodies, to suggest that their characteristics are irrelevant to our subjectivities; whereas, for example, the experiences of menstruation, childbirth, ejaculation, may be thought to play a constitutive role in the formation of gendered subjectivities.

Butler's account has also been challenged by some transsexual theorists. Transsexual experiences serve to trouble accounts of gender construction on both sides of the biological/cultural divide. A marker of transsexuality is clinically termed gender dysphoria. Transsexual subjects experience their gender identity in tension with their biological body, which would appear to undermine any naturalizing accounts; for here the biological body has not fixed the subjective gender identity. However, the widespread desire for *bodily* modification which is a marker of transsexual experience appears at odds with performative accounts of gender, frequently because such a desire is often expressed as a search for a real or coherent gender identity. On the kind of social constructionist account we have been considering, transsexuals can perform gendered bodily style of different kinds without respect to the actual shape of the body. The resort to surgery is just another manifestation of such a style, showing the flexibility of gendered performance. This is contested by some transsexual theorists who argue that coming to have bodies which approach those of biological males and females is a necessity for real gender identity. (We shall return to the work of such transsexual theorists briefly below and in chapter 9.)

In this chapter we aim to explore the role of the body in the production of gendered subjectivities. What we shall be working towards is an account which attempts to undermine the polarity between the biological and the cultural with relation to our sexed identities. That is, we need to recognize how central our embodiment is to our subjective sense of self, but none the less refuse to ground gender differences in purely biological ones.

Docile and Disciplined Bodies

Some of the earliest use which feminists made of the work of Foucault was in relation to the disciplining of the female body. Foucault had emphasized both the productivity of discourses, so that they bring into existence the phenomena they are apparently describing; and their link to an all-pervasive operation of power (see chapter 3). This account enables us to see the way in which the body is regulated by dominant discourses within the society which prescribe norms for the male but, more insistently, the female body. These norms work through the subjects whose attempt to regulate their bodies to conform to them is a key way of becoming constituted as masculine or feminine: 'through the organization and regulation of the time space and movements of our daily lives our bodies are trained, shaped and impressed with the prevailing historical forms of selfhood, desire, masculinity and femininity' (Bordo 1997: 91).

Feminists who make use of Foucault's work in this way emphasize the regimes of dieting, make-up, exercise, dress and cosmetic surgery by means of which women (and increasingly men) try to sculpt their bodies into acceptable shapes. Failure can lead to feelings of shame and alienation from and betrayal by one's body. Such acceptable shapes reflect hierarchies not only of gender but also of race and class. The attempt to straighten hair, the popularity of blue-tinted contact lenses and even of skin-whitening creams, together with the demands for surgical reconstructions of noses into pleasing Aryan shapes, are manifestations of the privileged position in which a certain kind of white body is placed. Femininity becomes constituted by the *surface presentation of the body*. Currently there is an insistence on a slender, athletic-looking female body, without bodily hair or wrinkled skin. The disciplining of our bodies extends to the way we move and sit and smile. Studies have shown how much women are routinely expected to smile for a good bit of their working day. Sandra Bartky (1997: 135) draws attention to the work of German photographer Marianne Wex, who has documented the different bodily postures of men and women, finding that women make themselves smaller, are loath to take up space, sit with their legs crossed, etc. Here discourses have material effects in shaping and moulding bodily forms.

Within the Foucauldian framework, of course, where there is power there is also resistance. The production of gendered subjectivities requires us to be subjected to such norms but also opens resistant possibilities. The work of queer theorists such as Judith Butler, with its recognition of the importance of parody and drag, makes clear that there are ways of producing our bodily identities which can undermine the disciplinary operation of dominant models of bodily masculinity and femininity. For most subjects compliance and resistance coexist in an uneasy conjunction.

The body, as it features in work of this kind, is being viewed as a product. It becomes the primary signifier of gendered identities. There is no sense that there is anything about the body itself which is playing any role in the femininity or masculinity which is produced. These become, in effect, bodily styles inscribed on a docile and blank surface (Foucault 1979: 138). Indeed, in the early work of Judith Butler, gender can seem to be quite disembodied. But for many theorists this does not capture adequately the role which our bodies play in our sense of self. Butler in her preface to a later work, *Bodies that Matter* (1993), reports a common response to her performative account of gender identity, a response captured in the question 'What about the materiality of the body, Judy? . . . an effort . . . to recall me to a bodily life that could not be theorized away', 'for surely bodies live and eat; eat and sleep; feel pain, pleasure; endure illness and violence; and these facts, one might skeptically proclaim, cannot be dismissed as mere construction' (1993: ix). The unease which is being expressed here is a recognition that (in the words of Kaja Silverman) 'our experience of "self" is always circumscribed by and derived from the body' (Silverman 1996) whose particular shapes and contours seem integral to it.

If, however, we want to give a role to the body with respect to our gendered subjectivities, in addition to that of the docile and disciplined body described above, what can that role be? How can we recognize the materiality of our bodies without falling back into seeing biology as the origin of our gendered identities, in the way in which we began this book by rejecting?

What about the Body, Judy?

Much contemporary theory, rather than taking up sides in the opposition between the biological and the cultural, is trying to undermine the opposition between them. Interestingly Butler sees her own work in this way. In *Bodies that Matter* she makes clear that her position was not an attempt to deny the importance of the materiality of the body but to undermine an opposition between such materiality and social construction.

The direction from which she undermines this opposition is to insist that materiality itself is a discursive effect. What we count as matter, as material, as nature or as given is itself a product of a particular mode of conceptualizing, modes of conceptualizing which are thereby tied up with relations of power. She quotes with approval Spivak's remarks: 'If one thinks of the body as such, there is no possible outline of the body as such. There are thinkings of the systematicity of the body, there are value codings of the body. The body, as such, cannot be thought, and I certainly cannot approach it' (Spivak, in Schor and Weed 1994: 177). We cannot therefore investigate the question of what differences there are in 'nature' as such, because our understanding of this nature is formed by our discourses. This does not mean that there is nothing outside discourse. But what there is cannot be approached other than through its formation in terms of our concepts. We cannot sensibly ask questions about what limits are set by something quite outside what we conceptualize. We can, however, explore the limits of conceptualization by trying to conceptualize otherwise.

Once we recognize this, for Butler there is no sense in concerning ourselves with the question how much of sexual difference is a given and how much constructed, for we recognize that any answer to that is itself formed from within our own power-laden discourses. Instead she argues we need to address a different question, namely how sexual difference is produced in such a way that it appears 'natural', appears to be a material fact, following from which we are to try to think sexual difference otherwise, outside of this naturalizing framework. It is just this which her performative theory of gender is addressing. Such 'natural facts' are the effects of normative ideals which establish what count as proper bodies (see chapter 4).

It is illuminating here to compare Butler's account of the body with those that are coming from theorists of disability, with which it initially appears to be in some tension. Within disability studies it was an important move to insist on the socially constructedness of the 'able' and 'disabled' body. This accompanied the recognition that what a body is able to do is very dependent on the situation it is in and the resources that are provided for it. In reaction to such social constructionist accounts, however, some writers have returned to the apparent bruteness of some bodily facts which no social modifications would seem to allow us to conceptualize away. Arms and legs cannot work, and pain is part of the daily reality for many. Nancy Mairs describes living with multiple sclerosis 'haunted by a . . . mean-spirited ghost . . . which trips you when you are watching where you are going, knocks glassware out of your hand, squeezes the urine out of your body before you reach the bathroom and weighs your body with a weariness no amount of rest can relieve . . . it's your own body' (Mairs 1997: 298).

Mairs's account here appears to be an articulation of a brute materiality which for Butler must always escape articulation. In providing such an articulation, Mairs may seem to be characterizing a limit set by the body itself to the way in which it can be conceptualized. Things are not so straightforward, however. Mairs admits experiencing shame of her body:

> it is a crippled body. Thus it is doubly other, not merely by the . . . standards of patriarchal culture but by the standards of physical desirability erected for everybody in our world. . . . my belly sags from loss of muscle tone, which also creates all kind of intestinal disruptions, hopelessly humiliating in a society in which excretory functions remain strictly unspeakable. (Mairs 1997: 299, 301)

Here it becomes clear that the way Mairs experiences her body is formed in relation to those very normalizing discourses which Butler refers us to; and in relation to which the 'crippled' body, in particular the 'desiring crippled body', is banished to the realm of the 'abject'. Butler's claim that there is no account of materiality which is not also a formation of that materiality seems vindicated.

None the less attention to Mairs's account stands in some tension to Butler's own. For Butler, 'there is a limit to constructedness' (Meijer, Costera and Prins 1998: 278), but this limit remains elusive. In her accounts of the political project of destabilizing our gendered categories there is therefore no sense of this limit as operating. This is, of course, crucial to her project, which is to make apparent that what had been taken to be a limit set by the natural body is no such thing, as we show by reconfiguring identities in ways which such a natural body is supposed to exclude. In Mairs's descriptions we both recognize the constructedness of experience and have a sense of the urgent need for reconceptualization, but we are also aware of the *limits* set by her body to what forms of conceptualizations would be coherent ones. We might be reminded here of the remarks of Biddy Martin, which we discussed in chapter 4, to be mindful of the 'drag' of the body and respectful of the limits it sets on conceptualization, even while we have no way of establishing in advance what these constraints are.

For Butler any attempted formation of such limits can be destabilized by the performance of what such formulations would render unthinkable. Whatever the bodily conditions may be, they exceed any account which can be provided of them, leaving open the possibility of alternative understandings. Some examples may perhaps make this clearer. Struck by the restrictions posed by certain bodies, we may articulate them as: men can't give birth, certain kinds of disabled bodies cannot run, do sport or be objects of desire. But Butler insists that there is always an excess to what is conceptualized, that the body outruns any way we might currently have of thinking about it. This opens the possibility of alternative conceptualizations in which pregnant men and desired and desiring Olympic paraplegics become thinkable.

The tensions here between the two approaches to theorizing embodiment are not direct oppositions. It is rather the case that if we are interested in theorizing the body we have to recognize the pull from both kinds of account. With Butler we have to be prepared to think the officially unthinkable in relation to them. We therefore need a way of thinking about the body which both recognizes its weightiness and accommodates the socially mediatedness of our experience of it. In this chapter we try to do this using the framework of the imaginary body.

Body Image and Imaginary Bodies

Recognizing the mediated nature of our relations to our bodies is, we will argue, compatible with giving a role to our embodiment over and above viewing bodies as simply signifiers of difference. It is to the work of theorists who are attempting to theorize this more substantial role that we now turn. Many gender theorists quote Freud's claim that that 'the ego is first and foremost a bodily ego' (Freud

1923: 26). What Freud is drawing attention to here is that our sense of self is a sense of a body, and involves an awareness of that body as having a certain shape or form. Elizabeth Grosz sees such an ego as a kind of 'psychical map' of the body (1994b: 33). The formation of ourselves as subjects is a formation of ourselves as embodied and involves something like an image of that body.

The concept of body image which is being invoked here has its origins in both phenomenological and psychoanalytic theory. For Merleau-Ponty, for example (Merleau-Ponty 1999), a subject is necessarily an embodied subject, but the body which constitutively forms such subjectivity is not that which would be offered to us by biological theory. The body we experience as *ourselves* is that which makes experience of other objects possible, rather than simply being another object among them. Embodiment is our mode of being in the world. This body in the world is an intentional body, apt for or engaged in projects. The mode in which our bodies inhabit the world is shown in habitual action. The body simply responds appropriately to the world by means of intentional acts, such as opening doors, picking up objects, scratching our nose, typing, playing an instrument. Iris Marion Young cites a passage from one of Tillie Olsen's short stories 'describing a kitchen dance in which a farm woman cans her tomatoes while mindful of the colicky baby she holds between her arm and her hip' (in Welton 1998: 289). Such actions do not require the issuing of conscious instructions to our bodies, but none the less require an awareness of their positionality. Our awareness of our bodies is yielded not simply through vision, but through inner sensation, sometimes termed 'proprioceptivity'. From this we gain a *corporeal or postural schema* or *body image* which is manifest in our habitual actions and responses and makes them possible.

In his discussion Merleau-Ponty focuses on cases of phantom limbs, where a subject retains a body image and consequent habitual dispositions even when the body as characterized by biology lacks the appropriate limb. Having a breast removed, for example, can leave one repeatedly attempting to rest one's arm in an empty space. If, as we argue here, embodiment is central to subjectivity, Merleau-Ponty's account explains why, for example, people grieve for parts of their body which are lost.

Our mode of experiencing our bodies is not brutal or unmediated. Our postural schemas or body images are already *morphologies*, that is mediated forms of organization. In Iris Marion Young's essay,

'Throwing Like a Girl' (in Young 1990b), she points out that the
habitual body schemas whereby physical negotiation of our environment becomes possible themselves reflect socially mediated gender
difference. Girls even throw balls in a different way from boys.

A danger here is that the concept of body image can suggest something like an inner mental map or picture which we have of our
bodies. This, however, separates the image from what it is supposed
to be an image of. It makes the image a mental representation of the
body and therefore separate from it. This is just what we need to
avoid. It is more accurate here to think of our body images as *modes
of experiencing our actual concrete body* such that we can operate in the
world as intentional and desiring agents. Such socially mediated ways
of experiencing our bodies should not be thought of as schemes of
interpretation thrown over a biological body, which in some sense
forms an objective given which we can experience in different ways.
On such a picture the biological body would remain as a foundational
or privileged account of the body as it is in itself. However, a biological account of our bodies is *also a socially mediated way of experiencing bodies*, different from that of the lived body we have been
considering, but no more fundamental. In the words of Moira Gatens,
the 'anatomical body is itself a theoretical object, for the discourse
of anatomy is produced by human beings in culture' (1996: 70). The
anatomical account of the body is therefore no more foundational
than the everyday accounts by means of which we experience our
bodies (see chapter 1).

Once we recognize that the phenomenological 'corporeal schema'
or 'body image' is itself a morphology, a mediated way of experiencing our bodies, then the transition to the notion of *the imaginary body*
with its links to psychoanalysis is straightforward. The important
contribution made by psychoanalysis here is to recognize that the
awareness we have of our bodies is not a neutral or purely cognitive
one. The way we have of experiencing our bodies invests *particular
contours* with emotional and affective salience. Some of our bodily
zones and shapes become significant to us, while others are barely
noticed. (One of our daughters was born with webbed toes, which
are only marginally significant to her, while the shape of her genitals
has become central to her subjectivity.) The neurologist and psychoanalyst Paul Schilder, for example, suggests: 'the touches of others,
the interests others take in the different parts of our bodies will be of
enormous importance in the development of the postural image of

the body' (Schilder, in Silverman 1996: 13). Freud's *Three Essays on the Theory of Sexuality* suggest the way in which erotic significance is attached to first one part and then another part of the body in the process of the development of an appropriately desiring gendered subjectivity (see chapter 2). The concept of the imaginary body, derived from psychoanalysis, and reworked in the contemporary writings of, among others, Elizabeth Grosz and Moira Gatens, is intended to capture the way the body is experienced as meaningful and salient both to the subject and to others who encounter it. Such meaning and salience is a consequence of social and cultural mediation. In the terms of Moira Gatens, the imaginary body is 'the social and personal significance of the body as lived' (1996: 11).

For such theorists the imaginary body is at the heart of accounts of gendered embodiment. Sexual difference, within such a framework, is constituted out of the imaginary investments in different bodily parts, the salience which we attach to them. Such gender theorists are attempting to capture how the body is to be woven into our account of lived sexual difference, while avoiding a crude biologism. The body, as it features in these accounts, is a body whose particular contours are laden with salience and significance, a body experienced not only cognitively but also affectively. The ways in which our bodies are experienced are a result of initiation into social and cultural norms, but also of the particular sets of emotional encounters which individual bodies have borne. Biddy Martin, as we noted in a previous chapter, while accepting the role of the social in the formation of the psyche, argued that our inner life could not be reduced to a moulding of the body by social norms. There is also, she insisted, a movement in the other direction, outwards from the psyche (see chapter 4). This lack of reducibility of the psyche to the social, she suggests, is a result of the temporal nature of subjectivity. We encounter situations carrying our history with us. This is the dimension recognized within a psychoanalytic theory that points out how the emotional salience of our bodily contours derives from the history of encounters in which that body has participated. This also goes some way to explaining the very different manners in which individuals can respond to social norms. These differences will be the result of particular familial and other emotional and desiring engagements which particular bodies have undergone and which inform the way in which those bodies are experienced as significant. This concept of the imaginary therefore goes some way to explaining both similarities and differences in our modes of experiencing our sexed bodies. Notice the differences in the imaginary investments of the painter and the sitter in the following poem.

A Nude by Edward Hopper

The light
drains me of what I might be, a man's dream
of heat and softness:
or a painter's
-breasts of cosy pigeons
arms gently curved
by a temperate noon

I am
blue veins, a scar,
a patch of lavender cells,
used thighs and shoulders;
my calves
are as scant as my cheeks,
my hips won't plump
small, shimmering pillows;

but this body
is home, my childhood
is buried here, my sleep
rises and sets inside,
desire
crested and wore itself thin
between these bones

Lisel Mueller, *The raving beauties* (1983)

The use of the concept of 'the imaginary' here therefore owes an acknowledged debt to psychoanalytic theory. Its use, however, can be more flexible than, for example, the strictly Lacanian notion (see chapter 2). The salience which our bodies have for us is not to be thought of as necessarily unconscious. Neither does the imaginary dimension need to be viewed as unchanging. Moreover, psycho-analysis gives us a particular account of the salience which is attached to different bodily contours. We do not, however, need to accept the universality of this account. We should remember, for example, that the Oedipal story is articulated in terms of a Greek myth, being utilized to articulate the emotional and erotic salience of particular kinds of bodily forms in the patients that Freud encountered. In other times and places the significance attached to such forms might be articulated in other terms. For Gatens, 'The imaginary body is socially and historically specific in that it is constructed by: a shared language; the shared psychical significance and privileging of various zones of the body . . . ; and common institutional practices and discourses (for example, medical, juridical and educational' (1996: 12).

We would also want to draw an important distinction between the way we want to use the notion of the imaginary body and the way it is used by Lacan. For Lacan the ego is phantasmatic. It is the body as it is reflected back to the subject by a mirror, or the gaze of others. The object with which the subject struggles to identify is thereby external and the subject's identification with it is in crucial respects illusory. Other writers, in reading Freud, however, make more of his claims that the image of the body involved in ego formation is prompted by bodily sensations (Prosser 1998: ch. 2), although these are given significance via our responses from significant others. Such a conception of the imaginary body is closer to the body image or corporeal schema which we find in phenomenological writers, for whom the body image is our way of experiencing concrete bodies rather than a phantasmatic image with which we struggle to identify. The conception of the imaginary body which we have been articulating tries to capture this point. Our gender identities are modes of experiencing our particular bodies and not simply an attempt to identify with something external.

The imaginary bodies which we inhabit and those of others which we encounter gain their salience from our social and personal histories. Such salience is learnt, and changes and develops through time. Our imaginary bodies are central to our identities as gendered human beings. Given that the significance which is at issue here includes emotional salience, recognition of the role of body image to the construction of identity goes some way to explaining the attachments we have to these identities. The way we experience our bodies as male or female is then a reflection both of personal history and of the culturally shared salience of certain bodily forms. In her later work Butler herself explores the emotional salience attaching to the categories in terms of which our subjectivities become constituted, although she persists in a predominantly negative view of this process, regarding it as 'one of the most insidious' (1997b: 6) of the operations of power (for a discussion of this later work, which we do not have space for here, see M. Lloyd 1998).

Here our interest in the imaginary body has been prompted by an interest in the production of gendered subjectivities. Its use, however, is not restricted to the issue of sexual difference. Skin colour, for example, as a visible bodily feature has become invested with a salience, an imaginary dimension, which partially constitutes the subjectivities of white and black bodies: 'the processes by which racial identities are produced work through the shapes and shades of human morphology, the size and shape of the nose, the breadth of the cheekbones, the texture of the hair, and the intensity of the pigment' (Alcoff 1999). Sara Ahmed in her book *Strange Encounters* (2000) quotes from Audre Lorde's account of a memory, which illustrates this process and Schilder's claim that our body image is formed out of the touch of others.

> The AA subway train to Harlem. I clutch my mother's sleeve, her arms full of shopping bags, christmas heavy. The wet smell of winter clothes, the trains lurching. My mother spots an almost seat, pushes my little snowsuited body down. On one side of me a man reading a paper. On the other, a woman in a fur hat staring at me. Her mouth twitches as she stares and then her gaze drops down, pulling mine with it. Her leather gloved hand plucks at the line where my blue snowpants and her sleek fur coat meet. She jerks her coat close to her. I look, I do not see what ever terrible thing she is seeing on the seat between us – probably a roach. But she has communicated her horror to me. It must be something very bad from the way she is looking, so I pull my snowsuit away from it, too. When I look up the woman is still staring at me, her nose holes and eyes huge. And suddenly I realize there is nothing crawling up the seat between us; it is me she doesn't want her coat to touch. (Lorde 1984: 147–8)

Alcoff (1999), in her discussion of the phenomenology of racial embodiment, makes a point which is relevant to all cases of imaginary embodiment, including that of gender. The imaginary investments of bodily shapes are ones we are initiated into. None the less the *material reality* of the features which are invested with significance enables the naturalizing of the meanings which are attached to them. They become experienced as simple responses to brute material features of the body.

It is important to note here that our body images, corporeal schemas, imaginary bodies are what enable us to act in the world. The imaginary dimension is central to our ways of experiencing ourselves, others and our world, signalling the desirability or undesirability of our options. Given that negative imaginaries will be our concern in the following section it is important here to register the positive and enabling possibilities of the imaginary. For bell hooks, for example, the skin of the man lying next to her 'soot black like my granddaddys skin' can return her to 'a world where we had a history . . . a world where . . . something wonderful might be a ripe tomato, found as we walked through the rows of daddy Jerry's garden' (hooks 1990: 33).

Damaging Social Imaginaries

Once attention is focused on the imaginary body, however, it becomes clear that many of the social imaginaries of, for example, the female body are negative. In *The Second Sex*, written in 1949 (it is interesting to note what changes there have been since then), Simone de Beauvoir gives an account of the young girl's experience of her body as she reaches puberty.

> At about the age of twelve or thirteen . . . the crisis begins . . . when the breasts and body hair are developing . . . she inspects herself with . . . astonishment and horror. . . . the enlargement of this . . . painful core, appearing under each nipple . . . this new growth in her armpits and middle transforms her into a kind of animal or alga. . . . at each recurrence [of her monthly annoyance] the girl feels the same disgust at this flat stagnant odour emanating from her – an odour of the swamp . . . disgust at this blood . . . there is no escape; she feels she is caught. (Beauvoir 1982: 33–4)

De Beauvoir contrasts with this the experience of the boy:

> it is true enough that at the moment of puberty boys also feel their bodies as an embarrassment, but being proud of their manhood from an early age . . . with pride they show each other the hair growing on their legs, a manly attribute; their sex organ is more than ever an object of comparison and challenge. (1982: 40)

In her discussion it becomes clear that, although de Beauvoir regards the female body as an obstacle to the possibility of participating fully in an active public and professional life, the problem is in no way a result of biology *per se*. The obstacle is a consequence of the way the body is experienced by the girl, and such experiences reflect responses to it from within her family as well as those which are found in public images and writings. The consequence is that her body feels to her in such a way that it inhibits certain kinds of agency.

In the Lacanian account, 'the female body in our culture . . . is often lived as an envelope, vessel or receptacle . . . a home for the penis and later for a baby . . . constructed as partial and lacking', whereas 'the male body image is that of a whole active subject' (Gatens 1996: 41). Moreover the female body has been imaged as 'leaking, uncontrollable seeping liquid' (Grosz 1994b: 205), a liquid that is soiling and shaming and messy. Regardless of the universality or exclusiveness of such accounts, such images certainly inform the way many women experience their bodies.

Such damaging social imaginaries are not restricted to ways of experiencing sexual difference. In this context Kaja Silverman (1996) invokes the accounts of Fanon of his arrival in France. In *Black Skins, White Masks* Fanon describes how 'assailed at various points [my pre-existing] corporeal schema crumbles. I [subject] myself to an objective examination, I [discover] my blackness, my ethnic characteristics; and I [am] battered down by tom-toms, cannibalism, intellectual deficiency fetishism, racial defects, slave ships and above all sho' good eating' (Fanon 1968: 112). Fanon's experiences here are comparable to those recounted by Lorde, above. Here her comforting bodily experiences, as wrapped in her snowsuit she presses up against a mother with Christmas-heavy bags, becomes transformed as she encounters the horror which her body has engendered in the fur-clad woman next to her. In both cases there is a severe disjuncture between their prior individual body image or corporeal posture, enabling habitual and unconscious negotiation of their world, and the social salience which, in a new context, they discover their bodies to have.

Similar accounts have been found in the recognition of a body reflected in the social imaginary as 'crippled'. The subject, with his/her body schema of habitual abilities and pleasurable and painful encounters derived from his/her everyday world, and accepting or rejecting relations with significant others, is reflected back as a body which is Not Able, a reflection which then forms the learnt salience attached to its contours. Rosemarie Garland Thomson discusses the 'cultural figures that haunt' the social imaginary attaching to the disabled body (Garland Thomson 1997: 288) in which the disabled body is reflected back as 'grotesque spectacle' (p. 285).

The response of the writers who recognize the damaging nature of such social imaginaries has been various. De Beauvoir sees the girl's way of experiencing her body as, given the society in which she lives, inevitable. The possibility of her participation in public life therefore requires her to transcend her body, distance her subjectivity from it to develop a sense of self in spite of its messy embodiment. Such a denial, she also recognized, carried with it emotional cost.

For Fanon the struggle was to keep his own body image, which enabled him to operate intentionally in the world, *separate* from the damaging social imaginings which he encountered. This is also the project which remains urgent for bell hooks. It informs much of her writings in which she attempts to link the diversity of contemporary black experience in America, back to historical roots in that southern black rural world. For hooks this is not an act of 'passive nostalgia . . . but a recognition that there were "habits of being . . . which we can re-enact", to provide ways of re-imagining black bodies in livable ways' (1990: 35). Nancy Mairs reimagines the disabled body with her claim 'as a cripple I swagger' (Mairs 1986: 90). Cheryl Marie Wade 'insists on a harmony between her disability and her womanly sexuality in a poem characterizing herself as "The Woman with Juice"' (Garland Thomson 1997: 285).

The reimagining adopted here as a strategy is also adopted by other feminist writers, with respect to the female body. Irigaray has been the most important influence here, insisting on the need to develop *different* imaginaries of the female body which would allow femininity to be lived in a less destructive way. Irigaray's project lovingly uses the contours and fluids of the female body to suggest ways of experiencing and living female bodies differently (Irigaray 1981, 1985a, 1985b). To this end Irigaray reimagines the female body in female terms, replacing the response to female sex organs as a lack or a hole with one which foregrounds the image of women's genitals as 'two lips touching'. 'Her sexuality, always at least double, goes even further; it is plural . . . the pleasure of the vaginal caress does not have to be substituted for that of the clitoral caress. They each contribute, irreplaceably to woman's pleasure. Among other caresses . . . fondling the breasts, touching the vulva, . . . pleasures which are misunderstood' if the female body is imagined as it is currently via the dominant male social imaginary (in Conboy, Medina and Stanbury 1997: 252). (We shall return to Irigaray in chapter 8.)

Corporeality

What we find in these writers who have made use of the notion of imaginary bodies, adapted from both phenomenological and psychoanalytic contexts, is a recognition of the corporeality of our gendered identities, of femininity and masculinity as ways of living differently shaped bodies. Our identities are formed as ways of giving significance to particular bodily forms. Gender is biology-as-lived. In this way such accounts are attempting to respect the materiality of our bodies and their central role in our sense of selves without reverting to a crude biologism. Rather the opposition between the material and the cultural is undermined. The conceptual resources of the imaginary body enable us to make sense of our embodied subjectivity without viewing the body as either a biological given or simply a signifier of a cultural phantasy of sexual difference.

Thinking which makes use of the concept of the imaginary body can also help to illuminate the importance of bodily modification to transsexual subjects. The body is not merely a signifier of gender identity. The phenomenology of gender, gender as lived, is partially constituted as a mode of experiencing certain material bodily features (though this mode can, of course, be variable). For the transsexual subject who desires gendered 'realness' (see chapter 9), such realness can require a bodily form. Moreover the social imaginaries attached to the bodily form with which they originally find themselves makes such an original form unlivable; impossible to integrate with a body image which makes possible intentional engagements in their world (Prosser 1998: ch. 2).

Attention to corporeality has, however, for some writers, led to a foregrounding of sexual difference as the *inevitable* frontier of biology-as-lived. It is to those writers that we turn next.

Sexual Difference

Egalitarian Feminism

Campaigns for women's emancipation have most commonly been conducted on the assumption that women's *difference* from men has been problematic. Differences in women's bodies and in the tasks which they most commonly perform have been perceived as obstacles to their taking part in the public world on the same terms that men do. Difference is here perceived as the origin of oppression. Within liberal feminist thought, one example of egalitarian feminism, the desired goal is to ensure that within the hierarchical structure of society men and women compete on the same terms. Women, it is thought, have been running the race with shackles and we must try to remove these shackles so that the competition is fair. It is such a vision that has motivated some of the key concerns of liberal feminism, with its central concept being that of equal opportunities. Legislation for equal access to education and non-discriminatory practices within education are designed to ensure that women are equipped in the same way as men to compete for jobs and not segregated into 'female' occupations with lower pay. Emphasis on assertiveness training encourages women to gain the skills which are required in a competitive setting. Sex discrimination legislation and equal pay laws are aimed at eliminating the obstacle of discrimination against women just because they are women. Campaigns addressing the way women are publicly represented have been justified on the basis that presenting women as sex objects makes it difficult to see them as equal workers and provides working environments in which women cannot work alongside men on an equal basis. The demand for freely available abortion tried to ensure that women are not being trapped into maternity without choosing it. The encouragement of business and local authorities to provide nurseries is also an attempt to free women from the obstacle of childcare which makes the competition for work and public office an unequal one (Jaggar 1983; Tong 1989).

In the attempt to ensure equality of opportunity for women within the liberal capitalist state certain tensions are set up. One tension is that in order to make women's lives like men's we are faced with a dilemma regarding the tasks that women commonly do, which prevent them from competing on an equal basis. These are most crucially the tasks of caring for children, the sick, the elderly. Within a liberal framework, which is an individualist one, these tasks are primarily conceived of as the responsibility of individual families (leading to such common attitudes as 'don't have children if you can't afford to keep them'). The campaign for public responsibility for care shifts perspective, to viewing society as a collectivity marked by mutual interdependence.

It is not only within liberal feminism that the route to women's emancipation is conceived of as consisting in bringing women's lives into line with those of men. Within Marxist feminism the goal for women has been to bring them into public production to work alongside men on the same terms. This is thought to do away with a division of labour between the public and private and the consequent economic inequalities which have allowed men to exercise power over women and capitalism to benefit from a division in its labour force. Within Marxism there was no tension involved in seeing the social order as a mutually interdependent collectivity and therefore of conceiving of those tasks which women commonly perform as being a public responsibility. Although put into practice only piecemeal in actually existent socialism, the domestic work, catering, care of children and the sick and elderly were conceived of as a public responsibility with state provision and public rather than private labour. Within this framework it is argued that once women's lives cease to be different from those of men the especial oppression which they experience will be removed and collectively, as workers, women and men can strive to overcome the oppressions of capitalism itself.

There are, however, difficulties with both of these approaches to female difference. Most centrally these approaches make it impossible to address issues which arise from the very specificity of women's experience. One way in which this is manifest is that these approaches find it difficult to address issues of embodiment and consequently to address questions of sexual and particularly reproductive relations. It is still women who take responsibility for reproduction and whose bodies are implicated in reproductive and contraceptive strategies. Maternity itself is often problematic for egalitarian feminists. Insistence on maternity leave, which is paralleled by an increasing demand for paternity leave, is barely a gesture in the direction of recognizing the significance of this differing mode of embodiment. It is, moreover, predominantly women who are raped and it is on women's bodies that rape is practised as a war crime, particularly within societies in which these female bodies are woven into a culture of honour and shame (Bracewell 1996; Seifert 1996). Again a stance that insists on an approach to equality which rests on sameness cannot adequately conceive what is at issue here.

The difficulties involved in addressing issues of embodiment are interconnected with a lack of attention which such approaches pay to issues of subjectivity. The direction of concern within both liberal and Marxist feminism is on the social roles or positions within which men and women are placed. What has not been centrally addressed is their ways of experiencing and understanding themselves as men and women (see chapter 3). This question of subjectivity is intimately tied to the question of embodiment. As we saw in the previous chapter, our subjectivity is partially constituted by our modes of experiencing our bodies. This in turn is mediated by the social imaginaries and symbolic order in which we are placed.

In the writings of Simone de Beauvoir, however, we find an egalitarian approach which recognizes the importance of embodiment, subjectivity and the social symbolic and imaginary orders in which we are placed. De Beauvoir famously claimed that we are not born women, we become women as a consequence of social processes (Beauvoir 1982). Part of this making, however, is the formation of a subjectivity in response to the cultural conceptions of what it is to be a woman. Within this conception woman is always 'other' to the male which forms the norm of the rational and the human. This otherness, difference, is conceived negatively. It is echoed in a conception of the female body as 'lacking', as not possessing that which is distinctive of the male body. Such otherness mediates the girl's experience of her body and thereby her sense of self. As we saw in the extracts from de Beauvoir in the previous chapter, it can yield an experience of female embodiment tinged with horror. The female body is in these circumstances an obstacle to the development of fully human faculties, to being fully rational and able to take a place in the public and intellectual world. De Beauvoir's analysis did not allow a solution to 'the woman problem' (the problem of women being different from men) by means solely of a reorganization of social role, since this did not address the issue of subjectivity and embodiment. Her own move, however, as we saw in chapter 7, was one of a struggle for transcendence. Women had to strive for a public life *in spite of their bodies*, by rising above the forms of experience which she ascribes to the girl at the time of puberty. For de Beauvoir this move of transcendence was required if women were to have access to universal properties of reason and reflective thought and action, the things which were most distinctive of being human. Not to attempt transcendence was to remain trapped by their bodies and the contingencies of their particular mode of existence (immanence). To accept our bodies as our fate was therefore a refusal to exercise freedom.

> Every subject plays his part as such specifically through exploits or projects that serve as a mode of transcendence: he achieves liberty only through a continual reaching out towards other liberties. There is no justification for present existence other than its expansion into an indefinitely open future. Every time transcendence falls back into immanence, stagnation, there is a degradation of existence onto the 'en-soi' – the brutish life of subjection, to given conditions – and of liberty into constraint and contingence. (quoted in Schor 1994: 47)

De Beauvoir, both later in *The Second Sex* and in other works, shows the costs involved to women of such a move to transcendence, a move which refuses to recognize embodied difference as having a role to play in intellectual life: 'she can become an excellent theoretician, can acquire real competence, but she will be forced to repudiate whatever she has in her that is "different"' (quoted in Schor 1994: 49). None the less she saw no alternative but for women to enter the public world on male terms.

De Beauvoir here illustrates the fundamental problem with the egalitarian approach. Within this approach men are taken as the norm. To reach equality women must strive to become like men. Men's working lives, men's education, men's bodies and men's forms of subjectivity are left untheorized and unproblematized. It is women's difference from men which is conceived of as problematic.

Equal or Different: Irigaray and Sexual Difference

Sexual difference theorists reject the negative conceptualization of difference implied by such egalitarian approaches. They insist, in contrast, on the importance of recognizing sexual difference in a positive rather than a negative way. 'What is at stake in the debate . . . is the positive project of turning difference into a strength, of affirming its positivity' (Braidotti 1994: 187). This project has two aspects. First, it insists on the difference of women from men. Secondly, it insists on the difference of real women from the 'women as other', which is the representation of women in male culture. Luce Irigaray refers to this as the 'double syntax'. The task is to ensure such real women can influence the content of the concept 'woman'. In this chapter we will pay most attention to the work of Irigaray, since all feminist theorists of sexual difference have been influenced by her work. But we will also pay attention to the positions of Rosi Braidotti and Elizabeth Grosz.

Irigaray, in discussing de Beauvoir, writes: 'Demanding equality, as women, seems to me to be an erroneous expression of a real issue. Demanding to be equal presupposes a term of comparison. Equal to what? What do women want to be equal to? Men? A wage? A public position? Equal to what? Why not to themselves?' For Irigaray as for other sexual difference theorists, difference is unavoidable. 'The human race is divided into *two genres* which ensure its production and reproduction. Trying to suppress sexual difference is to invite a genocide. . . . What is important, on the other hand, is defining the values of belonging to a sex specific *genre*' (Whitford 1992: 32). In insisting on the specificity of sexual difference in this way, Irigaray is opposing the very idea of a universal subject which de Beauvoir is claiming for women. Such an insistence, however, raises problems, not only for the egalitarian feminists who form her target when she is considering de Beauvoir, but also for certain strands of post-structuralist thought. A celebration of a multiplicity of differences and consequent aspects of identity and subjectivity, it can be argued, fails to give recognition to the specificity of *sexual* difference and does away with the possibility of doing justice to such a difference by allowing women themselves to define its content. This is a point to which we will return below.

The claim that sexual difference is unavoidable can mean different things, to which it is important to pay attention. One thing it can mean is that here and now women's and men's experiences of their embodiment are significantly distinct. Moreover, given the different cultural salience attached to male and female bodies, even similar kinds of behaviour will be read quite differently when issuing from a male or a female body. This is simply a reiteration and insistence that it matters to almost everything you do currently what shape your body is. This point is expressed by Gatens in the following way: 'masculinity and femininity as forms of sex appropriate behaviours are manifestations of an historically based, culturally shared phantasy about male and female biologies, and as such sex and gender are not arbitrarily connected' (Gatens 1996: 130). Gatens concludes from this that degendering proposals are utopian. The more urgent task is to rework our sexual imaginaries in less destructive ways. Gatens, however, does not go so far as to espouse an essential sexual difference as 'fundamental and immutable' (1996: 73). Something like this view does, however, seem to be that adopted by Irigaray, Rosi Braidotti and Elizabeth Grosz. Grosz insists on 'the irreducible specificity of women's bodies, the bodies of all women, independent of class, race and history' (Grosz 1994b: 207). This specificity is anchored in the bodily processes of reproduction (although Grosz accepts that the way these are experienced are in no way universal). But, while accepting that no articulation of sexual difference, no sexual identity, will be universal, she none the less claims that 'sexual difference is the horizon that cannot appear in its own terms but is implied in the very possibility of an entity . . . a difference that is originary and constitutive' (1994b: 209). Similarly Braidotti insists that being a woman 'pertains to the facticity of my being' (1994: 186). For Braidotti, however, 'the factual element that founds the project of sexual difference . . . is not biological, it is biocultural, historical.' None the less, 'being-a-woman is always already there as the ontological precondition for my existential becoming as subject' (1994: 187). It is because of such facticity that we can claim, as women, that the representations we find of ourselves are insufficient.

These sexual difference theorists are both indebted to and critical of the psychoanalytic tradition, most especially in its Lacanian formulation. Irigaray focuses on the differences between male and female subject positions interconnectedly in both symbolic and imaginary forms. She critiques these dominant cultural meanings for being *phallogocentric*, for presenting women as the 'other' to the rational man of Western thought, as the lack which forms the necessary and negative opposite to the plenitude of masculinity. Such symbolic meanings are matched with imaginary identifications in which female bodies are experienced as chaotic, formless and threatening. Irigaray recognizes, through her acceptance of the psychoanalytic framework, that such cultural symbolic and imaginary associations are constitutive of the formation of subjectivity. Subjects are initiated into the significance of bodily difference in the process of coming to be subjects at all. She departs from Lacan, however, in challenging the inevitability of such symbolic and imaginary structures and their resistance to change. She criticizes psychoanalysis for concentrating on the situation of the boy and consequently for being able to conceive of women only as lack, what is not male. It is in this context that Irigaray employs one of her most famous metaphors. If we look at women's bodies through the flat mirror (of the male gaze and consequent male theorizing), the distinctiveness of their sex can be viewed only as a hole, as an absence. If, however, we look at female bodies with the speculum (the curved mirror used by women for self-examination) we detect the specificity of their sexuality and the plenitude of their sexual organs (Irigaray 1981, 1985a).

Irigaray, therefore, along with other sexual difference theorists, recognizes that deconstructing contemporary discourses of sexual difference to highlight the oppositions and assumptions on which they are based is only part of the task. There has also to be a construction, a transforming of phallogocentric discourses of femininity, to develop an interconnected symbolic and imaginary which is liveable for women. In this she is attempting an account of women which is not simply that which is defined in relation to norms of the male. She is also seeking an account in which the experiences of real women can play a role in providing content to the term. This is, however, not an easy or straightforward project. As Margaret Whitford comments, 'There is no simple manageable way to leap to the outside of phallogocentrism, nor any possible way to situate oneself there, that would result from the simple fact of being a woman . . . she deliberately attempts to speak as a woman, from a non-existent place, which has to be created or invented as she goes along' (Whitford 1991: 124–5).

In the process we can never be sure when we are reinscribing the very oppositions which we seek to subvert.

Rosi Braidotti suggests that 'women's relative "nonbelonging" to the system can provide margins of negotiation for alternative subject positions. . . . These margins must however be negotiated through careful processes of undoing hegemonic discourses at work not only in dominant culture but within feminist theory itself' (in Jaggar and Young 1998: 302). Braidotti might have added here: not only within feminist theory but within the subjectivities of individual women. Transformations of dominant conceptions of 'woman' will not be available to mere acts of will. We cannot simply opt, as we might regard de Beauvoir of doing, for transcendence, and remove ourselves from the significance attached to our bodily form. The imaginary associations which condition our mode of experiencing our bodies are not easily transparent to consciousness and thereby not susceptible to such acts of will. It is because of this that Irigaray pays such attention to the domain of the imaginary. Our affective relations to our embodiment require transformation if our subjectivity is to be reconstructed in other than phallogocentric terms. This explains her loving rewriting of female anatomy that we highlighted in the previous chapter. Here Irigaray is insisting on the possibility of developing a distinctive female sexuality which does not rest on penetration but recognizes the plurality of female sexuality: 'a woman's erogenous zones are not the clitoris or the vagina, but the clitoris and the vagina, and the lips and the vulva, and the mouth of the uterus, and the uterus itself, and the breasts' (Fraser and Bartky 1992: 103); 'if we are to discover our female identity, I do think it important to know that, for us, there is a relationship with jouissance other than that which functions in accordance with the phallic model' (Whitford 1992: 45).

The desire to rewrite the 'house of language', to enable women to find themselves as female subjects, involves for Irigaray the reconception of relations between women. One step towards such a reconception is the recognition of our maternal origins. 'The relationship with the mother . . . is the "dark continent" *par excellence*. It remains in the shadows of our culture' (Whitford 1992: 35). We have to reconstruct the imaginary and symbolic relations with our mother: 'The imaginary and symbolic of intra-uterine life and of the first bodily encounter with the mother . . . where are we to find them / In what darkness, what madness, have they been abandoned' (p. 39).

Presently the mother/womb is 'fantasized by many men to be a devouring mouth, a cloaca or anal and urethral outfall, a phallic threat, or at best reproductive' (p. 41). This needs to be replaced by our inventing new words with which to recognize our relation to the body of the mother, 'sentences which translate the bond between her body, ours and that of our daughters' (p. 43). This is part of the process of asserting an autonomous sexuality and identity for women. Following from this Irigaray asserts the need to establish a female genealogy, a history of women, our mothers and grandmothers and forebears, so that we can define for ourselves a female position within the symbolic. The process of rethinking the relation to the female body, and of constructing a female genealogy, also make possible the redefinition of relations between women in contemporary life. Such relations have previously been mediated by relations to men and thereby have been marked by distrust and envy. Outside this phallic order and in the context of a female genealogy, relations between women can take on a new form: 'Let us also try and discover the singularity of our love for other women. . . . This love is necessary if we are not to remain the servants of the phallic cult, objects to be used by and exchanged between men, rival objects on the market, the situation in which we have always been placed' (p. 45). This project, as with Irigaray's project as a whole, remains fraught with difficulties, as she recognizes. For we remain formed within a phallic order, while we are attempting to reconstitute it, and the changes she is envisaging can take place only by collective working.

What kind of politics does this approach to sexual difference suggest? It is possible to read Irigaray as concerned primarily with personal transformations, with changing the way women experience their bodies and conceive of themselves. But the imaginaries which she is trying to transform are social imaginaries and have an interdependent relation to social practices. Social practices are informed by social imaginaries. Moreover transformation of those imaginaries requires changes to the social and material conditions within which women are working. A condition of political activism for Irigaray is the recognition of sexual difference, women consciously claiming an identity for themselves while they both deconstruct and reconstruct it: 'it is essential for women among themselves to invent new modes of organization, new forms of struggle, new challenges' (p. 10). In her later writings she pays more attention to material and social conditions, arguing for the recognition of women as a sex before the law with a distinctive civil status (p. 11). She herself has been active particularly in the development of the Italian women's movement which has developed particular social/symbolic practices to foreground transformation of relations between women and recognition of female genealogy (Milan Women's Bookstore Collective 1990).

The Critique of Gender

Rosi Braidotti, in defending an approach to theorizing the position of women which foregrounds sexual difference, contrasts it to approaches which foreground the concept of gender (Braidotti 1994, 1998). For Braidotti the emphasis on gender is found in much Anglo-American theorizing, in contrast to that found on the European continent. She sees this as partly a function of the languages concerned. The romance languages have no concept of 'gender' which can be distinguished from that of sex. The use of such a concept has, she suggests, led to a separation of sex and gender, with sex denoting a particular form of embodiment and gender capturing a social role.

One of Braidotti's concerns about the use of the term gender is that it concentrates on social and material factors and insufficiently on the symbolic and the semiotic. Another is that the division of sex and gender re-essentializes sex, by making it the domain of biology, while giving an account of gender which is unable to explain the importance of particular forms of embodiment. Within the work of sexual difference theorists, sexual difference cannot be divided into biological and social or symbolic elements; instead the material and the symbolic are indivisibly intertwined.[1]

Braidotti's main criticism of gender theory, however, is that it assumes a false symmetry between men and women. Both have a gender and the gender of both has been socially constructed, the gender of both is variable historically and cross-culturally, and the gender of both can be constricting on an individual basis. The apparent symmetry which is given by using gender as a category of analysis is, she claims, reflected in the political use to which the term has been put. In universities where women's studies and feminist studies have a clearly political agenda, gender studies appears bland and acceptable. Gender is symmetrical, so men get studied too. Men even are hired to teach on gender studies courses. The consequence, for Braidotti, is that differences in power and the point about male domination are lost. (In response to these points, see the Introduction.) In contrast to this apparent symmetry the approach of sexual difference theorists, she argues, highlights the asymmetry in the position of men and women: 'men, as the empirical referent of the masculine, cannot be said to have a gender: rather they are expected to carry the Phallus – which is something different. They are expected to exemplify abstract virility, which is hardly an easy task' (Braidotti with Butler 1994: 38). Women, in contrast, are those who cannot inherit the phallus. By recognizing this asymmetry, sexual difference theorists can respond to it by challenging the phallocentrism of culture.

With the difference in analysis goes a difference in political agendas. For gender theorists the goal is to change the processes of socialization so that there is no longer a clear binary division between masculinity and femininity. For sexual difference theorists, such a goal is both unachievable and undesirable. It is unachievable because sexual difference is unavoidable and undesirable because it deprives women of the opportunity of self-definition just at the moment when it becomes a possibility. (We return to the debate between sexual difference theorists and gender theorists below.)

The Essentialism Which is not One

The work of Irigaray and other sexual difference theorists has often been criticized on the basis that it requires an essentialist conception of 'woman'. There are many different claims that can be captured by the term essentialist, and the problems which critics have found with sexual difference theory usually concern essentialism in one of its forms. Naomi Schor defines essentialism in the context of feminism as 'the belief that woman has an essence, that woman can be specified by one or a number of inborn attributes which define across cultures and throughout history her unchanging being and in the absence of which she ceases to be categorized as a woman' (Schor and Weed 1994: 42). This is the form of essentialism which was under discussion in the first chapter of this book. There are passages in Irigaray's work which seem to suggest essentialism of just this form. For example: 'Your/my body doesn't acquire its sex through an operation. Through the action of some power, function, or organ. Without

any intervention, or special manipulation, you are a woman already'
(quoted in Fraser and Bartky 1992: 99). This leads to the accusation
of Toril Moi, in *Sexual/Textual Politics*: 'having shown that so far
femininity has been produced exclusively in relation to the logic of
the same, she falls for the temptation to produce her own positive
theory of femininity. But . . . to define "woman" is to essentialize her'
(1985: 139). Such accusations have been fuelled by the suggestion that
Irigaray is invoking biological essentialism in the accounts she gives
of the female body, both in her redescriptions of female sexuality and
her re-envisaging of the maternal function. For some readers she
appears to be evoking a female body, as it is, without the overlay of
patriarchal ordering, a pre-discursive pre-Oedipal body. This then
forms the basis of our reconceived 'woman'.

In key respects the accusation of biological essentialism does, however, seem to be a misreading. Irigaray does not suggest we could
have unmediated access to a female body. Rather her project is a
utopian one (Whitford 1991). She is attempting to allow women
to experience their bodies in a positive way. She is clear, however,
that the body she is describing is an imaginary one, in the sense
outlined in chapter 7. Her descriptions are explicit creative attempts
to mediate our affective relations to the body in a positive way. In
the words of Rosi Braidotti, 'The process is forward looking, not
nostalgic. It does not aim at recovering a lost origin' (Braidotti with
Butler 1994: 43). Irigaray is clear that the switch in the imaginaries
by which women experience their bodies is not something which
she can do alone. Nor, given that the dominance of male imaginaries
is a consequence of their social power, is it something which is
achievable without changes in the social relations between men and
women. Braidotti herself explicitly claims that the basis of sexual
difference is not biological and the content of the category 'woman'
variable. For Grosz, sexual difference is anchored in reproductive
differences, yet the content of 'woman' is not universal. There is then
some agreement that the content of the category 'woman' is fixed
at the imaginary and symbolic level, and though presently defined
phallocentrically is open to change and variation.

More problematically, however, for all theorists, we have the claim
that sexual difference itself is an originary difference. In relation to
this the question arises: what makes the division between the sexes
unavoidable? It is difficult to see what answer could be given to this
which did not invoke the body. We will return to this issue below.

Colonizing Gestures

The attempt to redesignate 'woman' and 'femininity' has, moreover, been subject to criticisms of ahistoricity and a false universalism on different grounds from that of biological essentialism. Irigaray remarks: 'A long history has put all women in the same sexual, social and cultural condition. Whatever inequalities may exist among women, they all undergo, even without realizing it, the same oppression, the same exploitation of their body, the same denial of their desire' (1985b: 164). In Irigaray's hands and those of other sexual difference theorists the enunciation of this shared position takes the form of woman being subject to the same oppressive imaginary and symbolic structures. Butler, and others, criticize such an approach for its 'globalizing reach'. She claims that 'the failure to acknowledge the specific cultural operations of gender oppression is itself a kind of epistemological imperialism . . . colonizing under the sign of the same those differences that might otherwise call that totalising concept into question' (1990a: 13).

The charge of universalism here is part and parcel of the charge of universalism discussed previously (see chapter 2) with regard to psychoanalytical thought in general. The reliance of sexual difference theorists particularly on the work of Lacan has made them targets of parallel anxieties. Some critics claim that the analysis of the symbolic and imaginary structures which inform sexual difference theory are therefore a response to particular philosophical and psychoanalytic theories, given prominence at a specific historical moment. They are not necessarily an account of the global situation of women. Their dominance may make them appropriate targets of deconstruction, but we should also recognize the existence historically, cross-culturally and within contemporary culture of other discourses in which, for example, women are not conceived of primarily in terms of lack (Nye and Leyland, in Fraser and Bartky 1992). We should, that is, not assume that our experience is entirely mediated by such patriarchal representations. We can 'embrace Irigaray's brilliant critical readings of specific androcentric texts while demurring from her global hypothesis about their collective input' (1992: 10).

Gayatri Spivak agrees that the critiques of the symbolic and imaginary orders, central to the writings of sexual difference theorists, make sense in the context of very particular strands of philosophical thought. She also expresses anxieties that exclusive attention to language and the imaginary can distract attention from the lived reality of political struggles. Recognizing the specificity of context of much of this writing, however, Spivak, interestingly, can also see some productivity in 'reaffirming the historically discontinuous yet common "object"-ification of the sexed subject as woman' (1987: 150). Drawing on the work of sexual difference theorists with regard to their descriptions of women's sexual pleasure, she discusses the importance of the erasure of the clitoris in the representation of sexuality: 'the precomprehended suppression or effacement of the clitoris relates to every move to define woman as sex object, or as means or agent of reproduction' (p. 151). Attention to the clitoris would force recognition that female sexual pleasure is outside the orbit of reproduction. Its erasure has made it possible to identify woman legally and socially with her reproductive function: 'all historical and theoretical investigation into the definition of woman as legal *object* – in or out of marriage; or as politico-economic passageway for property and legitimacy would fall within the investigation of the varieties of the effacement of the clitoris' (p. 151). The strength of Spivak's analysis here is a recognition that this effacement forms the basis of interdependently linguistic and social organization. What she terms 'uterine social organization', in terms of which woman is conceived as reproductive object, is manifest in diverse social forms: clitoridectomy, the dowried bride, the patriarchal family with its cult of home buying, the female wage slave 'with a body for exploitation', and many more. Here an insistence on the specificity of sexual difference and attention to the fact that women have been defined in male terms has allowed a scope of analysis which takes us outside of the debates within philosophy and psychoanalysis in France to provide insights into social organization with a global reach.

Spivak is more deeply critical, however, of the sexual difference project in its reconstructive phase. Here she sees the dangers of Western feminist thought reinventing itself as the universal woman: 'I see no way to avoid insisting that there has to be a simultaneous other focus: not merely who am I? but who is the other woman? How am I naming her? How does she name me? Is this part of the problematic I discuss?' (1987: 155). Spivak is insisting that the deconstructive techniques which feminists have applied to male definitions of woman should be applied with equal ruthlessness to feminist redefinitions – to make evident which women are being privileged by such accounts, and who is being excluded as not quite womanly enough: the 'other' or outside against which those with power position themselves.

Critics have noticed the absence of such questions in the work of Irigaray. Rosi Braidotti has, however, attempted to address them. Seeing the first stage of sexual difference theory as establishing women as different from men, the second stage for Braidotti is in engaging with and celebrating the difference within the category 'woman'. Women are united by being categorized as 'the second sex'. A starting point for feminist consciousness and a bond of commonality is the recognition of a difference between the way women are and the way they are represented. After this, however, comes a recognition that women are not all the same. 'This idea . . . stresses the importance of rejecting global statements about all women and of attempting instead to be as aware as possible of the place from which one is speaking' (1994: 163). For her the content of the term woman is one which will be variously filled by different women in different situations. There will be no single account. The different contents will reflect women's different positions, the fact that, as Nancy Fraser puts it, 'we position ourselves as "women" to be sure, but also as workers, as parents, as lesbians, as producers and consumers of culture, as people of color, and as inhabitants of a threatening biosphere' (Fraser and Bartky 1992: 30).

It remains the case, however, that for Braidotti, as for other sexual difference theorists, sexual difference is privileged. This in itself is the ground of a different charge of essentialism. Sexual identity – the fact of being embodied female – remains the primary site of both identification and resistance. The variation allowed in the content of the term 'woman' does not therefore answer the anxieties which both Spivak and Fraser are expressing, and which are also echoed in the criticism of Judith Butler that 'the "sexual difference" framework . . . makes sexual difference more hallowed, more fundamental, as a constituting difference of social life more important than other kinds of differences' (Braidotti with Butler 1994: 41). Different forms of racial embodiment remain different variations of being female. It is not that being female is simply a variation of racial embodiment. Sexual difference remains the primary site of struggle, and there will be no necessary relations between woman's struggles and anti-racist or other areas of political struggle (Grosz 1995: 54). Such necessary prioritizing of sexual identity at both the personal and the political level has, however, been challenged by many writers for whom other aspects of their identity may be equal or more important, personally and/or politically.

Spivak's remarks also highlight another issue here, which echoes comments of Judith Butler's discussed in previous chapters. It is not simply a question of ensuring that you have a variety of voices manifest in the articulations of what it is to be a woman. As soon as we engage in such a process at all we are drawing boundaries which will necessarily be exclusory, and thereby create as the excluded others who do not fit our definitions. While recognizing and providing an account of the role that sexed categories play in the construction of subjectivities, Butler none the less argues there is no way of using the categories 'man' and 'woman' without bringing into play what it is to be a proper man and woman, deviation from which produces social penalties, including violent assault. The norms privilege certain kinds of bodies that matter, those that conform, and leave the 'abject' bodies rejected (see chapter 4). The response of sexual difference theorists is that this is a risk we have to take. For without some way of recognizing our commonality as women we can have no basis for political organization and resistance. (We shall return to this debate in chapter 9.)

Gender versus Sexual Difference

The charges of essentialism against sexual difference theory can take the form of any or all of the anxieties expressed above. But the most fundamental essentialist aspect of its thinking is that sexual difference is unavoidable. It forms the horizon from which subjectivity and identity become possible at all. It is this which yields the privileged position in which it is placed both personally and politically. Such claims bring sexual difference theory into particular disagreement with the work of gender theorists such as Judith Butler, who argues that such a move reifies 'a social asymmetry as an eternal necessity' and then makes this the ground of feminist politics (Braidotti with Butler 1994: 39). It is to the debates between Butler, as a gender theorist, and those committed to the project of sexual difference that we turn next.

Judith Butler, when interviewing Rosi Braidotti for the journal *differences*, defends the use of the term 'gender' to make sense of the differing social position and subjectivities of man and woman.

Accepting Braidotti's argument that using the term gender can suggest a false symmetry between the positions of man and woman, she none the less defends it as freeing us from a perception of that asymmetry as 'irreducible and irreversible'. Use of the term gender enables us to free conceptions of masculinity and femininity from particular bodily forms and consequently undermine the division into binary genders and interdependently the division of bodily forms into binary sexes. For Butler it is the binary division which is a precondition to the asymmetry which Braidotti is highlighting.

At the heart, then, of the disagreement here is a difference concerning the irreducibility of sexual difference. Butler would simply insist that the question of a pre-ontological requirement of sexual difference is one that could simply never be decided (Jagger 1999). We simply cannot have access to something which is beyond discourse. Moreover we should be highly suspicious of any such claim once we become aware of the processes by means of which sexual difference is produced to take on the appearance of something which is simply given, and inevitable. We can thereby come to see sexual difference as an effect rather than as something originary. Moreover, by attempting to think gender outside the binary divisions of male and female, we can undermine the apparent gulf which is seen as impassable. The test of whether sexual difference is an inevitable horizon is to try to think outside it.

In the previous chapter we discussed the limitations of a purely performative account of gender identity with respect to the corporeality of the body. We suggested that viewing corporeality itself as a discursive effect, as Butler seemed to suggest, failed to answer to the weightiness and constraints which our bodily existence seemed to provide, and the role which our bodily experiences played within our subjectivities. Purely performative accounts interconnectedly seemed inadequate to the affective relations in which we stood to our bodies. We attempted to address both of these concerns by use of the concept of the imaginary body. Such a concept is put to work most prominently in the writings of sexual difference theorists, which prompts the question whether its use requires us to adopt such a stance. Attention to the imaginary body brings into prominence that here and now sexual difference is central to our mode of experiencing, mediated by 'culturally shared phantasy about male and female biologies' (Gatens 1996: 130). It is much less clear, however, that such imaginary relations are unavoidable.

What has become clear through attention to the imaginary, how-ever, is that thinking gender otherwise, in the way that Butler recom-mends, also requires imagining otherwise, changing the *affective salience* which differently shaped bodies currently carry. The degendering shift requires an imaginary shift. Performative strategies, such as those recommended by Butler, are clearly a contribution to this. The difficulties, however, are acute, once we recognize the irreducibility of the psyche to the social (see the discussion of Biddy Martin in chapter 4). The strength of performative strategies is in *denaturalizing* gender, in highlighting that there is no essential link between bodily forms and certain patterns of categorization. Such a recognition, how-ever, does not necessarily affect our attachments to certain bodily forms and the significance which gendered identifications play in our ways of experiencing them. It is recognition of just this point which prompted Irigaray to foreground imaginary shifts, as a creative project. The imaginary shifts which she explores, however, all operate within the framework of sexual difference. But if the degendering shift also requires an imaginary shift then theorists who prioritize reworking our sexual imaginaries may also need to look beyond the current binary divisions. When Irigaray insists we have to imagine 'woman' outside the logic of the 'other of the same', for gender theorists this will have to be read as re-imagining 'woman' *outside a binary structure* of male and female.

Butler's arguments in favour of gender theory are not all of the metaphysical kind described above. In discussion with Braidotti she sees 'the turn to gender' as a way of 'insisting that feminism expand its political concerns beyond gender asymmetry, to underscore the cultural specificity of its constitution as well as its interrelations with other politically invested categories, such as nation and race' (Braidotti with Butler 1994: 43). Sexual difference theorists prioritize gender over other aspects of subjectivity, and, in the words of Elizabeth Grosz, 'It is not clear, for example, that struggles against racism will necessarily be allied with women's struggles or, conversely, that feminism will overcome forms of racist domination' (1995: 54). Within a performative account of gender, however, gender is *mutually con-stituted* alongside other categories. There is no performance of gender that is not also a performance of race, class or dis/ability. Attention to the regulatory ideals constraining such performances draws our attention to the operations of power within them and the privileges and exclusions which retain them.

Whereas, for Braidotti, the turn to gender hid the asymmetries of sexual difference, for Butler an insistence on the perspective of sexual difference institutionalizes heterosexuality, making 'an affirmation of heterosexuality . . . the basis of linguistic intelligibility . . . exclusive or primary focus on sexual difference obfuscates or denies the asymmetry of the hetero/homo divide' (Braidotti with Butler 1994: 49). What for Braidotti is a threat – that women's studies becomes diluted by attention to gay sexuality – is, for Butler, a benefit of the turn to gender. It allows the concerns of feminism to be articulated alongside and in the context of an interrogation of sexuality. As we made clear in chapter 4, for Butler the binary division into male and female requires a heterosexual norm, and operates by a process of 'othering' of homosexual and lesbian desire. Butler is clear that an adequate account of lesbian desire cannot be provided within the framework of sexual difference, with its affirmations of a positive female sexuality. Although this might suggest to some writers (though not Irigaray) the desirability of female sexuality being explored independently of men, for Butler 'an emphasis on female specificity cannot suffice' to do justice to lesbian desire. What the perspective of sexual difference misses out is the importance within lesbianism of 'cross-identifications with *masculine* norms and figures' (emphasis ours). Indeed recognition of such cross-identifications within lesbian practice serves to destabilize binary divisions between male and female (see chapters 4 and 5).

From the title and approach of this book it is clear that we have thrown in our lot with the 'turn to gender' and for many of the reasons which Butler has articulated. It is not clear, however, that here and now we have to make a choice of either thinking gender differently, or working at reconfiguring damaging sexual imaginaries. Perhaps we can do both, interrogating our categories nervously even as we use them. Sexual difference theorists have insisted on the need for the category 'woman' to enable the specificity of female experience to be captured and to enable collective forms of political action. In the following chapter concentrating on the experiences of transsexual people we shall explore the need for our sexed categories to make sense of experience. In the final chapter we shall consider whether such categories are needed for political agency.

Borderlands and Gendered Homes

In this chapter we are concerned with the use of gendered and other categories, not only to constitute our identities performatively, but also as a means of *making sense of* our experiences. We will be paying attention particularly to the work of certain transsexual theorists and theorists of postcoloniality. Such theorists are often conceived of as drawing attention to those at the borderlands of identity categories, problematizing stable notions of gender or nation. We hope to undermine the opposition between the margins and the centre which such a formulation may suggest, using such writings to illuminate the role of gendered and other categories in making sense of subjective identity in general.

Doing justice to our experiences was a central concern of early feminist writings. It was recognized that much of what passes for theory had failed to pay attention to the lives and experiences of women. An anchorage in experience became a condition of feminist theorizing in general. With the increasing appropriation of post-modernist thought within feminist thought the category of experience became suspect. It was recognized that no experiences could be regarded as foundational for theory, because our experiences are themselves mediated by the cultural discourses which are available for us to make sense of ourselves with. Joan Scott, in a famous article 'Experience' (Butler and Scott 1992: 22–40), discusses a scene in Samuel Delaney's autobiography *The Motion of Light in Water* (1988), in which he describes his first visit to the St Mark's bathhouse in 1963. Standing on the threshold, he sees an 'undulating mass of male bodies, spread wall to wall'. 'What this experience said was that there was a population – not of individual homosexuals . . . not of hundreds, not of thousands, but rather of millions of gay men' (1992: 174). On one reading of Delaney's account this moment 'marked . . . a coming to consciousness of himself, a recognition of his authentic identity, one he had always shared, would always share with others like himself' (p. 34). It is the use of experience to ground such claims of authenticity which Scott finds particularly problematic: 'talking about experience in these ways leads us to take the existence of individuals for granted (experience is something which people have) rather than to ask how conceptions of selves are produced' (p. 27); 'it masks the necessarily discursive character of these experiences' (p. 31). 'Experience is at once always already an interpretation and in need of interpretation . . . it is always contested' (p. 37). Reflecting back on Delaney's account of what he views as 'a clarifying moment', Scott suggests we 'see this event not as the discovery of a truth (conceived of as the reflection of a prediscursive reality) . . . but as the substitution of one interpretation for another' (p. 35).

To reflect solely on the productive power of discourse, as we have done in previous chapters, and as Scott along with Butler recommends, is, however, to be in danger of leaving experience out altogether. We can fail to recognize uses of discourses not only to produce identities, but to do so in a way that makes sense of people's lives. In this chapter we shall be exploring the possibility of using discourse in this latter way, without falling back into the picture which Scott critiques, of viewing experiences as pre-discursive realities, grounding authentic identities which we are attempting to represent. All our experiences are interpretations and they can be replaced by other interpretations. But all interpretations are not equal here, and some make more sense, make lives more liveable than others.

Transgendering and Transsexuality: Feminist Responses

The reaction of the feminist movement to transsexuals has overall been less than welcoming. Characteristic of the most extreme response, Janice Raymond's *The Transsexual Empire: the making of the she male*, published in 1979, 'represents male to female transsexuals as agents of a medical empire sent out to colonise women's community'. This refusal to see male-to-female transsexuals as authentic women was repeated in women's spaces and events across Britain and America throughout the 1970s and 1980s. When transsexual autobiographies were first coming to public attention there were very few publicly available narratives of female-to-male transitions, and many feminists simply regarded transsexual women as impostors encroaching on their space. There were different kinds of reason for this hostility. Some groups were operating with notions of being an authentic woman grounded in possessing a female body from birth, which was indeed problematically essentialist. Others were responding to the kind of narratives which transsexuals were telling, which seemed to invest 'being female' with the very trappings of gender which feminist activists were in the process of trying to shake off. Here, for example, is Jan Morris in *Conundrum*, following transition: 'I feel small and neat. . . . My blouse and skirt are light. . . . My shoes make my feet look more delicate than they are, . . . besides giving me . . . a suggestion of vulnerability that I rather like . . . when I walk out into the street I feel ready for the world's appraisal, in a way I never felt as a man' (Morris 1974: 174). Similarly Hedy Jo Star in *I Changed My Sex*: 'I wanted the sensual feel of lingerie against my skin, I wanted to brighten my face with cosmetics. I wanted a strong man to protect me' (Star 1955, quoted in Stone 1997: 343). Such transsexual women were viewed as renaturalizing gender characteristics as constitutive of 'being a woman', the same gender characteristics which feminists were insisting were disposable social constructions.

The resistance to the acceptance of transsexual women within the category 'woman' was also found within the work of the sexual difference theorists discussed in chapter 8. Elizabeth Grosz claims:

> There will always remain a kind of outsideness or alienness of the experiences and lived reality of each sex for the other. Men, contrary to the fantasy of the transsexual, can never, even with surgical intervention, feel or experience what it is like to be, to live, as women. At best the transsexual can live out his fantasy of femininity – a fantasy that in itself is usually disappointed with the rather crude transformations effected by surgical and chemical intervention. The transsexual may look like a woman but can never feel like or be a woman. (Grosz 1994b: 208)

It is much more recently that the phenomenon of female-to-male transsexuality has gained a high public profile. This was helped by the 1996 documentary on Channel 4 television telling the stories of a group of female-to-male transsexuals, including their trips to Amsterdam to consider the surgical operations, and the transformations of their bodies as they took hormones. The documentary, *The Wrong Body*, included, perhaps most strikingly, the story of Fredd. Fredd, whose history was followed from nine to twelve years old, was a child with a biologically female body who laid claim to a male gender identity and was seeking help and hormone injections to stave off a female puberty which was viewed by him as catastrophic to his sense of his own gendered subjectivity.

Attention to the biographies of female-to-male transsexuals, however, also reveals a frequently troubled relationship to the feminist movement. Lesbian groups, where pre-transition FTMs (female-to-male transsexuals) often initially sought a community, were tolerant to different degrees of the manifestation of butch roles. For some lesbian communities influenced by particular forms of feminism, such forms of identification were regarded as a problematic incorporation of patriarchal norms. Other communities, however, accepted butchness as a sexual identity but were unhappy when it became clear that what was at issue was a desire for a change of sex/gender. Moving from a position as butch lesbian to (possibly heterosexual) man was regarded as going over to the enemy (Stone 1997).

Transgendering and Queer Theory

With the advent of queer theory and the emphasis on the performativity of gender, however, the 'trans' people became viewed as the vanguard in the war against a binary/heterosexist construction of gendered identity. In summer 1994, 'Camp Trans' was established outside the Michigan Womyns music festival, which explicitly refused entry to transsexual women: 'the presence of transsexuals on the borders of the festival posed a profoundly theoretical question about the symbolic borders of gender' (Prosser 1998: 172). Trans people of all kinds were portrayed as the 'gender outlaws' who were challenging the dominant categorization into male and female, making evident its constructedness, and opening up the possibility of both numerous forms of sex/gender/sexual identifications and radical indeterminateness in positioning in the sex/gender system. For Butler, in *Gender Trouble*, and other queer theorists the changes to embodiment which are sought by those seeking sex/bodily reassignment serves to make evident the constructedness of sexed identity which is also constitutive of apparently more stable gender identities, a constructedness which is displayed by other trans people in ways which do not require bodily modification.

Many trans people therefore regard the advent of queer theory, with its goal of destabilizing sexual binaries, as the theoretical framework whereby their own histories can be made sense of. Included among these are transsexual women and men who don't wish simply to pass but who desire their transsexual history to be evident. Sandy Stone, for example, argues: 'I am suggesting that in the transsexual's erased history we can find a story disruptive to the accepted discourses of gender. . . . For a transsexual, as a transsexual, to generate a . . . counter-discourse is to speak from outside the boundaries of gender, beyond the constructed oppositional nodes which have been predefined as the only positions from which discourse is possible' (1997: 351). 'In the transsexual as text we may find the potential to map the refigured body onto conventional gender discourse and thereby disrupt it, to take advantage of the dissonances created by such a juxtaposition to fragment and reconstitute the elements of gender in new and unexpected geometries' (p. 352).

The experiences of transgendered people can therefore be understood in terms of queer theory in two ways. First, they make evident that our current gender categories are in no way exhaustive. For here are people who cannot be understood in terms of them. This, however, might simply suggest we need new categories, something like a 'third sex' which historically and cross-culturally has been suggested (Herdt 1994). A more radical reading of queer strategies, however, makes problematic identity categories altogether, insisting that subjectivity is such that it can never be contained within them without the closure of possibilities. So Judith Butler responds, in an interview which asked her if she would identify herself as a 'butch dyke', 'What is clear is that I have an uneasy relationship to categorization. . . . the point of my work is not to figure out a proper or adequate mode of description for myself and I would hope to never come up with such a thing. I think it might be a certain kind of death to have actually achieved identity' (More and Whittle 1999: 286). It is this kind of challenge to identificatory categorization altogether which the transgendered person has come to symbolize within queer theory. So, in an early article by Judith Halberstam, transsexuality becomes the marker of the fictionality of all gender categories. 'We are all transsexuals except that the referent of the trans becomes less and less clear (and more and more queer). We are all cross-dressers but where are we crossing from or to what? There is no "other" side, no "opposite" sex, no natural divide to be spanned by surgery, by disguise, by passing' (Halberstam 1994: 212).

The Search for Gendered Realness: Finding a Home

There are transsexual theorists for whom the performative theory of gender, and the consequent project for queering gender and other identity categories, is profoundly unsatisfactory. For writers such as Jay Prosser (1998), the experiences of transsexuals reveal the limits of queer theories' discursive account of gendered identity. In his book *Second Skins* Prosser suggests the queer theorist cannot account for the transsexual's desire for sexed *embodiment* in terms other than a misguided naturalism about sexed identity, consequent on the hegemonic discourses in which they have been placed. The objection Prosser raises to such a view is that it fails to explain the bodiliness of our sexed identities, which gives to transsexual experience the characteristic desire for bodily modification. In response to Halberstam, Prosser replies that the suggestion that we are 'all transsexuals' is a way of 'not attending to the specificity of narrative' (1998: 15).

The Channel 4 documentary referred to above was entitled *The Wrong Body*. The sense of being born into the wrong body is a recurrent motif within transsexual narratives. Indeed it is the articulation of their experience in this way which is used by psychiatrists as the basis for diagnosis of 'gender dysphoria'. Such a diagnosis is needed if people are to be allowed access to surgery to alter their biological sex. The sense of being wrongly embodied is articulated, according to numerous autobiographies, at a very young age, sometimes as young as three, and the sense of alienation from found embodiment has resulted in a number of cases to self-destructive behaviour against the body: 'because my body was becoming more and more alien to me as I developed, there was an urge to rip off my own skin' (Thompson, quoted in Prosser 1998: 71). It leads to a desire to change the biological body to bring it into line with the 'real' gender identity which is felt to constitute the subjectivity of the person. Such a narrative is puzzling for a number of the theoretical positions on gender. Its insistence on gendered realness sits in tension with social constructionist accounts of gender, and certainly with the performative account associated with queer theory. A return to biological naturalness, however, is also problematic, given that the body at issue is experienced as the wrong body and therefore, far from fixing gendered realness, threatens to undermine it.

Trans people who provide such a narrative claim communality not with transgenderists, who celebrate the ambiguities of gender, but with biological males and females who comfortably inhabit their categories as men and women. Prosser therefore draws a distinction between those who inhabit the 'borderlands' of 'no gender' and those seeking such gendered 'homes'. In highlighting the longing of many transsexual men and women for a gender 'home', for a sense of belonging, he is drawing attention to a desire for a sexed realness which most people are able to take for granted. What remains as problematic, however, is what such gendered realness can consist in either for the transsexual or for born men and women, if it is supposed to outrun the performativity which formed the centre of Butler's account. What is unclear is what could *constitute* such gendered realness. It is, moreover, unsettling that characteristics which are stereotypical and culturally specific should appear, in many transsexual autobiographies, to be woven into such claims to authentic femininity and masculinity.

Prosser argues that what constitutes transsexual identity is the adoption of a particular kind of narrative about their life (1998: part 2). What is distinctive of the autobiographies of transsexuals is a narrative of transition. The lives which are revealed in these texts are represented as having a teleological shape with a trajectory towards a gendered home: 'transsexuality in fact appears as a narrative; a plot typically beginning in childhood recognition of cross-gendered difference and ending, again typically, with the transsexual achieving some marker of becoming, . . . some degree of closure' (Prosser 1999a: 90). Again typically the moments of becoming are associated with bodily transformations. There are certain recurrent themes and tropes within such a plot. One key element is the feeling of being trapped in the wrong body, which in the narratives offered is projected back into early childhood. Other elements include posited childhood feelings of difference, of not conforming to gender stereotypes: not being sporty, not liking rough and tumble games, wanting to play with dolls, liking dressing up; or being a tomboy, not liking dolls, etc. Prosser particularly identifies in such narratives the sense of a journey, a crossing over of borders, of reaching a stable destination (often marked in the autobiographies he discusses by literal journeys and literal crossing of borders). The narratives are, he emphasizes, an attempt to produce a coherent sense of self by means of the structure which is brought into the account of the life. What marks this structure most importantly is its telos, the reaching of a home of gendered realness, most commonly achieved by some degree of bodily modification which enables the possibility of social 'passing'. The sense of arrival, of reaching such a home, seems bound up with the very flesh of the new body. Given the account of gender identities in terms of 'biology as lived' explored in the last chapter, and by Prosser himself, the importance of the flesh is that it yields the possibility of shared bodily imaginaries as central to the shared gender identities which form the endpoints of such narratives.

What emerges here is people attempting to make coherent their apparently fragmented lives and experiences; weaving the profound unease which they have felt with the identities which have been attributed to them into some kind of sense, finding a 'home' in which they can rest. The identification as male or female, or in many cases as transsexual male or female, is one which makes sense of their lives. (We can, after all, it might be argued, only make sense of our lives in terms of the categories which are on offer.) Prosser argues for 'the ongoing centrality of sexual difference in our worlds [with] limits to its refigurability [which has the] consequence of many subjects yearning to relocate in relation to this difference' (1998: 204). On Prosser's account the 'realness' of the transsexual's gender, in common with the 'realness' of other genders, consists in the 'home' it provides by making the best sense around of the experiences of the subjects concerned.

The desire for a sense of belonging, a yearning for a home which enables us to make sense of our lives, is a theme found in other accounts of identity. bell hooks, for example, talks about the meaning of 'homeplace' for black people. She describes the journey to her grandmother's house: 'we would have to pass that terrifying whiteness – those white faces on the porches staring us down with hate. . . . Oh that feeling of safety, of arrival, of homecoming when we finally reached the edges of her yard' (hooks 1990: 41). She argues for the need for such a homeplace: 'that space where we return for renewal and self-recovery, where we heal our wounds and become whole' (1990: 49).

There is never a suggestion in Prosser's work that transition can provide quite this sense of safety (and see below for later shifts in his thinking). It can, however, be, he suggests, from the perspective of the subject, the location from which they hope to heal their wounds and become whole.

The Dangers of Home

A number of problems can be raised with Prosser's early account of transsexual identity. All relate in some way to his theorization of gender identities as 'homes'.

1   One problem concerns the suggestion that there is some kind of common shape to transsexual narrative, which is the basis for transsexual identity claims. Sandy Stone (1997) had earlier challenged the apparent communalities which serve to unite transsexual narratives around the motif of 'the wrong body'. First, she points out that the production of such a narrative is required if medical support is to be gained, and this is known by those seeking transformative surgery. Secondly, this way of articulating transsexual experience surfaced in an early text which many transsexual people read en route to finding a way of expressing their own unease with their gendered identification. Rather than expressive of a shared common experience, this phrase has come to be productive of a shared classification which is masking underlying diversity: 'the berdache and the stripper, the tweedy housewife and the mujerado, the mah'un and the rock star, are still the same story after all, if we only try hard enough' (1997: 349). E. Probyn makes a similar point, though in a different context, when she discusses the danger of narratives becoming 'an exchange of calling cards', in which important differences and specificities of experience become invisible as, anxious for a recognizable narrative to be provided of our lives, we too quickly rush to a 'me too' response to those accounts which have entered the public domain (Probyn 1996: 23). The critique here, if applied to Prosser's work, would be that Prosser assumes there is a homogeneity within the category of transsexual, and generally within gendered categories,

which seems to belie the specificity and diversity of people's experiences of gender.

2   The anxiety that Prosser's account over-homogenizes transsexual lives is linked to a further problem raised by Judith Halberstam (1998: ch. 5). In Halberstam's reading of Prosser the transsexual experience of gender 'relies on a belief in the two territories of male and female, divided by a flesh border and crossed by surgery and endocrinology' (p. 164). The transsexual shares with the non-transgendered male and female a secure habitation of one of these territories. In contrast the 'queer' transgendered subject remains inhabiting the borderlands. For Halberstam such a picture falsifies the continuities and discontinuities between a range of gendered and sexed identities, for example the link between the experiences of FTM transsexuals and butch lesbians who don't consider transitioning. Many of the recurrent motifs listed above as common to transsexual narratives appear in the life histories of lesbian and straight people who never think of transitioning. In the words of Jordy Jones, a FTM performance artist from San Francisco,

> not everyone who experiences gender dysphoria experiences it in the same way, and not everyone deals with it in the same way. Not all transgendered individuals take hormones and not everyone who takes hormones is transgendered. I have a (genetically female) friend who identifies as male and passes perfectly. He's never had a shot. I certainly know dykes who are butcher than I could ever be, but who wouldn't consider identifying as anything other than women. (pp. 148–9)

3   Halberstam also claims that within this account there is a sense of the 'closure' of the categories male and female, such that following transition the transsexual has reached a determinate place, shared with biological males and females. Masculinity and femininity are represented as endpoints of a continuum, with biological males and then transsexual males at one end and biological females and then transsexual females at the other. Masculine-identified females who do not transition are thereby portrayed as lacking the gendered realness of those who cross. In contrast to such a model, Halberstam suggests that there is a patchwork of overlapping similarities and differences which makes such a linear model impossible to apply. Masculinity and femininity are not endpoints of a continuum but categories which are being continually constituted, contested and negotiated in the subjectivities of us all.

4   In line with such anxieties, Halberstam also challenges the dominant narrative of the *wrong body*. Who, Halberstam wants to know, has the 'right body'? 'Such rhetoric . . . assumes that the proper solution to "painful wrong embodiment" (Prosser) is moving to the right body, where "rightness" may as easily depend on whiteness and class privilege . . . as it does on being regendered. Who, we might ask, can afford to dream of a right body? Who believes such a body exists?' (Halberstam 1998: 172). Here we might be reminded of the aspirations of Venus Xtravaganza (in the film *Paris is Burning*), who aspires to be 'a rich white girl'. Her body is wrong not only for being male but for being poor and Latino. The questions which Halberstam is raising here link to those we considered at the end of our previous discussion of the imaginary body. In terms of the social imaginaries attaching to bodies, which, as Butler points out, operate by reference to normalizing ideals that it is impossible to actualize, none of us can possibly have the right body. People can spend different amounts of money in an attempt to bring their bodies close to an actualization. If the concept of wrong and right bodies is understood in this way then it is difficult to make the transsexual decision to seek body modification look different from that of those seeking cosmetic surgery in an attempt to make their body right.

Halberstam is not here simply repeating the accusation that those who seek body modification are in some sense 'gender dupes'. She is rather problematizing the articulation of that modification as a route to the 'right body' (connected to problematizing it as reaching a 'gender home'). People change their bodies to different degrees to make their lives liveable, and to make those bodies ones which they are able to live with and make (some) sense of. This is not necessarily to be thought of as a crossing from the 'wrong' body to the 'right' one.

5   Central to Halberstam's whole discussion of Prosser is resistance to an articulation of identities as 'homes', stable places where subjects can rest, having finally managed to weave a coherent narrative out of their lives. Halberstam draws a comparison here with work in postcolonial studies, where 'the politics of migration have been fiercely debated, and what has emerged is a careful *refusal* of the dialectic of home and border' (1998: 164). One strand of this refusal comes from a recognition that homes find it difficult to tolerate difference and change, and are constructed by the erection of barriers of exclusion and intolerance. Minnie Bruce Pratt in her autobiography

describes a moment in which her father takes her to climb a tower to look around the town 'to position her in relation to it', a positioning which she becomes aware excludes the people living on the wrong side of the tracks: 'what emerges is the consolidation of the white home in response to a threatening outside' (Martin and Mohanty 1986: 204). Gloria Anzaldua describes her home as unable to tolerate her lesbianism and her refusal to conform to the range of possibilities on offer to women: 'to this day I'm not sure where I found the strength to leave the source, the mother, disengage from my family, *mi terra, mi gente*, and all that picture stood for. I had to leave home so I could find myself' (Anzaldua 1987: 16).

Borderlands and Postcolonial Precedents

The apparent stand-off between Halberstam, with an account of identity categories which shares affinities with the queer goal of destabilization, and Prosser, who sees the need for such categories to make sense of our subjectivities, need not, however, be as polarized as this presentation thus far has suggested. Here we can get help by looking at the work of theorists such as Gloria Anzaldua, to undermine the starkness of the opposition we seem to have created.

The challenge to identificatory categorization which the transgendered person has come to symbolize within much contemporary theory is a position which is shared by the migrants and border dwellers who have become the focus and producers of much postcolonial writing. The focus of discussion of identity within the postcolonial context has focused on the impossibility of 'pure identities' of a nationalist or cultural type. The colonial encounter itself resulted/ results in the emergence of so-called 'native' identities, constructed as the 'other' in relation to which the colonizers could/can place themselves (Said 1978) (and incidentally justify their colonial enterprise). Even the process of reclaiming such identities for anti-imperialist purposes cannot escape a solely constructed homogeneity which is a consequence of their original colonial purpose. Reference back to imagined pure identities of a pre-colonial past are of no help here. Neither the colonized nor the colonizer is unchanged by the colonial experience or the reappropriations of identity which have been the result of independence movements. The margins (of empire) are no longer, if ever, a pure space, despite the fact that claims to such purity fuel escalating numbers of nationalist wars throughout the world.

These consequences of colonialism are intertwined with the movements of peoples, so that migration has become the mark of late twentieth-century and early twenty-first-century living. World travelling (Lugones 1987) or living on the borderlands (Anzaldua 1987) has thereby come to symbolize the inadequacy of nationalist/cultural/ ethnic categories, in just the way that the experiences of transgendered people have come to symbolize the inadequacy of our binary sex/ gender system. In the words of Gloria Anzaldua:

To live on the Borderlands means you

are neither *hispana india negra espanola*
ni gabacha, eres mestiza, mulata, half breed
caught in the cross fire between camps
while carrying all five races on your back
not knowing which side to turn to, run from
(1987: 194)

In her own work Anzaldua has used the image of *mestiza* consciousness to explore notions of identity and subjectivity which rejects discrete categorization: 'the new *mestiza* copes by developing a tolerance for contradictions, a tolerance for ambiguity. She learns to be an Indian in Mexican culture, to be Mexican from an Anglo point of view. She learns to juggle cultures. . . . She has a plural personality, nothing is thrust out . . . not only does she sustain contradictions, she turns the ambivalence into something else' (1987: 79).

Such critiques have not, however, meant that the concept of home is totally rejected. There is no attempt by Anzaldua to deny what her past has been and the way in which it is informing her present. She writes 'lo mexicano is in my system. I am a turtle, wherever I go I carry "home" on my back' (1987: 21).

Moreover, the opposition between home and borders becomes destabilized with the recognition that for many people home is a borderland. Anzaldua was raised '*en el Valle del Rio grande* in South Texas – that triangular piece of land wedged between the river *y el golfo* which serves as the Texas–US/Mexican border' (1987: 35). Here indigenous Indian, Spanish, European American and black American peoples have lived and interrelated to produce a *mestiza* culture whose very distinctiveness is a product of this particular kind of history.

Notable in much postcolonial writing is a strong sense of located-ness, an anchorage of narratives in specific locations with very specific histories. The *mestiza* consciousness which Anzaldua is articulating is both an attempt to make sense of a very specific history and a meta-phoric exploration of the nature of subjectivity to make evident the *mestiza* possibilities in the consciousness of others. There is a refusal of strict categories. But such a refusal allows the articulation of very specific histories.

This enables us to reflect back on the strategy of 'queering'. There is very evidently in the work of Butler a political goal of making evident the constructed nature of our gender categories, in order to break a normative ordering of biology, gender and sexuality, and open up a proliferation of possibilities presently rendered invisible. Con-spicuous gender 'playfulness' can thereby be a political act directed at these ends. The critique of the gender binary division, however, is both its closure (of possibilities) and its violence, its exclusions – in short its failure to *make sense of* the specific subjectivities of us all. In the *mestiza* consciousness which Anzaldua recommends we find *both* the challenge to categorization *and* the resources for articulating very specific subjectivities. Moreover these subjectivities are anchored in particular places with distinctive histories.

Belongings

In more recent work Prosser has revised his account of the 'realness' of transsexual gender (Prosser 1999b). Whereas in *Second Skins* such real gender was held out as the telos of the transsexual narrative, marked by bodily transition, in his later article the achievement of a 'real' gender is a necessarily unachievable object of desire. What marks transsexual identity is 'the failure to be real' (1999b: 85). Here Prosser emphasizes that there is no home to form the telos of the transsexual narrative. The transsexual body retains the marks of surgery, and some trace or remnant of what cannot be reassigned. In place of a telos there is rather a continually renegotiated desire, a yearning to be what is necessarily unattainable. In his discus-sion Prosser does not address the question of the realness of non-transsexual gender. His discussion might suggest that the 'real' gender is unattainable only to transsexual men and women. Its logic, however, leads elsewhere. 'Real women' and 'real men' are fantasies which, as Butler realized, we may aspire to but can never realize.

The emphasis on desire, which is found in Prosser's recent work, is linked to the rejection of an endpoint or resting point in the negotiation of subjective identities. Identity is no longer a matter of arriving at a determinate destination but is instead a continual process of negotiation. Both aspects have parallels in other contemporary work. For Elspeth Probyn, for example, the concept of identity has been replaced by that of belonging (1996). Probyn argues that where we concern ourselves with identity categories we can only be concerned with articulating characteristics which attach to those who fall under the categories. What we cannot capture as a feature of subjectivity is the yearnings people have to belong, and the way these yearnings can be anchored to particular times and places, can change and can bring us into connection with very different groups of people, in a way that constitutes the singularity of our own subjectivity.

Probyn discusses, like Prosser, the use of narratives of childhood and past to articulate subjectivity. She resists narratives of lives in which there 'is only one line of movement, one that goes from the present to the past in order to justify the present', seeing the present only as the effect of past causes (1996: 112). Rather, 'images from childhood pull us back to a space that cannot be revisited, they throw us into a present becoming, profoundly disturbing any chronological ordering of life and being' (p. 103). The transsexual narratives which Prosser discusses in *Second Skins* would on this account be seen not as an exploration of the past to reveal that the subject has always been of the desired gender, but as a reading of the past to articulate the *present* desire to modify one's body, to belong to particular communities of men or women.

Probyn explores the networks of relationships, connections and aspirational belongings in Montreal where she was living at the time of writing. What emerges from her text is the extent to which the possibilities for belonging are anchored in the specificity of place, climate, history and political structures in which people are operating. These make possible certain forms of social interactions which, 'driven by desire, produce unexpected connections as they rub against each other' (1996: 35). Belonging is something which is conducted within limits. What Probyn's account shares with that of Prosser is the recognition of yearnings to belong, in accounts of subjectivity. It has in common with Prosser's later work the refusal of a telos, a stable home to give coherence to these yearnings. Rather, relations of sameness and difference, continuity and rupture are continually renegotiated.

Making Sense of Ourselves

Current debates on identity are often posed in terms of stark oppositions. Such oppositions are found in discussions of identity in terms of gender, nation, culture, sexuality, and to some extent class and able-bodiedness. On the one hand we have the defenders of stable identity categories, reference to which is needed if we are to give an account of people's subjectivities. (And, it is argued, to make possible political agency. This strand of argument we will pick up in the following chapter.) Here the assumption is that membership of the category rests on some shared characteristics, whether these are biological, material subjectification to a common set of social norms or the sharing of certain experiences or desires. On the other is posed queer theory with its attempts to destabilize such categories, insistence that they cannot capture the diversity and fluidity of people's experiences, and that they are inevitably interwoven with relations of power and privilege.

In this chapter so far we have explored this opposition in terms of the metaphors of home and borderlands. Attention to some postcolonial writers has, however, suggested a way of negotiating these positions so that 'home' and 'borderlands' are not placed in opposition to each other but rather in dialectical relation. Prosser's insistence on the need for gendered categories to make sense of, to provide a narrative of, subjectivity is compatible with rejecting the problematic associations of 'home' highlighted by Halberstam. The need to use gendered categories to provide narratives of the self can be defended without having recourse to any set of characteristics shared by all people who use the categories 'male' and 'female', 'man' and 'woman' in the stories they tell about themselves. Prosser accepts that 'transsexuality is not a question of immediate or singular crossing but a question of local reading' (Prosser 1999a: 95). So what different transsexuals take to be constitutive of the gender for which they yearn can vary according to the discursive accounts of gender which they have available to them. Prosser, even in his early work, when defending the right of transsexuals to a stable gendered home, none the less recognizes the *mythical* status of such a place. Its mythical status is what becomes predominant in his later writings. This makes the transsexuals' account of their identities closer to the yearnings to belong which are articulated in Probyn. To 'become man' or 'become woman' is invested with an imaginary dimension (see chapter 7), the specific salience of which will vary for different subjects, making identity, as Prosser admits, a matter of 'local readings'. The 'becoming woman' which features in the autobiography of Jan Morris, with its associations of smallness and lightness and vulnerability, will bear little comparison with the 'african royalty' which inspires the eight-year-old mentioned by Probyn.

> In 'Jonnieruth', Becky Birtha's story of growing up black and queer . . . the protagonist . . . is eight when she 'spied this lady. . . . She ain't nobodies mama – I'm sure. And she ain't wearing Sunday clothes. She got on blue jeans and a man's shirt, with the tail hanging out. She got patches on her blue jeans, and she still got her chin stuck out like she some kinda african royalty.' (Probyn 1996: 109)

When such an insistence on local readings is added to the recognition that subjectivity is in a continual process of constitution and negotiation then it is possible that the gendered categories in terms of which we articulate it can shift. Patricia Zavellas reports the narrative of Maria Perez. Maria, growing up in Mexico and coming to desire women, articulates her subjectivity as 'male', and adopts the macho lifestyle which goes along with it. Later, moving to the US, and finding lesbian communities with a range of gendered possibilities, she sees herself as a woman, and allows her bodily shape to change, to become rounder (Lancaster and Leonardo 1997). In Jackie Kay's novel *Trumpet* (1998), in the glory of playing, Joss can accept, as a man, the girl that he has been: 'he is himself again, years ago, skipping along the railway line with a long cord his mother has made into a rope. In a red dress' (1998: 135). The possibility of such shifts, however, is not to be associated with the suggestion that our gendered identities are *styles* which are open to voluntary modification. (This is an accusation which we noted in chapter 4 is often quite inappropriately directed at Butler's account.) Attention to the imaginaries which constitute our affective relations to our bodies and those of others makes evident the extent to which such imaginary modes of experiencing our bodies are constitutive of our subjectivities (see chapter 7). Such imaginaries are 'deep', not susceptible to voluntary modification.

In the search to make sense of ourselves we do not have to appeal to foundational experiences which validate certain kinds of narratives and rule out others. We can agree with Scott that what is involved here is a reinterpretation of what is already interpreted. Moreover there will be differing narratives which may offer differing interpretations, made by a person about themselves at different times or simultaneously and made by others about them. In Jackie Kay's novel a range of different people are presented who make different judgements about Joss the protagonist. Not all narratives are equal, however. They have to make sense (which is perfectly compatible with being contradictory) of the lives they are both constructing and representing. In cases of subjective identity, authority is usually given to the narrative provided by the subject themselves. But this is not without constraint. There is at least an implicit requirement that its appropriateness could be recognized by (at least some) others.

Importantly, even in his early work, Prosser is prepared to allow the possibility of a range of gendered homes outside the locations 'male' and 'female'. He admits continuities of experiences between, for example, butch identities and those of FTM transsexuals. This becomes clear in his discussion of the protagonist Jess, in Leslie Feinberg's novel *Stone Butch Blues* (Feinberg 1993). Jess at a certain point in the book begins the process of transition with hormones and contemplates surgery. S/he draws back, however, and continues hir existence in a masculine-identified female body. Jess fails to feel comfortable in any of the communities with which s/he interacts. S/he does not feel able to deny the history of her female body and become a straight man. But neither does s/he fit easily into a lesbian community increasingly informed by a feminism celebratory of women. Jess in Halberstam's terms finally decides to *make a home* in the body s/he has (Halberstam 1998: 168), a process which is also referred to by Prosser. Jess's home, however, lacks many of the characteristics which Halberstam found problematic in Prosser's earlier use of the term. It is not comfortable, it does not place Jess within a community with shared characteristics. It is not a closed and static endpoint but a continual process of renegotiation.

What early Prosser recognizes in Feinberg's story, which enables him to place it with the transsexual autobiographies he had been discussing, is the sense of a subject painfully negotiating a gendered identity which best approximates to making sense of hir life and desires. In the writers we have been discussing, for whom the metaphor of the borderlands is pivotal, we find an insistence on narrative specificity. For Anzaldua it is exactly the need to make sense of the specificity of her own experiences which requires the development of the *mestiza* consciousness. What becomes evident is that such specificity cannot be accommodated within the framework of static categories of either gender or culture which are otherwise on offer. Rather these categories need to be reconfigured so they give a larger range of locations than male and female, American or Indian, gay or straight. We also find in Probyn that the kinds of belonging to which she draws attention only make sense in particular kinds of context. They emerge out of possible modes of sociability anchored in very specific locations. Without the reference point of those locations they would not be coherent.

What emerges are complex and multiple configurations of inter-dependent genders, sexualities and cultural locations in terms of which people not only constitute themselves (as Butler's performativity captures) but also strive to make some sense of themselves (an aspect which Butler and Scott's account seems to marginalize and which Prosser brings insistently to the fore). Such identities will be multiple, they may or may not include bodily modification, and they will form overlapping networks of similarities and differences which for all of us are important markers of our specificity. What we can recognize, however, is that people are negotiating their identities in an increasingly diverse discursive context, as a result of the visibility of explicit transgendered and transsexual activism, with its political destabilization of the binary categories of sex and the writings of postcolonial people who provide a parallel challenge to our conceptions of nation and ethnicity.

Prosser concludes his later article with a telling quote from Lejeune which seems to capture what has emerged here. 'Telling the truth about the self, constituting the self as a complete subject – it is a fantasy. In spite of the fact that autobiography is impossible, this in no way prevents it from existing' (Prosser 1999b).

Gender and the Politics of Identity

In the previous chapters we have examined the diverse and varied modes of theorizing gender. On one level gender can be used as a lens through which to analyse theory; employed as a means to illustrate the strengths and weaknesses of various theoretical positions and to consider the ways in which the analysis of gender may serve to re-evaluate or rewrite theoretical ideas. However, our interest in gender theory is not merely an interest in it as an academic exercise. Although we recognize the important contribution gender theory has made to the development of social theory more generally, our interest in gender theory is rooted in a desire not only to understand more fully the ways in which gender is constructed but also to develop and implement strategies to reconstruct/deconstruct gender in a less damaging fashion. In short we are concerned with the politics of gender.

It is the aim of this chapter to consider in more depth the political implications of various modes of theorizing gender, in particular the implications of the turn towards queer theory for gender-based political activism (see chapter 4). The current anti-essentialist mood within gender theory, fuelled by the recognition of differences between women as well as the insights of deconstructionism and queer analysis, challenges the very foundations of identity-based political movements, such as the feminist women's movement, and therefore raises crucial questions about political agency and intervention. Indeed, the tension between maintaining a space for feminism both academically and at the grassroots level and eschewing any charges of essentialism or false universalization shapes the content and direction of much contemporary feminism. As illustrated previously, race, sexuality, ethnicity, age, class, able-bodiedness, geographical location and historical time period are just some of the factors that construct women's lives differently. The recognition of differences amongst women has questioned the validity of a political campaign based on the assumption of women's shared experiences. 'In some instances, questioning feminism's claim to speak for all women has led to fears that dismantling the identity "woman" may well lead to the dissolution of feminism itself' (Hennessy 1993: xi).

Additionally, contemporary shifts in feminist theorizing, most notably the moves to deconstruct the subject, have undermined the idea of a fixed, unified self which in turn challenges the basis of a politics grounded in identity. Our subjectivities – our sense of self – are characterized as fluid, shifting and in conflict. Subjectivity is interpreted as 'an ongoing construction, not a fixed point of departure or arrival from which one then interacts with the world' (Lauretis 1984: 159). On the one hand feminists have been drawn to the idea that subjectivity is not immutable but fluid, as it indicates the potential for transformation at the level of the individual. It also enables us to conceptualize more fully the complexities and contradictions of subjective identity – woman, man, black, white, etc., are all shifting, plural and unstable, and how we make sense of ourselves and others via discourses is intensely variable. At the same time, however, the destabilization of the subject poses a key dilemma for an identity-based movement such as feminism. How can one organize as and on behalf of women when the subject 'woman' is itself so unstable, itself a fiction? As di Stefano (1990) points out, as feminism is based entirely on 'subject-centred inquiry', to lose the subject 'woman' or even 'women' is to undermine the foundations of feminist thought and action. If 'women' is a constantly shifting signifier, variable according to the discourse in which it is located, how can we conceptualize 'women's interests', let alone defend them? As Ransom points out, 'What threatens to disappear is the hook on which to hang our feminism' (1993: 126).

This chapter thus deals with the problems and possibilities of identity politics and their implications for gender. In chapter 9 we considered the need for categories to give an account of subjective identity. Here we consider the implications of either maintaining or deconstructing categories for political action. Debates on identity and identity politics, as suggested previously, are often polarized, split between those who argue that stable identity categories are needed not only to give an account of people's subjectivities but also as a basis for political action, and those who contend that categories cannot relay the fluidity and multiplicity of people's experiences, never fully describing or representing that which they name (Webster 2000): in short, a divide between the 'boundary-defenders' and the 'boundary-strippers' (Gamson 1996), between category-supportive and deconstructive political strategies. A third way is sometimes sought in an attempt to reconcile the two positions 'to negotiate the tension between theoretical vision and pragmatic policy' (Squires 1999: 69–70), often with the aim of working with the categories in order to deconstruct or remould them. As Aziz aptly remarks: 'If a feminism of difference is to compete with reactionary forces for the spaces caused by political schisms, it needs to incorporate both the deconstruction of subjectivity and the political necessity of asserting identity' (1997: 77).

Identity Politics

Identity-based political movements, like women's liberation, the gay and lesbian movement and the black civil rights movement, have hinged upon the understanding that we can talk about women, gay men, lesbians, and black men and women as groups with certain shared experiences; that there are recognizable identities – for example, female, male, gay, black – around which we can collectively group. The 'rights' mode of political activism has traditionally been based on the assumption and assertion of collective identities, whether they be gendered, sexual, ethnic, racial, religious or national identities, and the use of corresponding categories – for example, female, black, gay, Indian, British, and so on. If we take the example of the 1970s women's liberation movement, activism centred upon improving the rights of women in relation to equal pay, domestic violence, sexual discrimination, self-determination over reproductive matters, and so on. Women came together to battle against gender-specific discrimination in the public and private spheres, to assert and defend 'women's interests'. Pivotal to their struggle was the recognition and assertion that women formed a group with certain shared experiences, that as a group they were disadvantaged and that as a group they could act collectively to tackle the structural inequalities that underpinned a gender hierarchy.

For some feminist writers the urgent task still is to get sexual differences recognized and properly legislated for in the public sphere. For many the retention of the category 'woman' is deemed vital to fighting against gendered forms of violence, such as rape and domestic violence, or to securing gender-specific rights regarding maternity leave and reproductive choice. Irigarary, for example, argues for 'the necessity of sexuate rights' (see chapter 8 for a fuller discussion of Irigaray). For her, women's civil rights should be thought of in terms of sexual difference rather than equality; what is needed, she suggests, is 'the recognition that there are different rights for each sex and that equality of status can only be established when these rights have been codified by the civil powers' (Whitford 1991: 207). Similarly, Pateman argues for a 'sexually differentiated' formulation of citizenship, which makes the particular experiences of women, for example their experiences as mothers, politically significant. Pateman contends that the present notion of citizenship is patriarchal, separating as it does the public from the private. By consequence our understanding of equality is based on a male model in which women, their lives and their experiences remain devalued (Pateman 1988, 1989).

The idea of shared female experience as a basis for collective action presumes a commonality amongst women. It assumes that, even if women are divided according to ethnicity, class, age, and so on, there is still some sameness based on gender, some common ground or experiences to unite them. Soper, for example, contends that 'Feminism, like any other politics, has always implied a banding together, a movement based on the solidarity and sisterhood of women, who are linked by perhaps very little else than their *sameness* and "common cause" as women' (quoted in Mouffe 1997: 542).

As a consequence identity politics are usually construed as relying on essentialist constructions of gender, implying a unity amongst women arising from biology, structural location or discursive construction. As Squires points out, 'Essences can be materially and symbolically as well as biologically given' (1999: 66). We have discussed biological essentialism in chapter 1, symbolic essentialism as found in Lacan in chapter 2 and material essentialism in chapter 3. Such essentialist positions were followed by a move to a discursive account of the construction of subjectivity, appropriating the ideas of Foucault, and later built on with the work of Butler and the emergence of queer theory. Such discursive accounts recognize the multiplicity of meaning attached to our categories and thus attempt to resist any of the preceding essentialisms.

Identity politics therefore run against the current anti-essentialist trend in gender theory. The notion of shared experience, of some sameness bringing women together as political actors, is incongruent with the deconstruction of 'woman' and 'women' as stable, fixed, coherent categories. Iris Marion Young's article 'The ideal of community and the politics of difference' (1990a) is useful here in exploring tensions that have emerged in relation to the notion of shared experience and the premise that political action can be founded on a sense of commonality (for example, sisterhood or brotherhood). Young argues that a desire for unity, of finding commonality underpins movements such as feminism, and this automatically 'generates borders, dichotomies and exclusions' (Young 1990a: 301) (see also the discussion of Butler in chapter 4). In so doing it suppresses the recognition and flourishing of difference. While understanding the yearning for 'relationships of mutual identification, social closeness and comfort', she suggests that those pursuing political strategies based on the ideal of community 'tend to suppress differences among themselves' and/or 'exclude from their political groups persons with whom they do not identify' (1990a: 300). Within this framework, unity takes precedence over difference and heterogeneity is curbed. This idea is taken up elsewhere by other authors. Bernice Johnson Reagon (1983) also points to the exclusions created by identity categories. The illusion of sameness, she argues, provides a space for a form of political action but the focus on commonality ignores difference. After an 'initial necessary period of consolidation' the preoccupation with sameness proves exclusionary. What is needed, she argues, is a politics based on coalitions (see chapter 3). Returning to Young's analysis, the ideal of community is presented as problematic not just because the pressure of unity forces the disregard and suppression of differences but also because it presumes that individual subjectivities are both unified and fixed. Young contends that the ideal of shared subjectivities, which underpins the pursuit of community, is unrealizable, as individual subjects are themselves so complex, multi-layered, dynamic and incoherent they cannot ever fully comprehend or grasp their entirety – in other words, they are not even transparent to themselves. How is the sharing of subjectivities possible when one cannot fully understand one's own subjectivity? 'If the subject is heterogeneous process, unable to present to itself, then it follows that subjects cannot make themselves transparent, wholly present to one another. If each subject escapes its own comprehension and for that reason cannot fully express to one another its needs and desires, then necessarily each subject also escapes sympathetic comprehension by others' (Young 1990a: 311).

The ideal of community, a yearning for 'mutual identification', often proves unworkable. Many of us have probably found ourselves in situations where we become perplexed or disappointed when those with whom we assume we identify and share experience, as women, men, gay, Hindu, etc., either misunderstand us or are not understandable to us and solidarity is not reached. Young argues that feminist groups, while recognizing and discussing difference, are still held back by the 'continuing desire for mutual identification and reciprocity' (1990a: 312).

Indeed, while the legitimacy of identity-based movements can be challenged at the level of theory, their effectiveness can also be questioned at the level of practice. Within grassroots activism identity movements have often foundered and fractured over issues of differences, experiencing at the levels of organization and ideas the ways in which the assertion of category-supportive politics and the pursuit of the 'ideal of community' homogenize and exclude. As illustrated previously in chapter 3, the women's movement in the West has come under fire for its white, middle-class, heterosexual, Western perspective, for operating primarily with a construct of woman which was exclusionary, partial, homogenizing and normative, universalizing as it did the experiences of the white, middle-class, heterosexual and Western elite within the movement (see, for discussion, Riley 1988; hooks 1990). This is not to undermine the effectiveness of the feminist women's movement in challenging the material and structural subordination of certain women (low pay, sex discrimination, domestic violence) or in exposing the cultural entrenchment of gendered division and inequality. The differences debate within the feminist movement does, however, demonstrate the potential problems of organizing around the notion of a shared identity (here, the shared identity 'female') and of formulating and acting upon shared political interests and goals. In a movement founded primarily on the premise of shared experience, the issue of women's differences was viewed often as a threat from within. How to deal with the question of differences and the associated problems of working with the category 'woman' have stymied political action, imploding the women's movement. The movement foundered, it could be argued, not because of differences *per se*, but because of the failure adequately to negotiate such differences.

Parallels can be found within other identity-based political movements. Within gay politics the question of differences has emerged with black and working-class gay men contesting the universalization of a white, middle-class gayness within the movement (Mercer and Julien 1988). Moreover, the foundations of the movement, based as it is upon the premise that sexual preference can form identity, that men and women with same-sex desire have a shared experience and standpoint, has been called into question. The gay and lesbian movement has been built around an *'ethnic/essentialist* politic' (Gamson 1996: 396) operating on the basis that there exist clear identity categories 'gay' and 'straight'. The boundaries between gay and straight are not necessarily so clear-cut. Many men who engage in homosexual practices do not necessarily self-identify as gay or even bisexual. However, gay men and women in the ethnic/essentialist model of sexuality are perceived and characterized as clearly defined minority groups who have claim to the same rights as the 'majority' straight population. As is argued in more detail below, the emergence of queer politics as a challenge to the conventional gay and lesbian movement explodes this strategy of assimilation politics, stressing instead that 'It is socially produced binaries (gay/straight, man/woman) that are the basis of oppression', a key problem being that 'fluid, unstable experiences of self become fixed primarily in the service of social control' (Gamson 1996: 396). If we understand the creation of the category 'homosexual' to be a social act and part and parcel of the subordination, discrimination and persecution of homosexual desire then operating with the categories, even reinforcing them through events such as the gay Olympics, is at odds with the process of deconstruction.

Similar dilemmas are encountered within the black civil rights movement and within black feminist activism. Although race is defined as a social rather than a natural category, as discrimination operates with fixed racial categories activists are left with the predicament that organizing collectively around, for instance, the category 'black' serves to fortify the notion of racial division. Here again we can see that operating with fixed-identity categories excludes and homogenizes. In Britain the concept 'Black' has been adopted as a political stance within anti-racist struggles with the aim of including a diverse range of peoples who are marginalized and excluded within our white-dominated culture (Kanneh 1998) – a kind of strategic essentialism, an issue which we return to below. Yet while aiming to be inclusive the concept constructs its own boundaries. Ang-Lygate (1997) argues, for instance, that the particular experiences of Chinese and Filipina women living in Britain are invisible within the concept 'Black identity'. The binary dualism black–white, she argues, 'inevitably undoes the possibility of difference' (1997: 172). As Aziz (1997: 72) suggests, the categories 'black' and 'white' 'take on a deceptive air of internal coherence', thereby suppressing similarities between women across-category and differences of women within-category (see chapter 3).

The Political Challenge of Queer

Butler's work radically challenges the ways in which we conceive political action, contesting as it does the case for identity-based politics. As illustrated in chapter 4, in Butler's account calls to unite as women, disabled, gay, etc., become questionable because they are based upon the existence of stable and unified identities. Butler insists that identities are constituted through the repetition of acts, deeds and corporeal styles, and that there is no stable, coherent subject in existence prior to entry into culture. As she puts it, there is no doer behind the deed; instead the doer is constituted through the doing. The subject is thus never complete or fixed but in a constant, ongoing process of negotiation and transformation. In this sense, identity movements, rather than representing the interests of a pre-existing group, actually form part of the performance – the repetition of acts – which serve to create the illusion of essential categories. By consequence political movements that coalesce around the categories 'woman', 'gay', 'black', etc., paradoxically serve to compound and cement the problems the group may face by reinforcing the very categories which restrict, subordinate and exclude. As Butler remarks: 'If there is a fear that, by no longer being able to take for granted the subject, its gender, its sex, or its materiality, feminism will founder, it might be wise to consider the political consequences of keeping in their place the very premises that have tried to secure our subordination from the start' (1992: 19).

In Butler's account, the deconstruction of identity does not, however, mean the end of politics – far from it. Instead it lends itself to rethinking new forms of political action. Here Butler argues that the destabilization of identity, the exposure of the artificiality of gender, for example, is a politically subversive act. Drag can be perceived as political in that it undermines our perceptions of gender as natural by putting on display the act of gender. Within the realm of queer politics a male bank manager going to work in a pink tutu is as political an act as demonstrating in front of Number 10 Downing Street or collecting signatures for a petition. Queer politics, for example the cultural-political movement in the US Queer Nation (see chapter 4), focus on disrupting the sexual and gender norms which dominate culturally and challenging the taken-for-grantedness of heterosexual desire. Queer Nation aims to expose and destabilize the heteronormativity through the tactics of visibility – by inserting 'gay spectacle into the centres of straight consumption' (Hennessy 1995: 160), like shopping centres and straight bars. The aim is not to assimilate but to directly challenge the predominance of heterosexuality by bringing queer from the margins into the centre. Unlike the gay and lesbian political movement which was based on sexual preference as a source of shared identity, queer politics brings together a broader, looser coalition of people who are 'unified only by a shared dissent from the dominant organization of sex and gender' (Duggan, quoted in Phelan 1995: 350). Unlike the civil rights approach of the gay and lesbian movement, which sought to extend rights to lesbians and gay men, queer activists do not seek to work from within the system. 'Queer does not so much rebel against outsider status but revel in it' (Gamson 1996: 402).

The political potential and effectiveness of Butler's analysis and queer activism more generally have, however, been challenged. It is suggested that Butler and queer activists have 'overestimated the emancipatory potential of such gender-bending performance in everyday life' (Fraser 1995: 163). Perhaps we should not inflate the extent to which the destabilization of the codes of normative gender threatens and undermines overarching relations of inequality. For example, in recent years some heterosexual men have resisted dominant conventions of masculinity by appropriating androgynous or feminine styles of dress – by wearing make-up, earrings, etc. Although such acts can be interpreted as political in that they can be seen to rearticulate the political signifier 'man', it does not mean that they will have recurring or profound significance beyond their immediate context. Culturally we seem to have absorbed this rearticulation without considerable impact upon the material lives of men and women – occupational segregation according to sex, pay differentials between men and women, and so on, continue. Anne McClintock, while discussing a related point, raises the question, 'if ambivalence is everywhere, at what point does it become subversive?' (1995: 65). (This is an issue on which Butler does not give a clear-cut answer, because she does not think there is one to give (see chapter 4). McClintock, discussing cross-dressing, argues that the fact that it 'disrupts stable social identities does not guarantee the subversion of gender, race, or class power. When the marines in the United States army deck themselves in drag or put on white faces white power is not necessarily subverted nor is masculinity thrown into disarray' (1995: 67).

In turn, the effectiveness of queer politics to induce change within our current political environment, grounded as it is in the workings of interest group representation, has been called into question. As our political institutions and culture operate according to interest group politics, perhaps, it has been suggested, it is necessary to work within the system to afford change. As Gamson contends, the categories may be the basis for repression and discrimination but therefore form 'a logical basis for resistance'. The debate over Colorado's Amendment 2 in the USA serves as a timely reminder of how the absence of categories can serve to limit the rights of marginalized people. Amendment 2 disallows 'the state or any of its subdivisions from outlawing discrimination against gay men, lesbians, or bisexuals'. The solicitor-general has, however, argued in opposition that 'We don't have a group that is easily confinable.' This statement has potentially enormous material repercussions. If the groups are not defined in law they would then become ineligible for state protection and legal benefits (Gamson 1996: 410).

Butler does, however, recognize the strategic and political importance of identity-based politics within our present political system. Although she recognizes that the category 'woman' is problematic she does not disallow the political usefulness and necessity of operating with the category in certain instances, while retaining an understanding of the subject as decentred, unstable, not fixed. In Butler's framework we need to reconfigure the political space and what we mean by politics instead of trying to adapt our political strategies to fit within the existing parameters of political life. Parallels can be found elsewhere, for instance, in postcolonial theory. Spivak, for example, supports 'strategic essentialism' under certain political conditions, although like Butler warns of the potential dangers. Spivak cautions, for example, that 'The strategic use of essentialism can turn into an alibi for proselytizing academic essentialisms' (cited in Segal 1999: 31).

Political Agency

The destabilization of the subject central to Butler's work is taken by many as irreconcilable with feminism. However, despite Butler's theoretical reflections on the instability of the category 'woman', others see within Butler's conceptual framework a positive rework-ing of the radical democratic aims at the heart of feminism (Webster 2000). Webster (2000) provides a useful analysis of the politics of Butler's work that is pertinent to the discussion here. In her article 'The politics of sex and gender: Benhabib and Butler debate sub-jectivity' Webster analyses the exchange between Butler and Seyla Benhabib in the book *Feminist Contentions*, focusing in part upon the two theorists' different approaches to the question of agency (Benhabib et al. 1995). One of the criticisms made by Benhabib of Butler is that her account of performative gender does not allow for the type of agency necessary for a feminist politics. Benhabib argues that a prerequisite for a feminist politics – like other identity-based polit-ical movements – is a stable subject and that certain forms of post-modernism, Butler's work included, by dispensing with the notion of a stable subject, render feminism untenable. Additionally she suggests that Butler's work is incompatible with feminism as it is over-deterministic in that it sees the subject as so determined by its cultural and social context that it does not allow for self-reflection, self-determination or autonomy, capacities which she regards as vital for feminist political action. Webster suggests that Butler and Benhabib disagree in three main ways over issues of agency, 'how to under-stand the origins and operation of agency', how agency 'does or ought to operate in the political domain' and 'the implications for a feminist politics of particular conceptions of agency' (2000: 13). (See also the criticisms from McNay in chapter 4.)

In her account of Butler's work, Webster suggests that Butler, contrary to Benhabib's claims, does provide an account of agency, albeit differently conceptualized than in Benhabib's work. Crucially

Butler does not believe that the subject has to be stable, fixed or pre-existing culture to have agency. Indeed, in Butler's account it is the very instability and openness of the category that forms the location of agency – because political signifiers/categories are not fixed or determined there is space for rearticulation and transformation (for example, the reworkings of the concepts of 'home' and 'kinship' as discussed in chapter 4). As Webster explains, "The critical force of the political signifier' ('woman' is an example of a political signifier) 'consists in its failure, ultimately, to fully or comprehensively describe or represent that which it names' (2000: 10). Because our subjectivities/identities are never complete but engaged in an ongoing process of renegotiation and transformation then agency (to resist) is possible. Webster suggests that, contrary to Benhabib's claim that Butler's account is deterministic, Butler sees the cultural context as constituting, not determining the subject, thus allowing space for resistance and agency.

By consequence a feminist politics (or at least a politics compatible with the aims of feminism) appears possible within Butler's theoretical framework because the instability of the category 'women' allows for political resistance. 'For Butler,' Webster suggests, 'the problematic character of that category is itself constitutive of its democratizing potential. Leaving that category open, and so never understanding it to have a fixed and determinate set of references, will leave it open to challenge and therefore open to the sort of change, transformation, and resignification which feminism might seek' (2000: 14). Yet while Webster does not see Butler's theory as totally at odds with feminist aims she retains reservations about the effectiveness of Butler's account as a political strategy. 'While Butler cannot be accused of *disallowing* agency or wholly undermining the basis for feminist political action, we are nevertheless justified in considering her conception of agency *inadequate* to explain or provide an account of the *actual practice* of freedom by subjects or groups of subjects in the political arena' (p. 18). Interpreting the practical political potential of Butler's work is, as Webster contends, problematic because she never details a 'programmatic vision' within her work. However, Webster contends that the conceptualization of agency within Butler's work retards large-scale political transformation, since agency is defined primarily as agency to resist. Drawing on Wendy Brown's work on agency, Webster suggests that resistance is not sufficient in itself to undermine or redraw power structures, lacking as it does political direction and *strategies* of collective action. Indeed, a detailed programmatic vision is impossible within Butler's theoretical framework. While Butler's account allows for political agency through resistive subversion, the reconfigurations of gender which may emerge are wholly unpredictable (see chapter 4). What seems missing therefore in Butler's account is the possibility of a certain kind of reflexivity. Reflexive agency, we would argue, is not simply a consequence of a coming together on the basis of shared subjectivity or commonality. It is rather the *conscious* adoption of a shared grouping to campaign politically for changes to those material, structural and discursive features which are leading to oppressive social relations. Such groupings are based on a reflexive understanding of what these features are. We explore such a possibility further below.

A Third Way?

A key dilemma articulated by many feminists is how to harmonize the two positions outlined above, how to reconcile the rejection of the binary male–female with a woman-based politics, and in so doing simultaneously deconstruct and claim the female identity. Segal notes in relation to Ann Snitow's 'Gender Diary' that the writer was torn both intellectually and personally between 'needing to value and organize around being a "woman", and needing to reject the very category "woman", and all its baggage' (Segal 1999: 53). On a theoretical basis at least these two positions are 'profoundly antithetical' (Squires 1999: 135). Feminist identity politics, as argued above, have been constructed on the basis that there is an essential difference between men and women. The project of deconstruction, however, challenges the very use of the categories 'male', 'female', 'men' and 'women', exposing the fiction of stable, immutable identity positions. In reality, however, many feminists who espouse a deconstructive conceptualization of gender, in principle, retain reservations about the breadth of its political potential and embrace the necessity of some form of identity politics in practice (Squires 1999), a form of what was referred to above as operational or strategic essentialism. How do we challenge the structural and material inequalities that many women face if we do not operate on some basis at least with the category 'woman', even if while utilizing the term we remain cognizant of its fictitious and unstable foundations? We can take the case of the UN

Women's Conference in Beijing as an example. An international conference to debate issues and formulate policies in relation to women assumes first and foremost that women exist as a distinct category. On the one hand the use of the category 'women' threatens to exclude and overlook the inherent diversity of women. How can international policy directives be formulated when women constitute such a diverse range of people? On the other hand, the conference highlights and attends to the very real suffering and subordination of many women world-wide. The formulation of rights, which the participating countries signed up to, could have a real effect on the lived experiences of many women, and this would have been impossible without the political usage of the category 'women'.

Many theorists have endeavoured to develop new frameworks that avoid the inconsistency of both deconstructing and claiming identities, a kind of third way. Braidotti, for example, makes the useful distinction between 'political subjectivity' as a conscious and wilful position and subjective identities that are anchored in unconscious, imaginary dimensions to explain the potential mismatch between individual subjectivity and collective agency (1994). Collective agency as a reflexive political choice therefore need not assume shared subjectivity, but can rather be a consequence of shared political analysis of the features leading to oppressive power relations. So that a man from a wealthy black family who has attended an English public school and developed a passion for Jane Austen can still get stopped regularly for driving an expensive Mercedes and be unable to see close family members because they are refused visas for entry. A masculine-identified woman living in Ireland is still at risk of rape, and if pregnant will be unable to obtain an abortion. The various subjectivities manifest here can still permit reflexive identification as 'black' or 'female' for the purposes of collective and strategic organizing.

Iris Marion Young also offers an approach to conceptualizing links between women which avoids assuming commonalities of experience. Drawing on Sartre, she makes the distinction between a group and a social series. A group, she suggests, is a 'self-consciously, mutually acknowledging collective with a self-conscious purpose' whereas a series is a 'social collective whose members are unified passively by the objects around which their actions are oriented or by the objectified results of the material effects of the actions of others' (1995: 199). Young uses Sartre's example of radio listening to exemplify what is

meant by seriality. Although one listens to the radio often in isolation the radio listener is aware of him/herself as listening alongside
others linked via the medium of the radio. Likewise people waiting
for a bus are part of a series linked as they are by the conventions of
waiting for a bus, although they may share no other commonalities.
A series can become a group. If for example the group of people
waiting for the bus become fed up because the bus is late, exchange
their frustrations verbally, perhaps decide to take the train instead,
then the series has become a group. Seriality, Young contends, acts
as a 'prereflective background to action' (1995: 203). She suggests
that we should see gender as seriality, albeit a more complex series
than radio listening or bus waiting. This, Young argues, means that
we have the tools to look upon women as a social collective without
having to fall back on essentialism or defining women as a homogen-
ous group: '"Woman" is a serial collective defined neither by any common identity nor by a common set of attributes that all the individuals
in the series share, but, rather, it names a set of structural constraints
and relations to practico-inert objects that condition action and its
meanings' (1995: 212). Women are serialized via the bodily processes
and social conventions of menstruation, pregnancy, our gendered language, the gendering of clothes, spaces, objects. How each individual
woman relates to the structures of gender will differ, leading to variable subjectivities. However, she will be unable to avoid these structures; this creates a passive unity. This does not mean that political
action as women is ruled out. Women can and do choose actively to
refigure the structures that have united them as a series – for example,
women's campaigns against domestic violence, low pay, etc. At this
point women become a group or groups as well as a series.

Young's account offers us a way of conceptualizing links between
women in relation to societal structure and material practices. Her
account serves as a reminder that there is a material reality to our
world, that gender is constructed through our relation to social structures and practices and not just constructed via cultural representations.
Young's account needs supplementing, however, to pay more attention to the way that discursive structures can themselves be oppressive; a recognition that makes the deconstructive strategies of Butler
themselves a manifestation of reflexive agency.

Chantal Mouffe's account of identity (Mouffe 1997), like Young's,
aims to offer an account which does not resort to essentialism. But her
account, rather than dealing with the structural world, draws instead

on the notion of discourse. It develops a narrative of identity, which, she argues, not only avoids the coupling of identity with essential-ism, but also allows the scope for political agency on behalf of an identity, even though this identity is both partial and transient. Mouffe suggests that each individual is an 'ensemble of "subject positions"'. By this she is suggesting that each subject is constituted by a range of discourses. These discourses are not necessarily connected but at the same time do not merely coexist but overdetermine and subvert each other. Additionally, there is no automatic, *a priori* link between dif-ferent subjects, that is between women (no passive unity as in Young's account). In Mouffe's analysis this does not mean that points of common interest will not emerge between social agents. On the contrary, 'partial fixations can take place and precarious forms of identification can be established' (pp. 542–3). The claiming of an identity does not therefore rest upon an essential core; it is instead momentary and dependent upon the discursive context and the agency of individuals (there are parallels here with the work of Probyn discussed in chapter 9). In her framework, feminist action is not based on the struggle for rights for women but instead at the 'trans-formation of all the discourses, practices, and social relations where the category "woman" is constructed in a way that implies subordina-tion'. 'Feminism' is, she argues, 'the struggle for the equality of women. But this should not be understood as a struggle for realizing the equality of a definable empirical group with a common essence and identity, women, but rather as a struggle against the multiple forms in which the category "woman" is constructed in subordina-tion' (p. 543). Mouffe's account, like those above, suggest that ident-ities that are claimed for political purposes (whether that be a gendered identity, an identity based around sexual preference, or an ethnic or racialized identity) are not straightforward expressions of a unified, fixed subjectivity. On the contrary, our subjectivities are character-ized as complex, multiple and dynamic, never fitting neatly with the political identities claimed.

We would conclude therefore that we do not need to choose between the politics of identity and the deconstructive strategies advocated by Butler. We can see identity politics as an open and potentially shifting set of allegiances born, not necessarily, of shared subjectivities, but of reflective political analysis. This analysis, in making evident the oppressive nature of discursive constructions, can also require just the kind of deconstructive strategies to which Butler points us. Here our views are parallel to those of Rosemarie Garland Thomson, expressed in relation to disability politics.

> Both constructionism and essentialism then become theoretical strategies – framings of the body – invoked when useful to achieve specific ends in the political arena, to liberate psychologically subjects whose bodies have been narrated to them as defective, or to facilitate imagined communities from which a positive identity politics can emerge. Thus, a strategic constructionism destigmatizes the disabled body, locates difference relationally, denaturalizes normalcy and challenges appearance hierarchies. A strategic essentialism, by contrast, validates experience and consciousness, imagines community, authorizes history and facilitates self-naming. The identity 'disabled' operates then as a pragmatic narrative, what Susan Bordo calls a 'life enhancing fiction' grounded in the materiality of the particular embodiment and perspective embedded in specific social and historical contexts. (Garland Thomson 1997: 283)

Resisting Polarities

The resolution we have attempted to broker on the question of identity politics is in line with the strategy which we have tried to adopt throughout this book of resisting polarities and recognizing the importance of different strands of thought in constructing an adequate theory of gender. This is not, of course, to deny that there are still some irresolvable tensions.

One criticism which we have discussed in chapters 3 and 4 was the claim that discursive accounts of gender formation privilege 'the local, the discrete, and the specific' (Fraser 1995: 163); in other words they focus primarily on the micro-level and in doing so do not address institutional, structural and systemic inequalities and injustices (Fraser 1995; Hennessy 1995; Gamson 1996). Hennessy, for example, argues that 'a radical sexual politics . . . needs a way of explaining how the sexual identities we can see are systemically organized. We need a way of understanding visibility that acknowledges the local situations in which sexuality is made intelligible as well as the ties that bind knowledge and power to commodity production, consumption, and exchange' (Hennessy 1995: 177). Within this approach the strategies of queer activists such as Queer Nation are criticized for not taking into account the broader contexts of social and political relations and for paying too little attention to the material inequalities that make certain forms of political action possible. In short, while queer activism concentrates on subversive gender performance, it pays little attention to economic and other structures which make such performance possible. Fraser suggests that Butler in her account of gender performance 'missed its susceptibility to commodification, recuperation and depoliticization – especially in the absence of strong social movements' (1995: 163). Hennessy takes this point further. She argues that the politics of queer visibility, centring as it does on exposing the heteronormative desires at the foundation of consumption, does not deal with the question of how those commodities are produced and is thus guilty of their fetishization. In other words queer activism does not engage with the relations of labour and social hierarchies which make the production of commodities possible. She argues that 'while Queer Nation's tactics attend to the commodity, the framework in which the commodity is understood is similar to the informing framework of queer theory. It is, in short, a cultural one in which the commodity is reduced to ideological icon' (Hennessy 1995: 161). Queer, it is suggested, fits well with the consumerism of late capitalism where identities have become lifestyles contingent upon certain consumer practices, for example, the labels we wear. By not engaging with the inequalities produced by capitalist production it is not able to engender large-scale social transformation.

There are elements in this critique which seem misplaced. The suggestion that queer activism colludes with consumerism and lifestyle choices is to fail to appreciate the extent to which our categorical practices are themselves part of the oppressive structures whereby gender inequalities are reproduced. Moreover, such practices make life literally unliveable for those who cannot live neatly within such categories. The violent deaths referred to in earlier chapters of Venus Xtravaganza and Brandon Teena, documented and dramatized respectively in *Paris is Burning* and *Boys Don't Cry*, are extreme examples of the practices and consequences of social exclusion. In the face of this, the suggestion that queer activism is simply consumerist is insulting. None the less the insistence from materialist feminist critique on the need to attend to material and structural features as central to the construction of gender is an important and central one. Materialist feminists, as we have seen in chapter 3, recognize that what it is to be gendered in our society is conditioned by material and structural features. The different kinds of paid work undertaken by, and the inequalities in pay between, women and men are examples of such material factors, as are the distinctive kinds of labour undertaken by men and women at home, especially in relation to care. Moreover the material fact that so many women carry and care for children conditions the social possibilities available to them in quite a different way from the occasion of parenthood for men, as do the gendered nature of public and social institutions. Such materialist accounts of gender go hand in hand with materialist accounts of class and race. For example, if we want to understand what it is to be black or male in this society then the materialist would argue that we have to pay attention to these structural features and patterns. Our individual gendered positions are then viewed as constituted by our being placed at the intersection of such multiple structures.

We must be careful, however, not to be pushed into accepting a false dichotomy between material and discursive accounts. Accepting such dualism is to oversimplify a situation constituted by a complex play of interdependencies. First, once we have moved away from naturalizing accounts, the material and structural divisions are, despite their materiality, social practices based on practices of social categorization. They are only possible because people engage in certain kinds of social acts. As emphasized in chapter 1, all actions are mediated through meaning. Material gendered divisions are no exception and are dependent on our having the categories 'men' and 'women' within which to place people and on the meanings which we attach to such categories. Changes in these understandings (allowing for instance the possibility of pregnant men) have the consequence that the material divisions cannot function in the same way.

Secondly, we have to recognize that the material and institutional factors do have brute causal effects that have to be recognized and appropriate action taken to promote or to avoid them. If you have little money there is a whole range of possibilities which are not open to you. If your housing is damp you may contract certain illnesses. If certain drugs or equipment are not made available you may die in childbirth. That is, we need to recognize that the world does not simply work according to the logic of meaning (McNay 2000). As Coole (1996) asks, 'are the mute and gnawing pains of real deprivation not to be counted or politicized if they find no adequate means among the poor for self-representation'. In Coole's analysis of class she suggests that attention solely or predominantly to discourse cannot fully account for structured economic inequality (see also Hennessy 1993).

Thirdly, however, the material practices themselves operate as 'signifying practices' (see McNay 2000). Not only do they have brute (i.e. unmediated) causal effects. They also have effects that are mediated through meaning. The complex set of things which it means to be male or female in a society derives at least in part from what men and women typically do and what characteristically happens to them in the social order. Transformation and destabilization of such meanings come not only from changes explicitly at the level of cultural representation, but also from material changes in which, for example, men change nappies and women drive trucks, or in which wells are put into villages or income is invested in certain forms of co-operative income generation.

The construction of gendered and other subjectivities takes place as a complex negotiation of such public meanings, derived both from cultural representation and signifying material practices. What has become evident from our discussions is the multiplicity, contrariness and complexity of the meanings available. Moreover the work of Butler, in particular, has made evident their inherent instability and susceptibility to change, 'the boundary maintaining images of base and superstructure . . . , or material and ideal, never seemed more feeble' (Haraway 1991a: 165).

In a similar vein we have insisted on the need to integrate psychoanalytic and discursive accounts to provide an adequate account of the significance attached socially and individually to particularly shaped bodies. While problematizing the universalism of some psychoanalytic accounts, key concepts such as the unconscious, the symbolic and the imaginary seem indispensable in providing a theory of gendered identity. We have also avoided choosing between attempts to imagine sexual difference in less damaging ways and destabilizing the gender binaries. Further we have insisted on paying attention to subjective experience while also recognizing its discursive construction.

There are remaining tensions, of course. Materialists and certain political activists require an analysis of the link between causes and effects, including discursive and non-discursive factors, which post-structuralist theorists believe to be in principle unpredictable. Psychoanalytic theorists and sexual difference theorists place a foundational role on gender identity which others resist. On these as on many other issues raised in the book, we recognize that debates will continue. We simply hope that our discussion has helped clarify what are the issues at stake, within these debates.

Notes

Introduction

1   The Editorial Board of *The Journal of Gender Studies* is still based in Hull. The University of Hull continues to run undergraduate and postgraduate programmes in Gender Studies.
2   Often race is written as 'race' to denote the non-biological, constructed nature of racial categories. While fully endorsing this position we have, however, decided not to write race in inverted commas. We also challenge the biological foundations of sex, gender, sexuality and class. It would be too clumsy to write all of these in inverted commas throughout the text and have therefore also chosen not to write race this way, despite our recognition of race as a socially constructed phenomenon.
3   Harding develops a similar framework through which to explore gender, identifying three distinct but interrelated processes – gender symbolism, gender structure and individual gender (Harding 1986).
4   Evans does not argue explicitly the case for sexual difference as a term over gender but her criticisms of the study of gender and the institutionalization of gender studies suggests implicitly a concern with the adequacy of gender as a concept to explore inequalities between men and women.
5   This book has been collaborative throughout. The three authors have been involved in the development and mapping of ideas and arguments and the drafting and redrafting of chapters. No chapter is written entirely in one hand. We have, however, individually taken responsibility for certain chapters – Rachel Alsop for the introduction, chapters 6 and 10, Annette Fitzsimons for chapter 5, and chapter 3 jointly with Kathleen Lennon, and Kathleen Lennon additionally for chapters 1, 4, 7, 8 and 9. The first draft of chapter 2 was written by Ros Minsky, our guest

contributor. Sadly, Ros died before the completion of this book. We dedicate this book to Ros, in memory of her outstanding contribution to the study of psychoanalysis and gender and in thanks for her contribution to our project.

Chapter 1   Natural Women and Men

1   It is important to note that many of the ways in which we use the term 'natural' have overtones, which go beyond what has so far been articulated. When people argue that same–sex desire is unnatural they are not simply saying that it is not a necessary feature of the world which is given to us. They are expressing disapproval – the kind of disapproval which might also be expressed when someone claims that it is not natural for women to be rally car drivers. The disapproval is assumed to have a certain kind of justification, however. The suggestion is not only that these forms of behaviour do not constitute a necessary feature of the world but that to engage in them is somehow to be setting oneself against the natural order, with dire results. This kind of argument is problematic, however. For, if there is a world with a fixed structure and laws of working which conditions what we can do, then we would not be able to act in ways it rendered impossible. We cannot, after all, fly unassisted. If we are able to act in certain ways then this must be at least compatible with the natural order; and the claim that it is unnatural needs some further justification.
2   We must be tempted to see the same mechanisms at work in contemporary research on sex differences in the corpus callosum, when researchers unable to detect differences in volume or area detected a difference in what they called the bulbosity coefficient of the splenium, a shape feature representing the percentage by which the average width of the splenium exceeds the average width of adjacent regions.

Chapter 2   Psychoanalysis and Gender

1   Those writers who see Freud's work as simply a theory of biological determinism include feminist psychoanalysts such as Karen Horney (1967) and feminist critics such as Shulamith Firestone (1979) and Kate Millett (1970). But as Juliette Mitchell emphasized in her powerful defence of Freud's value for feminists in *Psychoanalysis and Feminism* (Mitchell 1975) those feminists critical of Freud's ideas often failed to appreciate the meaning of the unconscious and what the child unconsciously constructs out of its bodily drives and sensations.

Chapter 3   The Social Construction of Gender

1   Although we will be primarily concerned with a Foucauldian model of discourse, discourse theory and analysis can take a variety of forms. See: Cameron (1985, 1990), McConnell-Ginet, Borker and Furman (1980), Henriques et al. (1984), Lakoff (1975), Tannen (1994), Wilkinson and Kitzinger (1995).

Chapter 5   Gender and Sexuality

1   From a different direction the links between sexuality and patriarchy have also been challenged by heterosexual women who argue for the possibility of heterosexual sexual practices which do not buy into or support heterosexuality as an institution.

Chapter 8   Sexual Difference

1   We shall return to evaluate these claims below. It is worth noting here that the overemphasis on the material as opposed to the symbolic is a criticism that clearly has more bearing on materialist models of the social construction of gender than on discursive ones. Also the dangers of the sex/gender distinction, as noted in several of our earlier chapters, has been highlighted by gender theorists themselves. With regard to embodiment chapter 7 has signalled the need to employ theoretical resources beyond those of social construction to provide an account of embodiment. We will discuss further below if this also requires a commitment to sexual difference.

Bibliography

Aaby, P. (1977) Engels and women. *Critique of Anthropology, Women's Issue,* 9 and 10, 3, 25–53.

Abbott, P., and Wallace, C. (1990) *An Introduction to Sociology: feminist perspectives.* London and New York: Routledge.

Abbott, P., and Wallace, C. (eds) (1991) *Gender, Power and Sexuality.* Basingstoke: Macmillan.

Abelove, H., Barale, M. A., and Halperin, D. M. (eds) (1993) *The Lesbian and Gay Studies Reader.* New York: Routledge.

Adkins, L. (1992) Sexual work and the employment of women in the service industries. In M. Savage and Anne Witz (eds), *Gender and Bureaucracy,* Oxford: Blackwell, 207–29.

Adkins, L. (1994) *Gendered Work: sexuality, family and the labour market.* Bristol: Open University Press.

Afshar, H., and Maynard, M. (eds) (1994) *The Dynamics of 'Race' and Gender: some feminist interventions.* London: Taylor & Francis.

Ahmed, S. (2000) *Strange Encounters: embodied others in post-coloniality.* London and New York: Routledge.

Alcoff, L. (1999) Towards a phenomenology of racial embodiment. *Radical Philosophy,* 95, 15–22.

Alexander, M. J., and Mohanty, C. T. (eds) (1997) *Feminist Genealogies, Colonial Legacies, Democratic Futures.* London and New York: Routledge.

Alexander, S., and Taylor, B. (1982) In defence of patriarchy. Repr. in Mary Evans (ed.), *The Woman Question: readings on the subordination of women,* London: Fontana, 80–3.

Altman, D. (1971) *Homosexual: oppression and liberation.* London: Outerbridge & Dienstfrey.

Amos, V., and Parmar, P. (1984) Challenging imperial feminism. *Feminist Review*, 17, 3–19.

Angelou, M. (1984) *I Know Why the Caged Bird Sings*. London: Virago.

Ang-Lygate, M. (1997), Interpreting gender. In L. Nicholson and S. Seidman (eds), *Social Postmodernism beyond identity politics*, Cambridge: Cambridge University Press, 168–86.

Anzaldua, G. (1987) *Borderlands/La Frontera: the new mestiza*. San Francisco: Spinsters/Aunt Lute.

Appiah, K. W., and Gates, H. L. (eds) (1995) *Identities*. Chicago: University of Chicago Press.

Appignanesi, L., and Forrester, J. (1992) *Freud's Women*. London: Weidenfeld.

Aziz, R. (1997) Feminism and the challenge of racism: deviance or difference? In H. S. Mirza (ed.), *Black British Feminism: a reader*, London and New York: Routledge, 70–81.

Barker, M. (1981) *The New Racism*. London: Junction Books.

Barrett, M. (1980 and 1988) *Women's Oppression Today: problems in Marxist feminist analysis*. London: Verso Books.

Barrett, M. (1984) *Women's Oppression Today*: a reply. *New Left Review*, July–August, 146, 123–8.

Barrett, M. (1991) *The Politics of Truth: from Marx to Foucault*. Cambridge: Polity.

Barrett, M. (1992) Words and things: materialism and method. In M. Barrett and A. Phillips (eds), *Destabilizing Theory: contemporary feminist debates*, Cambridge: Polity, 201–19.

Barrett, M., and McIntosh, M. (1979) Christine Delphy: towards a materialist feminism? *Feminist Review*, 1, 1, 95–105.

Barrett, M., and Phillips, A. (eds) (1992) *Destabilizing Theory: contemporary feminist debates*. Cambridge: Polity.

Bartky, S. Lee (1990) *Femininity and Domination: studies in the phenomenology of oppression*. New York: Routledge.

Beauvoir, S. de (1982) *The Second Sex*. Harmondsworth: Penguin.

Beechey, V. (1977) Some notes on female wage labour in capitalist production. *Capital and Class*, 3, 45–66.

Beechey, V. (1978) Women and production: a critical analysis of some sociological theories of women's work. In A. Kuhn and A. M. Wolpe (eds), *Feminism and Materialism: women and modes of production*, London: Routledge & Kegan Paul, 155–79.

Beechey, V. (1979) On patriarchy. *Feminist Review*, 3, 66–82.

Beechey, V. (1987) *Unequal Work*. London: Verso Books.

Beechey, V., and Whitelegge, E. (eds) (1986) *Women in Britain Today*. Milton Keynes: Open University Press.

Bell, V. (ed.) (1999) *Performativity and Belonging, Special Issue: Theory, Culture and Society*. London: Sage.

Benhabib, S., Butler, J., Cornell, D., and Fraser, N. (eds) (1995) *Feminist Contentions: a philosophical exchange*. London and New York: Routledge.

Benjamin, J. (1990) *The Bonds of Love*. London: Virago.

Bion, W. (1967) *Second Thoughts: selected papers on psychoanalysis*. New York: Aronson.

Blachford, G. (1981) Male dominance and the gay world. In K. Plummer (ed.), *The Making of the Modern Homosexual*, London: Hutchinson.

Bleier, R. (1984) *Science and Gender: a critique of biology and its theories on women*. New York: Pergamon.

Bly, R. (1990) *Iron John: a book about men*. Reading, Mass.: Addison-Wesley.

Bollas, C. (1992) *Being a Character: psychoanalysis and self experience*. London: Routledge.

Bordo, S. (1993) *Unbearable Weight: feminism, Western culture and the body*. Berkeley: University of California Press.

Bornstein, K. (1994) *Gender Outlaw: on men, women and the rest of us*. New York: Routledge.

Bowie, M. (1991) *Lacan*. London: Fontana.

Bowlby, J. (1963–80) *Attachment and Loss*, 3 vols. London: Hogarth Press; New York: Basic Books.

Bracewell, W. (1996) Women, motherhood and contemporary Serb nationalism. *Women's Studies International Forum*, 19, 1/2, 25–33.

Brah, A. (1992) Difference, diversity and differentiation. In J. Donald and A. Rattansi (eds), *Race, Culture and Differentiation*, London: Sage.

Brah, A. (1996) *Cartographies of Diaspora: contesting identities*. London: Routledge.

Braidotti, R. (1994) *Nomadic Subjects: embodiment and sexual difference in contemporary feminist theory*. New York: Columbia University Press.

Braidotti, R. (1998) Sexual difference theory. In A. Jaggar and I. M. Young (eds), *A Companion to Feminist Philosophy*, Oxford: Blackwell, 298–307.

Braidotti, R., with Butler, J. (1994) Feminism by any other name. *differences*, 6, 27–61.

Brando, M., and Lindsey, R. (1994) *Songs My Mother Taught Me*. London and New York: Random House.

Brennan, T. (ed.) (1989) *Between Feminism and Psychoanalysis*. London: Routledge.

Brennan, T. (1991) *History after Lacan*. London: Routledge.

Brennan, T. (1992) *The Interpretation of the Flesh: Freud and femininity*. London: Routledge.

Brenner, J., and Ramas, M. (1984) Rethinking women's oppression. *New Left Review*, March–April, 144, 33–71.

Bristow, J. (1997) *Sexuality*. London: Routledge.

Bristow, J., and Wilson, A. R. (1993) *Activating Theory*. London: Lawrence & Wishart.

Brittan, A. (1989) *Masculinity and Power*. Oxford: Blackwell.

Brod, H. (1987) A case for men's studies. In M. S. Kimmel (ed.), *Changing Men: new directions in research on men and masculinities*, Newbury Park, Cal.: Sage.

Brod, H. (1994) Some thoughts on some histories of some masculinities: Jews and other others. In H. Brod and M. Kaufmann (eds), *Theorizing Masculinities*, Thousand Oaks, Cal.: Sage, 82–96.

Brown, W. (1995) *States of Injury: power and freedom in late modernity*. Princeton, NJ: Princeton University Press.

Bruegal, I. (1982) Women as a reserve army of labour. In M. Evans (ed.), *The Woman Question: readings on the subordination of women*, London: Fontana, 273–88.

Bubeck, D., and Klaushoper, A. (eds.) (1998–9) *Women's Philosophy Review*, 20.

Burris, V. (1982) Dialectic of women's oppression. *Berkeley Journal of Sociology*, 27, 51–74.

Butler, J. (1982) Lesbian S & M: the politics of dis-illusion. In R. R. Linden, D. R. Pagano, D. E. H. Russell and S. L. Star (eds), *Against Sadomasochism: a radical feminist analysis*, East Palo Alto, Cal.: Frog in the Wall, 169–75.

Butler, J. (1990a) *Gender Trouble: feminism and the subversion of identity*. New York and London: Routledge.

Butler, J. (1990b) Gender trouble, feminist theory and psychoanalytic discourse. In L. Nicholson (ed.), *Feminism/Postmodernism*, New York and London: Routledge, 324–41.

Butler, J. (1991) Imitation and gender insubordination. In D. Fuss (ed.), *Inside/Out: lesbian theories, gay theories*, New York and London: Routledge, 13–31.

Butler, J. (1993) *Bodies that Matter: on the discursive limits of 'sex'*. New York and London: Routledge.

Butler, J. (1994) Against proper objects. *differences*, 6, 2 and 3, 1–27.

Butler, J. (1995) Contingent foundations: feminism and the question of 'postmodernism'. In S. Benhabib, J. Butler, D. Cornell and N. Fraser (eds), *Feminist Contentions: a philosophical exchange*, London: Routledge, 35–57.

Butler, J. (1997a) *Excitable Speech: a politics of the performative*. New York and London: Routledge.

Butler, J. (1997b) *The Psychic Life of Power*. Stanford, Cal.: Stanford University Press.

Butler, J. (1998) Merely cultural. *New Left Review*, 227, 33–44.

Butler, J., and Scott, W. J. (eds) (1992) *Feminists Theorize the Political*. New York and London: Routledge.

Califia, P. (1980) *Sapphistry: the book of lesbian sexuality*. New York: Naiad Press.

Cameron, D. (1985) *Feminism and Linguistic Theory*. London: Macmillan.

Cameron, D. (ed.) (1990) *The Feminist Critique of Language: a reader*. London: Routledge.

Canaan, J. E., and Griffin, C. (1990) The new men's studies: part of the problem or part of the solution. In J. Hearn and D. Morgan (eds), *Men, Masculinities and Social Theory*, London: Unwin Hyman.

Caplan, P. (ed.) (1987) *The Cultural Construction of Sexuality*. London and New York: Routledge.

Carby, H. (1982) White women listen! Black feminism and the boundaries of sisterhood. In Centre for Contemporary Cultural Studies (ed.), *The Empire Strikes Back: race and racism in 70's Britain*, London: Hutchinson.

Carpenter, E. (1894a) *Marriage in a Free Society*. Manchester: The Labour Press Society.

Carpenter, E. (1894b) *Sex-Love: its place in a free society*. Manchester: The Labour Press Society.

Carpenter, E. (1894c) *Woman, and Her Place in a Free Society*. Manchester: The Labour Press Society.

Carrigan, T., Connell, R. W., and Lee, J. (1985) Toward a new sociology of masculinity. *Theory and Society*, 14, 551–604.

Castoriadis, C. (1987) *The Imaginary Institution of Society*. Cambridge: Polity.

Cavendish, R. (1982) *Women on the Line*. London: Routledge & Kegan Paul.

Chauncey, G. (1994) *Gay New York*. New York: Basic Books.

Chodorow, N. (1978) *The Reproduction of Mothering: psychoanalysis and the sociology of gender*. Berkeley, Cal.: University of California.

Chodorow, N. (1989) *Feminism and Psychoanalysis*. Cambridge: Polity.

Chodorow, N. (1994) *Femininities, Masculinities, Sexualities*. London: Free Association Books.

Cixous, H. (1976) The laugh of the Medusa. Trans. K. Cohen and P. Cohen. *Signs*, 1, 4, 875–93.

Clarke, G. (1998) Queering the pitch and coming out to play: lesbians in physical education and sport. *Sport, Education and Society*, 3, 2, 145–60.

Clement, C. (1987) *The Weary Sons of Freud*. London: Free Association Books.

Cockburn, C. (1983) *Brothers: male dominance and technological change*. London: Pluto Press.

Cockburn, C. (1985) *Machinery of Dominance: women, men, and technological know-how*. London: Macmillan.

Cockburn, C. (1988) The gendering of jobs. In S. Walby (ed.), *Gender Segregation at Work*, Milton Keynes: Open University Press, 29–42.

Cockburn, C. (1991) *In The Way of Women: men's resistance to sexual equality in organisations*. London: Macmillan.

Coltrane, S. (1994) Theorizing masculinities in contemporary social science. In H. Brod. and M. Kaufmann (eds), *Theorizing Masculinities*, Thousand Oaks, Cal.: Sage, 39–60.

Conboy, K., Medina, N., and Stanbury, S. (eds) (1997) *Writing on the Body: female embodiment and feminist theory.* New York: Columbia University Press.

Connell, R. W. (1983) *Which Way is Up? Essays on sex, class and culture.* Sydney: George Allen & Unwin.

Connell, R. W. (1985) Theorising Gender. *Sociology*, 19, 2, 260–72.

Connell, R. W. (1987) *Gender and Power.* Cambridge: Polity.

Connell, R. W. (1992) A very straight gay: masculinity, homosexual experience, and the dynamics of gender. *American Sociological Review*, 57, 735–51.

Connell, R. W. (1993) The big picture: masculinities in recent world history. *Theory and Society*, 22, 597–623.

Connell, R. W. (1995) *Masculinities.* Cambridge: Polity.

Conway-Long, D. (1994) Ethnographies and masculinities. In H. Brod and M. Kaufmann (eds), *Theorizing Masculinities*, Thousand Oaks, Cal.: Sage, 61–81.

Coole, D. (1996) Is class a difference that makes a difference? *Radical Philosophy*, 77, 17–25.

Coulson, M., Magas, B., and Wainwright, H. (1975) The housewife and her labour under capitalism – a critique. *New Left Review*, 89, 59–71.

Coward, R. (1983) *Patriarchal Precedents.* London, Boston and Henley: Routledge & Kegan Paul.

Crompton, R., and Mann, M. (eds) (1986) *Gender and Stratification.* Cambridge: Polity.

Crowley, H., and Himmelweit, S. (1992) *Knowing Women.* Milton Keynes: Open University Press; Cambridge: Polity.

Daly, M. (1978) *Gyn/Ecology: the metaethics of radical feminists.* Boston, Mass.: Beacon Press.

Davies, A. (1981) *Women, Race and Class.* New York: Random House.

Davies, A. (1989) *Women, Culture and Politics.* New York: Kandan.

Davies, K. (1997) *Embodied Practices.* London: Sage.

Davis, L. J. (1997) *The Disability Studies Reader.* London: Routledge.

Dawkins, R. (1976) *The Selfish Gene.* Oxford: Oxford University Press.

Delaney, S. (1988) *The Motion of Light in Water: sex and science fiction writing in the East Village 1957–1965.* New York: New American Library.

Delphy, C. (1977) *The Main Enemy.* London: Women's Research and Resources Centre.

Delphy, C. (1984) *A Materialist Analysis of Women's Opression.* London: Hutchinson.

Delphy, C. (1992) Mother's Union. *Trouble and Strife*, 24, 12–19.

Delphy, C. (1993) Rethinking sex and gender. *Women's Studies International Forum*, 16, 1, 1–9.

D'Emilio, J. (1992) Capitalism and gay identity. In J. D'Emilio, *Making Trouble: essays on gay history, politics, and the university*, New York: Routledge.

Deutsch, H. (1944) *The Psychology of Women*. Vol. 1. New York: Grune & Stratton. Vol. 2. London: Research Books.

Diamond, I., and Quinby, L. (eds) (1988) *Feminism and Foucault: reflections on resistance*. Boston, Mass.: Northeastern University Press.

Dinnerstein, D. (1978) *The Rocking of the Cradle and the Ruling of the World*. London: Souvenir Press.

Diprose, R. (1994) *The Bodies of Women: ethics, embodiment and sexual difference*. London: Routledge.

Donaldson, M. (1993) What is hegemonic masculinity? *Theory and Society*, 22, 643–57.

Dreyfus, H., and Rabinow, P. (1982) *Michel Foucault: beyond structuralism and hermeneutics*. Chicago: Chicago University Press.

Duberman, M. B., Vicinus, M., and Chauncey, G. (eds) (1989) *Hidden from History: reclaiming the gay and lesbian past*. New York: New American Library.

Dworkin, A. (1989) *Pornography: men possessing women*. New York: E. P. Dutton.

Ebert, T. L. (1996) *Ludic Feminism and After: postmodernism, desire and labor in late capitalism*. Ann Arbor: University of Michigan Press.

Edholm, F., Harris, O., and Young, K. (1977) Conceptualizing women. *Critique of Anthropology, Women's Issue*, 9 and 10, 3, 101–30.

Edley, N., and Wetherell, M. (1995) *Men in Perspective: practice, power and identity*. Hemel Hempstead: Prentice Hall/Harvester Wheatsheaf.

Edwards, P. N. (1990) The army and the microworld: computers and the politics of gender identity. *Signs*, 16, 1, 102–27.

Edwards, T. (1990) Beyond sex and gender: masculinity, homosexuality and social theory. In J. Hearn and D. Morgan (eds), *Men, Masculinities and Social Theory*, London: Unwin Hyman, 110–23.

Eisenstein, H. (1984) *Contemporary Feminist Thought*. London: Allen & Unwin.

Eisenstein, Z. R. (ed.) (1979) *Capitalist Patriarchy and the Case for Socialist Feminism*. New York: Monthly Review Press.

Ellis, H. (1933) *Psychology of Sex*. London: William Heinemann.

Engels, F. (1972) [1884] *The Origins of the Family, Private Property and the State*. London: Lawrence & Wishart.

Epstein, C. F. (1988) *Deceptive Distinctions, Sex, Gender and the Social Order*. New Haven and London: Yale University Press.

Epstein, S. (1987) Gay politics, ethnic identity: the limits of social constructionism. *Socialist Review*, 17, 3–4, 9–56.

Evans, M. (1990) The problem of gender for women's studies. *Women's
Studies International Forum*, 13, 5, 457–63.

Faderman, L. (1981) *Surpassing the Love of Men: romantic friendship and
love between women from the Renaissance to the present.* New York:
Morrow.

Fanon, F. (1968) *Black Skin, White Masks.* London: MacGibbon & Kee.

Fausto-Sterling, A. (1992) *Myths of Gender: biological theories about women and
men.* New York: Basic Books.

Fausto-Sterling, A. (1993) The five sexes: why male and female are not
enough. *The Sciences*, 33, 2, 20–5.

Fausto-Sterling, A. (2000) The five sexes: why male and female are not
enough. In Tracy E. Ore, *The Social Construction of Difference and Inequality:
race, class, gender and sexuality*, Mountain View, Cal.: Mayfield Publishing,
113–19.

Feinberg, L. (1993) *Stone Butch Blues: a novel.* New York: Firebrand.

Feinberg, L. (1996) *Transgender Warriors: making history from Joan of Arc to
RuPaul.* Boston, Mass.: Beacon Press.

Feminists against Censorship (1991) *Pornography and Feminism: the case against
censorship.* London: Lawrence & Wishart.

Firestone, S. (1979) *The Dialectic of Sex.* London: Women's Press.

Flax, J. (1990) *Thinking Fragments.* Berkeley: University of California Press.

Foucault, M. (1972) *The Archaeology of Knowledge.* London: Tavistock.

Foucault, M. (1978) *The History of Sexuality, vol. 1: An Introduction.* London:
Penguin.

Foucault, M. (1979) *Discipline and Punish.* New York: Vintage.

Foucault, M. (1985) *The Uses of Pleasure.* Trans. R. Hurley. Harmondsworth:
Penguin.

Foucault, M. (1986) *The Care of the Self.* Trans. R. Hurley. Harmondsworth:
Penguin.

Fox Keller, E., and Longino, H. (eds) (1996) *Feminism and Science.* Oxford:
Oxford University Press.

Frankenberg, R. (1993) *White Women, Race Matters: the social construction of
whiteness.* London: Routledge.

Fraser, N. (1989) *Unruly Practices: power, discourse and gender in contemporary
social theory.* Cambridge: Polity.

Fraser, N. (1995) Pragmatic feminism and the linguistic turn. In S. Benhabib,
J. Butler, D. Cornell and N. Fraser (eds), *Feminist Contentions: a philosophical exchange*, New York: Routledge.

Fraser, N., and Bartky, S. (1992) *Revaluing French Feminism: critical essays
on difference, agency and culture.* Bloomington and Indianapolis: Indiana
University Press.

Freud, A. (ed.) (1986) *Sigmund Freud: The Essentials of Psychoanalysis.* Harmondsworth: Penguin.

Freud, S. (SE) (1953–65) *The Standard Edition of the Complete Psychological Works of Sigmund Freud.* 24 vols, trans. James Strachey et al. London: Hogarth Press and the Institute of Psycho-Analysis.

Freud, S. (PFL) (1973) *Pelican Freud Library.* Harmondsworth: Penguin.

Freud, S. (1905) *Three Essays on the Theory of Sexuality.* SE, 7: 123–45. PFL, 7.

Freud, S. (1908) On the sexual theories of children. SE, 9: 205–26. PFL, 7.

Freud. S. (1915) A case of female paranoia. SE.

Freud, S. (1920a) *Beyond the Pleasure Principle.* SE, 18. PFL, 2.

Freud, S. (1920b) A case of homosexuality in a woman. In SE.

Freud, S. (1923) *The Ego and the Id.* SE, 19. PFL, 2.

Freud, S. (1925) Some psychical consequences of the anatomical distinction between the sexes. SE, 19: 243–58. PFL, 7.

Freud, S. (1933) Femininity. *New Introductory Lectures on Psychoanalysis.* SE, 22. PFL, 2.

Fuentes, A., and Ehrenreich, B. (1983) *Women in the Global Factory.* Boston, Mass.: South End Press.

Fuss, D. (1989) *Essentially Speaking: feminism, nature and difference.* London: Routledge.

Gallop, J. (1982) *Feminism and Psychoanalysis: the daughter's seduction.* London: Macmillan.

Gallop, J. (1990) *Thinking Through the Body.* London: Routledge.

Gamson, J. (1996) Must identity movements self-destruct? A queer dilemma. In S. Seidman (ed.), *Queer Theory/Sociology*, Oxford: Blackwell, 395–420.

Garber, M. (1992) *Vested Interests: cross dressing and cultural anxiety.* London: Routledge.

Garber, M. (1995) *Vice Versa: bisexuality and the eroticism of everyday life.* London: Hamish Hamilton.

Gardiner, J. (1975) Women's domestic labour. *New Left Review*, 89, 47–58.

Garland Thomson, R. (1997) *Extraordinary Bodies: figuring physical disability in American culture and literature.* New York: Columbia University Press.

Gatens, M. (1996) *Imaginary Bodies: ethics, power and corporeality.* London and New York: Routledge.

Gatens, M., and Lloyd, G. (1999) *Collective Imaginings: Spinoza, past and present.* London and New York: Routledge.

Gilligan, C. (1982) *In a Different Voice.* Cambridge, Mass.: Harvard University Press.

Gilman, S. L. (1985) *Difference and Pathology: stereotypes of sexuality, race, and madness.* Ithaca, NY: Cornell University Press.

Gilroy, P. (1993) *The Black Atlantic: modernity and double consciousness.* London: Verso.

Goldberg, S. (1973) *The Inevitability of Patriarchy*. New York: William Morrow.

Gordon, C. (ed.) (1980) *Michel Foucault: Power/Knowledge, selected interviews and other writings 1972–77 by Michel Foucault*. London: Harvester Wheatsheaf.

Greenstein, B. (1993) *The Fragile Male*. London: Boxtree.

Grosz, E. (1990a) Contemporary theories of power and subjectivity. In S. Gunew (ed.), *Feminist Knowledge*, London and New York: Routledge, 59–120.

Grosz, E. (1990b) *Jacques Lacan: a feminist introduction*. London: Routledge.

Grosz, E. (1994a) Refiguring lesbian desire. In L. Doan (ed.), *The Lesbian Postmodern*, New York: Columbia University Press, 67–84.

Grosz, E. (1994b) *Volatile Bodies: towards a corporeal feminism*. Bloomington and Indianapolis: Indiana University Press.

Grosz, E. (1995) *Space, Time and Perversion*. New York and London: Routledge.

Halberstam, J. (1994) F2M: the making of female masculinity. In L. Doan (ed.), *The Lesbian Postmodern*, New York: Columbia University Press, 210–28.

Halberstam, J. (1998) *Female Masculinity*. Durham, NC: Duke University Press.

Hamilton, R., and Barrett, M. (1986) *The Politics of Diversity*. London: Verso.

Hamner, J. (1990), Men, power and the exploitation of women. In J. Hearn and D. Morgan (eds), *Men, Masculinities and Social Theory*, London: Unwin Hyman.

Haraway, D. (1989) *Primate Visions: gender, race and nature in the world of modern science*. New York and London: Routledge.

Haraway, D. (1991a) Cyborgs at large: interview with Donna Haraway. In C. Penley and A. Ross (eds), *Technoculture*, University of Minnesota Press, Minneapolis, 1–25.

Haraway, D. (1991b), *Simians, Cyborgs and Women: the reinvention of nature*. New York and London: Routledge.

Haraway, D. (1997) *Modest_Witness@Second_Millennium.FemaleMan©_ Meets_OncoMouse™: feminism and technoscience*. New York and London: Routledge.

Harding, S. (1986) *The Science Question in Feminism*. Ithaca, NY: Cornell University Press.

Harding, S. (1992) *Whose Science, Whose Knowledge? Thinking from women's lives*. Ithaca, NY: Cornell University Press; Milton Keynes: Open University Press.

Harding, S. (ed.) (1993) *The 'Racial' Economy of Science: towards a democratic future*. Bloomington: Indiana University Press.

Harding, S. (1998) *Is Science Multi-Cultural? Postcolonialisms, feminisms and epistemologies*. Bloomington and Indianapolis: Indiana University Press.

Hargreaves, J. (1994) *Sporting Females: critical issues in the history and sociology of women's sports.* London: Routledge.

Hartmann, H. (1981) The unhappy marriage of Marxism and feminism. In L. Sargent (ed.), *Women and Revolution*, Boston, Mass.: South End Press, 1–42

Hartmann, H. (1982) Capitalism, patriarchy and job segregation by sex. In A. Giddens and D. Held (eds), *Classes, Power and Conflict*, Basingstoke: Macmillan, 446–69.

Hartsock, N. (1990) Foucault on power: a theory for women. In L. J. Nicholson (ed.), *Feminism/Postmodernism*, New York and London: Routledge, 157–75.

Hausman, B. (1995) *Changing Sex: transsexualism, technology and the idea of gender.* Durham, NC: Duke University Press.

Hawkesworth, M. (1997) Confounding gender. *Signs*, 22, 3, 649–85.

Hearn, J. (1989) Reviewing men and masculinities – or mostly boys' own papers. *Theory, Culture and Society*, 6, 4, 665–89.

Hekman, S. J. (1990) *Gender and Knowledge: elements of a postmodern feminism.* Cambridge: Polity.

Hennessy, R. (1993) *Materialist Feminism and the Politics of Discourse.* New York and London: Routledge.

Hennessy, R. (1995) Queer visibility in commodity culture. In L. Nicholson and S. Seidman (eds), *Social Postmodernism: beyond identity politics*, Cambridge: Cambridge University Press, 142–83.

Henriques, J., Hollway, W., Urwin, C., Venn, C., and Walkerdine, V. (1984) *Changing the Subject: psychology, social regulation and subjectivity.* London and New York: Methuen.

Herdt, G. (ed.) (1994) *Third Sex, Third Gender: beyond sexual dimorphism in culture and history.* New York: Zone.

Hill Collins, P. (1990) *Black Feminist Thought.* Boston, Mass.: Unwin Hyman.

Hite, S. (1976) *The Hite Report: a nationwide study of female sexuality.* New York: Macmillan.

Holland, J., Ramazanoglu, C., Sharpe, S., and Thomson, R. (1998) *The Male in the Head: young people, heterosexuality and power.* London: Tufnell Press.

Hollway, W. (1984a) Gender difference and the production of subjectivity. In J. Henriques et al. (eds), *Changing the Subject: psychology, social regulation and subjectivity*, London: Methuen, 227–63.

Hollway, W. (1984b) Women's power in heterosexual sex. *Women's Studies International Forum*, 7, 63–8.

Hondagneu-Soleto, P., and Messner, M. A. (1994) Gender displays and men's power: the 'new man' and the Mexican immigrant man. In H. Brod and M. Kaufmann (eds), *Theorizing Masculinities*, Thousand Oaks, Cal.: Sage, 200–18.

hooks, b. (1984) *Feminist Theory: from margin to centre*. Boston, Mass.: South End Press.

hooks, b. (1990) *Yearning: race, gender, and cultural politics*. Boston, Mass.: South End Press.

Horney, K. (1967) *Feminine Psychology*. London: Routledge & Kegan Paul.

Hoy, D. (ed.) (1986) *Foucault: a critical reader*. Oxford, Blackwell.

Humphries, M. (1985) Gay machismo. In A. Metcalf and M. Humphries (eds), *The Sexuality of Men*, London: Pluto Press.

Inahara, M. (2000) Fetish and self-image: exploration of physical disability. Unpublished article.

Irigaray, L. (1981) This sex which is not one. Trans. Claudia Reeder. In E. Marks and I. de Courtivan (eds), *New French Feminisms*, Brighton: Harvester, 96–106.

Irigaray, L. (1985a) *Speculum of the Other Woman*. Trans. G. Gill. Ithaca, NY: Cornell University Press.

Irigaray, L. (1985b) *This Sex Which is not One*. Trans. C. Porter with C. Burke. Ithaca, NY: Cornell University Press.

Irigaray, L. (1993) *Je, Tu, Nous*. Trans. A. Martin. London: Routledge.

Jackson, S. (1995) Gender and heterosexuality: a materialist feminist analysis. In M. Maynard and J. Purvis (eds), *(Hetero)sexual Politics*, London: Taylor and Francis, 11–26.

Jackson, S. (1996a) *Christine Delphy*. London: Sage.

Jackson, S. (1996b) Heterosexuality, power and pleasure. In S. Jackson and S. Scott (eds), *Feminism and Sexuality: a reader*, Edinburgh: Edinburgh University Press, 175–9.

Jackson, S. (1999a) Feminist sociology and sociological feminism: recovering the social in feminist thought. *Sociological Research Online*, 4, 3. http://www.socresonline.org.uk/4/3/jackson.html

Jackson, S. (1999b) *Heterosexuality in Question*. London: Sage Publications.

Jackson, S., and Jones, J. (1998) *Contemporary Feminist Theories*. Edinburgh: Edinburgh University Press.

Jackson, S., and Scott, S. (eds) (1996) *Feminism and Sexuality: a reader*. Edinburgh: Edinburgh University Press.

Jaggar, A. M. (1983) *Feminist Politics and Human Nature*. Brighton: Harvester.

Jaggar, A. M. (ed.) (1995) *Living with Contradictions*. Boulder, Colo.: Westview Press.

Jaggar, A., and Young, I. M. (eds) (1998) *A Companion to Feminist Philosophy*. Oxford: Blackwell.

Jagger, G. A. (1999) Feminism and deconstruction: towards a theory of embodied subjectivity. Ph.D., Hull University.

James, S., and Busia, A. P. A. (eds) (1993) *Theorizing Black Feminisms: the visionary pragmatism of black women*. London and New York: Routledge.

Jardine, A. (1985) *Gynesis: configurations of women and modernity.* Ithaca, NY: Cornell University Press.

Jeffreys, S. (1990) *Anticlimax.* London: The Women's Press.

Johnson, M. (1997) *Beauty and Power: transgendering and cultural transformations in the Southern Philippines.* Oxford: Berg.

Johnson Reagon, B. (1983) Coalition politics: turning the century. In B. Smith (ed.), *Home Girls: a black feminist anthology,* New York: Kitchen Table Women of Color Press, 356–68.

Jordanova, L. (1989) *Sexual Visions: images of gender in science and medicine between the eighteenth and twentieth centuries.* Madison: University of Wisconsin Press.

Kaluzynska, E. (1980) Wiping the floor with theory – a survey of writings on housework. *Feminist Review,* 6, 27–54.

Kanneh, H. (1998) Black feminisms. In S. Jackson and J. Jones (eds), *Contemporary Feminist Theories,* New York and Edinburgh: NYU Press, 86–97.

Katz, J. N. (1983) *Gay American Almanac: a new documentary.* New York: Harper Colophon.

Kaufmann, M. (1994) Men, feminism and men's contradictory experiences of power. In H. Brod and M. Kaufmann (eds), *Theorizing Masculinities,* Thousand Oaks, Cal.: Sage, 142–63.

Kay, J. (1998) *Trumpet.* London: Picador.

Kelly, J. (1979) The doubled vision of feminist theory. *Feminist Studies,* 5, 216–27.

Kimmel, M. S. (1987) Rethinking 'masculinity': new directions in research. In M. S. Kimmel (ed.), *Changing Men: new directions in research on men and masculinities,* Newbury Park: Sage.

Kimmel, M. S. (1994) Masculinity as homophobia: fear, shame and silence in the construction of gender identity. In H. Brod and M. Kaufmann (eds), *Theorizing Masculinities,* Thousand Oaks, Cal.: Sage, 119–41.

Kimmel, M. S., and Kaufmann, M. (1994) Weekend warriors: the new men's movement. In H. Brod and M. Kaufmann (eds), *Theorizing Masculinities,* Thousand Oaks, Cal.: Sage.

Klein, M. (1931) *The Psychoanalysis of Children.* London: Hogarth Press.

Klein, M. (1961) *Narrative of a Child Analysis.* London: Hogarth Press.

Kristeva, J. (1977) *About Chinese Women.* London: Marion Boyars.

Kristeva, J. (1980) *Desire in Language.* Trans. L. S. Roudiez. Oxford: Blackwell.

Kristeva, J. (1981) Women's time. Trans. A. Jardine and H. Blake. *Signs,* 7, 1, 13–15.

Kristeva, J. (1982) *Powers of Horror: an essay on abjection.* New York: Columbia University Press.

Kristeva, J. (1984) *Revolution in Poetic Language.* Trans. M. Waller. New York: Columbia University Press.

256 *Bibliography*

Kuhn, A., and Wolpe, A. M. (eds) (1978) *Feminism and Materialism*. London, Boston, Mass., and Henley: Routledge & Kegan Paul.

Lacan, J. (1966) *Ecrits*. Paris: Seuil.

Lacan, J. (1977) *Ecrits: a selection*. Trans. Alan Sheridan. London: Tavistock.

Lacan, J. (1978) *The Four Fundamental Concepts of Psycho-Analysis*. Ed. Jacques-Alain Miller. Trans. Alan Sheridan. New York: W. W. Norton.

Lakoff, R. (1975) *Language and Women's Place*. New York: Harper & Row.

Lancaster, R. N., and Leonardo, M. di (1997) *The Gender Sexuality Reader*. New York and London: Routledge.

Landry, D., and MacLean, G. (1993) *Materialist Feminisms*. Oxford: Blackwell.

Laplanche, J., and Pontalis, J. B. (1985) *The Language of Psychoanalysis*. London: Hogarth Press.

Laqueur, T. (1990) *Making Sex: body and gender from the Greeks to Freud*. Cambridge, Mass.: Harvard University Press.

Lauretis, T. de (1984) *Alice Doesn't: feminism, semiotics, cinema*. Bloomington: Indiana University Press.

Lauretis, T. de (ed.) (1986) *Feminist Studies/Critical Studies*. Bloomington: Indiana University Press.

Lauretis, T. de (1987) *Technologies of Gender: essays on theory, film, and fiction*. Basingstoke: Macmillan.

Leonard, D., and Adkins, L. (eds) (1996) *Sex in Question: French materialist feminism*. London: Taylor & Francis.

LeVay, S. (1996) *Queer Science: the use and abuse of research into homosexuality*. Cambridge, Mass.: MIT Press.

Linden, R. R., Pagano, D. R., Russell, D. E. H., and Star, S. L. (eds) (1982) *Against Sadomasochism: a radical feminist analysis*. East Palo Alto, Cal.: Frog in the Wall.

Livingston, J. (dir.) (1990) *Paris is Burning*. Miramax.

Lloyd, G. (1993) *The Man of Reason*. 2nd edn. London: Routledge.

Lloyd, M. (1998) Review of *The Psychic Life of Power: theories in 'subjection'*. *Women's Philosophy Review*, 18.

Locke, J. (1690) *An Essay Concerning Human Understanding*. London. 2.31, 3.3, 3.6, 3.10, 4.6 and 13.6.

Looby, C. (1997) As thoroughly black as the most faithful philanthropist could desire: erotics of race in Higginson's *Army Life in a Black Regiment*. In H. Stecopoulos and M. Uebel (eds), *Race and the Subject of Masculinities*, Durham, NC, and London: Duke University Press, 71–115.

Lorde, A. (1982) *Zami: a new spelling of my name*. Trumansburg, NY: Gossing Press.

Lorde, A. (1984) *Sister Outsider*. Freedom, Cal.: The Crossing Press.

Lugones, M. (1987) Playfulness, 'world' travelling, and loving perception. *Hypatia*, 2, 3–19.

Lupton, D., and Barclay, L. (1997) *Constructing Fatherhood: discourses and experiences*. London: Sage.

Mac an Ghaill, M. (1994) The making of black English masculinities. In H. Brod and M. Kaufmann (eds), *Theorizing Masculinities*, Thousand Oaks, Cal.: Sage.

McClintock, A. (1995) *Imperial Leather: race, gender and sexuality in the colonial contest*. London: Routledge.

Maccoby, E., and Jacklin, C. (1974) *The Psychology of Sex Differences*. Stanford: Stanford University Press.

McConnell-Ginet, S., Borker, R., and Furman, N. (eds) (1980) *Women and Language in Literature and Society*. New York: Praeger.

McDonough, R., and Harrison, R. (1978) Patriarchy and relations of production. In A. Kuhn and A. M. Wolpe (eds), *Feminism and Materialism*, London, Boston, Mass., and Henley: Routledge & Kegan Paul, 11–41.

McDowell, D. E. (1997) Pecs and reps: muscling in on race and the subject of masculinities. In H. Stecopoulos and M. Uebel (eds), *Race and the Subject of Masculinities*, Durham, NC, and London: Duke University Press, 361–85.

McIntosh, M. (1993) Queer theory and the war of the sexes. In J. Bristow and A. R. Wilson, (eds), *Activating Theory*, London: Lawrence & Wishart, 30–52.

McIntosh, M. (1996) The homosexual role. In S. Seidman (ed.), *Queer Theory/Sociology*, Oxford: Blackwell, 33–40.

MacKinnon, C. A. (1982) Feminism, Marxism, and the state: an agenda for theory. S, 7, 515–44.

MacKinnon, C. A. (1983) Feminism, Marxism, method, and the state: toward feminist jurisprudence. *Signs: Journal of Women in Culture and Society*, 8, 4, 635–58.

MacKinnon, C. A. (1992) Pornography, civil rights and speech. In Catherine Itzin (ed.), *Pornography: women, violence and civil liberties*, Oxford: Oxford University Press, 456–511.

MacKinnon, C. A. (1993) *Only Words*. Cambridge, Mass.: Harvard University Press.

Mackintosh, M. (1977) Reproduction and patriarchy: a critique of Meillassoux, 'Femmes, Greniers et Capitaux'. *Capital and Class*, 2, 119–27.

Mackintosh, M. (1981) The sexual division of labour and the subordination of women. In K. Young, C. Wolkowitz and R. McCullagh (eds), *Of Marriage and the Market: women's subordination in international perspective*, London: CSE Books, 1–15.

McMahon, A. (1993) Male readings of feminist theory: the psychologization of sexual politics in the masculinity literature. *Theory and Society*, 22, 675–95.

McNay, L. (1992) *Foucault and Feminism*. Cambridge: Polity.

McNay, L. (1994) *Foucault*. Cambridge: Polity.

McNay, L. (2000) *Gender and Agency*. Cambridge: Polity.

Mairs, N. (1986) On being a cripple. *Plaintext Essays*, Tucson: University of Arizona Press.

Mairs, N. (1997) Carnal acts. In K. Conboy, N. Medina and S. Stanbury (eds), *Writing on the Body: female embodiment and feminist theory*, New York: Columbia University Press, 293–309.

Mama, A. (1995) *Beyond the Masks: race, gender and subjectivity*. London: Routledge.

Marks, E., and de Courtivan, I. (eds) (1981) *New French Feminisms*. Brighton: Harvester.

Martin, B. (1988) Feminism, criticism and Foucault. In I. Diamond and L. Quinby (eds), *Feminism and Foucault: reflections on resistance*, Boston, Mass.: Northeastern University Press, 3–19.

Martin, B. (1992) Sexual practices and changing lesbian identities. In M. Barrett and A. Phillips (eds), *Destabilizing Theory*, Cambridge: Polity, 93–120.

Martin, B. (1994a) Sexuality without gender and other queer utopias. *Diacritics*, 24, 2–3, 104–21.

Martin, B. (1994b) Extraordinary homosexuals and the fear of being ordinary. *differences*, 6, 2 and 3, 100–25.

Martin, B., and Mohanty, C. (1986) Feminist politics: what's home got to do with it? In de Lauretis (ed.), *Feminist Studies/Critical Studies*, Bloomington: Indiana University Press, 191–212.

Martin, E. (1987) *The Woman in the Body: a cultural analysis of reproduction*. Milton Keynes: Open University Press.

Martin, L., Gutman, H., and Hutton, P. (eds) (1988) *Technologies of the Self: a seminar with Michel Foucault*. London: Tavistock.

Masters, W. H., and Johnson, V. E. (1966) *Human Sexual Response*. Boston, Mass.: Little, Brown.

Maynard, M. (1990) The re-shaping of sociology? Trends in the study of gender. *Sociology*, 24, 2, 269–90.

Mead, M. (1949a) *Coming of Age*. New York: Mentor.

Mead, M. (1949b) *Male and Female: a study of the sexes in a changing world*. New York: Morrow.

Meijer, Costera I., and Prins, B. (1998) How bodies come to matter: an interview with Judith Butler. *Signs*, 23, 2, 275–86.

Meillassoux, C. (1975), *Maidens, Meal and Money: capitalism and the domestic community*. Paris: Malpeso.

Mercer, K., and Julien, I. (1988), Race, sexual politics and black masculinity: a dossier. In R. Chapman and J. Rutherford (eds), *Male Order: unwrapping masculinity*, London: Lawrence & Wishart, 97–164.

Merleau-Ponty, M. (1999) *Phenomenology of Perception*. Trans. C. Smioth. London and New York: Routledge.

Messner, M. A. (1997) *Politics of Masculinities: men in movements*. Thousand Oaks, Cal.: Sage.

Metcalf, A., and Humphries, M. (eds) (1985) *The Sexuality of Men*. London: Pluto Press.

Middleton, C. (1983) Patriarchal exploitation and the rise of English capitalism. In E. Gamarnikow, D. Morgan, J. Purvis and D. Taylorson (eds), *Gender, Class and Work*, London: Heinemann, 11–27.

Milan Women's Bookstore Collective, The (1990) *Sexual Difference: a theory of social-symbolic practice*. Bloomington and Indianapolis, Indiana University Press.

Mill, J. S. (1869) The subjection of women. In A. Rossi (ed.) (1970) *Essays on Sex Equality*. Chicago and London: University of Chicago Press.

Miller, A. (1983) *Towards a New Psychology of Women*. Harmondsworth: Penguin.

Miller, A. (1987) *The Drama of Being a Child*. London: Virago.

Millett, K. (1970) *Sexual Politics*. London: Rupert Hart-Davis.

Minsky R. (ed.) (1996) *Psychoanalysis – Gender*. London: Routledge.

Mirza, H. S. (ed.) (1997) *Black British Feminism: a reader*. London and New York: Routledge.

Mitchell, J. (1971) *Women's Estate*. Harmondsworth: Penguin.

Mitchell, J. (1974) *Psychoanalysis and Women*. Harmondsworth: Penguin.

Mitchell, J. (1975) *Psychoanalysis and Feminism: Freud, Reich, Laing and women*. London: Allen Lane.

Mitchell, J. (1979) *Psychoanalysis and Feminism*. Harmondsworth: Penguin.

Mitchell, J., and Rose, J. (eds) (1982) *Jacques Lacan and the École Freudienne: feminine sexuality*. London: Macmillan.

Mohanty, C. T. (1988) Under Western eyes: feminist scholarship and colonial discourses. *Feminist Review*, 30, 61–87.

Mohanty, C. T. (1992) Feminist encounters: locating the politics of experience. In M. Barrett and A. Phillips (eds), *Destabilizing Theory: contemporary feminist debates*, Cambridge: Polity, 74–93.

Mohanty, C. T., Russo, A., and Torres, L. (eds) (1991) *Third World Women: the politics of feminism*. Bloomington: Indiana University Press.

Moi, T. (1985) *Sexual/Textual Politics: feminist literary theory*. London and New York: Methuen.

Moi, T. (ed.) (1987) *French Feminist Thought: a reader*. Oxford: Blackwell.

Money, J., and Ehrhardt, A. (1972) *Man and Woman, Boy and Girl: differentiation and dimorphism of gender identity from conception to maturity*. Baltimore: Johns Hopkins University Press.

More, K. (1999) Never mind the bollocks: Judith Butler on transsexuality, an interview. In K. More and S. Whittle (eds), *Reclaiming Genders:*

transsexual grammars at the fin de siècle, London and New York: Cassell, 285–303.

More, K., and Whittle, S. (ed.) (1999) *Reclaiming Genders: transsexual grammars at the fin de siècle*. London and New York: Cassell.

Morgan, R. (ed.) (1984) *Sisterhood is Global*. London: Penguin.

Morris, J. (1974) *Conundrum*. New York: Harcourt Brace Jovanovich.

Morris, J. (ed.) (1996) *Encounters with Stranger Feminism and Disability*. London: The Women's Press.

Morris, M., and Patton, P. (eds) (1979) *Michel Foucault: power, truth, strategy*. Sydney: Feral Publications.

Mouffe, C. (1997) Feminism, citizenship and radical democratic politics. In D. Tietjens Meyers (ed.), *Feminist Social Thought: a reader*, New York and London: Routledge.

Mueller, L. (1983) The raving beauties. In *In the Pink*, London: The Women's Press.

Munt, S. (1998) (ed.) *Butch/Femme: inside lesbian gender*. London: Cassell.

Nardi, P. M. (ed.) (2000) *Gay Masculinities*. Thousand Oaks, Cal., and London: Sage.

Nayak, A., and Kehily, M. J. (1996) Playing it straight: masculinities, homophobias and schooling. *Journal of Gender Studies*, 2, 211–30.

Nestle, J. (1987) *A Restricted Country*. Ithaca, NY: Firebrand Press.

Nestle, J. (ed.) (1992) *The Persistent Desire: a femme–butch reader*. Boston, Mass.: Alyson Publications.

Newton, E. (1979) *Mother Camp: female impersonators in America*. Chicago: Chicago University Press.

Nicholson, L. (ed.) (1990) *Feminism/Postmodernism*. London: Routledge.

Nicholson, L. (1995) Interpreting gender. In L. Nicholson and S. Seidman (eds), *Social Postmodernism: beyond identity politics*, Cambridge: Cambridge University Press, 39–67.

Oakley, A. (1974) *The Sociology of Housework*. London: Martin Robertson.

Oakley, A. (1985a) *Housewife*. Harmondsworth: Penguin.

Oakley A. (1985b) *Sex, Gender and Society*. Aldershot: Arena.

O'Brien, M. (1981) *The Politics of Reproduction*. London, Henley and Boston, Mass.: Routledge & Kegan Paul.

Ortner, S. B. (1974) Is female to male as nature is to culture. In M. Z. Rosaldo and L. Lamphere (eds), *Woman, Culture and Society*, Stanford: Stanford University Press, 67–87.

Osborne, P., and Segal, L. (1994) Gender as performance: an interview with Judith Butler. *Radical Philosophy*, 67, 32–9.

Oudshoorn, N. (1994) *Beyond the Natural Body: an archaeology of sex hormones*. London: Routledge.

Parker, R. G., and Gagnon, J. H. (eds) (1995) *Conceiving Sexuality: approaches to sex research in a postmodern world*. New York and London: Routledge.

Pateman, C. (1988) *The Sexual Contract*. Stanford: Stanford University Press.

Pateman, C. (1989) *The Disorder of Women: democracy, feminism and political theory*. Cambridge: Polity.

Pearce, L., and Stacey, J. (1995) *Romance Revisited*. London: Lawrence & Wishart.

Phelan, S. (1995) The space of justice: lesbians and democratic politics. In L. Nicholson and S. Seidman (eds), *Social Postmodernism: beyond identity politics*, Cambridge: Cambridge University Press.

Phoenix, A. (1987) Theories of gender and black families. In G. Weiner and M. Arnot (eds), *Gender under Scrutiny*, London: Hutchinson/Open University, 50–63.

Pleck, I. (1987) American fathering in historical perspective. In M. S. Kimmel (ed.), *Changing Men: new directions in research on men and masculinities*, Newbury Park, Cal.: Sage, 83–97.

Plummer, K. (1981) Homosexual categories: some research problems in the labelling perspective of homosexuality. In K. Plummer (ed.), *The Making of the Modern Homosexual*, London: Hutchinson.

Probyn, E. (1996) *Outside Belongings*. London: Routledge.

Prosser, J. (1998) *Second Skins: the body narratives of transsexuality*. New York: Columbia University Press.

Prosser, J. (1999a) Exceptional locations: transsexual travelogues. In K. More and S. Whittle (eds), *Reclaiming Genders: transsexual grammars at the fin de siècle*, London and New York: Cassell, 83–117.

Prosser, J. (1999b) A palinode on photography and the transsexual real. *Autobiography Studies*, 14, 1.

Rabinow, P. (ed.) (1984) *The Foucault Reader*. Harmondsworth: Penguin.

Ramazanoglu, C. (1989) *Feminism and the Contradictions of Oppression*. London: Routledge.

Ramazanoglu, C. (1993) *Up Against Foucault*. London: Routledge.

Ransom, J. (1993) Feminism, difference and discourse: the limits of discursive analysis for feminism. In C. Ramazanoglu (ed.), *Up Against Foucault*, London: Routledge, 123–47.

Raymond, J. G. (1979) *The Transsexual Empire: the Making of the She Male*. London: The Women's Press.

Reiter, R. R. (1975) *Toward an Anthropology of Women*. New York and London: Monthly Review Press.

Reiter, R. R. (1977) The search for origins. *Critique of Anthropology, Women's Issue*, 9/10, 3, 5–24.

Reynolds, T. (1997) (Mis)representing the black (super)woman. In H. S. Mirza (ed.), *Black British Feminism: a reader*, London and New York: Routledge, 97–113.

Rich, Adrienne (1993) Compulsory heterosexuality and lesbian existence. In H. Abelove, M. A. Barale and D. M. Halperin, (eds), *The Lesbian and Gay Studies Reader*, London and New York: Routledge, 227–54.

Richardson, D. (ed.) (1996) *Theorising Heterosexuality*. Buckingham: Open University Press.

Richardson, D., and Robinson, V. (1994) Theorizing women's studies, gender studies and masculinity. *The European Journal of Women's Studies*, 1, 11–27.

Richardson, D., and Robinson, V. (eds) (1997) *Introducing Women's Studies, Feminist Theory and Practice*. 2nd edn. Basingstoke: Macmillan.

Riley, D. (1988) *Am I that Name? Feminism and the category of 'women' in history*. London and New York: Macmillan.

Robinson, V. (1996) Heterosexuality and masculinity: theorising male power or the wounded male psyche. In D. Richardson (ed.), *Theorising Heterosexuality*, Buckingham: Open University Press, 109–24.

Rosaldo, M. Z. (1974) 'Woman, culture and society: a theoretical overview. In M. Z. Rosaldo and L. Lamphere (eds), *Woman, Culture and Society*, Stanford: Stanford University Press, 18–42.

Rose, J. (1986) *Sexuality in the Field of Vision*. London: Verso.

Rose, S., Lewontin, R., and Kamin, L. (1984) *Not in our Genes: biology, ideology and human nature*. New York: Pantheon.

Roseneil, S. (2000) Queer frameworks and queer tendencies: towards an understanding of postmodern transformations of sexuality. *Sociological Research Online*, 5, 3.

Rowbotham, S. (1982) The trouble with patriarchy. Repr. in M. Evans (ed.), *The Woman Question: readings on the subordination of women*, London: Fontana, 73–9.

Rowbotham, S. (1992) *Women in Movement*. New York and London: Routledge.

Rowbotham, S., Segal, L., and Wainwright, H. (1979) *Beyond the Fragments: the making of socialism*. London: Methuen.

Rubin, G. (1975) The traffic in women: notes on the 'Political Economy of Sex'. In R. Reiter (ed.), *Towards an Anthropology of Women*, New York: Monthly Review Press, 157–210.

Rubin, G. (1993) Thinking sex: notes for a radical theory of the politics of sexuality. In H. Abelove, M. A. Barale and D. M. Halperin (eds), *The Lesbian and Gay Studies Reader*, London and New York: Routledge, 3–44.

Rubin, G., with Butler, J. (1994) Sexual traffic. *differences*, 6, 2 and 3, 62–100.

Said, E. (1978) *Orientalism*. New York: Pantheon Books.

Sargent, L. (ed.) (1981) *Women and Revolution*. London: Pluto Press.

Sawicki, J. (1988) Identity politics and sexual freedom: Foucault and feminism. In I. Diamond and L. Quinby (eds), *Feminism and Foucault: reflections on resistance*, Boston, Mass.: Northeastern University Press, 177–91.

Sawicki, J. (1991) *Disciplining Foucault: feminism, power and the body*. London: Routledge.

Schor, N. (1994) This essentialism which is not one: coming to grips with Irigaray. In N. Schor and E. Weed (eds), *The Essential Difference, Brown University and differences*, 40–63.

Schor, N., and Weed, E. (eds) (1994) *The Essential Difference*. Brown University and *differences*.

Scott, J. W. (1988) *Gender and the Politics of History*. New York: Columbia University Press

Seccombe, W. (1974) The housewife and her labour under capitalism. *New Left Review*, 83, 3–24.

Sedgwick, E. K. (1990) *Epistemology of the Closet*. Berkeley: University of California Press.

Sedgwick, E. K. (1993) *Tendencies*. Durham, NC: Duke University Press.

Segal, L. (1990) *Slow Motion: changing masculinities, changing men*. London: Virago.

Segal, L. (1994) *Straight Sex: the politics of pleasure*. London: Virago.

Segal, L. (1999) *Why feminism? Gender, psychology, politics*. Cambridge: Polity.

Seidler, V. J. (1989) *Rediscovering Masculinity: reason, language and sexuality*. London: Routledge.

Seidman, S. (ed.) (1996) *Queer Theory/Sociology*. Oxford: Blackwell.

Seifert, R. (1996) The Second Front: the logic of sexual violence in wars. *Women's Studies International Forum*, 19, 1–2, 35–43.

Seymour, W. (1988) *Remaking One Body: rehabilitation and change*. London: Routledge.

Silverman, K. (1992) *Male Subjectivity at the Margins*. London: Routledge.

Silverman, K. (1996) *The Threshold of the Visible World*. New York and London: Routledge.

Smith, P. (1978) Domestic labour and Marx's theory of value. In A. Kuhn and A. M. Wolpe (eds), *Feminism and Materialism*, London, Boston, Mass., and Henley: Routledge & Kegan Paul, 198–219.

Smith, P. (ed.) (1996) *Boys: masculinities in contemporary culture*. Boulder, Colo.: Westview Press.

Snitow, A., Stansell, C., and Thompson, S. (eds) (1984) *Desire: the politics of sexuality*. London: Virago.

Soper, K. (1995) *What is Nature*. Oxford: Blackwell.

Spelman, E. (1990) *Inessential Woman: problems of exclusion in feminist thought*. London: The Women's Press.

Spivak, G. C. (1987) *In Other Worlds: essays in cultural politics*. New York and London: Methuen.

Spivak, G. C. (1988) Can the subaltern speak? In C. Nelson and L. Grossberg (eds), *Marxism and the Interpretation of Culture*, Urbana: University of Illinois Press, 271–313.

Spivak, G. C. (1993) *Outside in the Teaching Machine*. London: Routledge.

Spivak, G. C., with Rooney, E. (1994) In a word: interview. In N. Schor and E. Weed (eds), *The Essential Difference*, Brown University and *differences*, 151–85.

Squires, J. (1999) *Gender in Political Theory*. Cambridge: Polity.

Stacey, J. (1993) Untangling feminist theory. In D. Richardson and V. Robinson (eds), *Introducing Women's Studies, Feminist Theory and Practice*. 1st edn. Basingstoke, Macmillan.

Staples, R. (1982) *Black Masculinity: the black male's role in American society*. San Francisco: Black Scholar Press.

Staples, R. (1995) Stereotypes of black masculinity: the facts behind the myths. In M. S. Kimmel and M. Messner (eds), *Men's Lives*, Boston, Mass.: Allyn & Bacon.

Star, H. J. (1955) [Carl Rollins Hammonds] *I Changed my Sex*. [Publisher unknown.]

Stefano, C. di (1990) Dilemmas of difference: feminism, modernity and postmodernism. In L. J. Nicholson (ed.), *Feminism/Postmodernism*, London: Routledge, 63–83.

Stein, A. (1997) Sisters and queers: the decentering of lesbian feminism. In R. N. Lancaster and M. di Leonardo (eds), *The Gender Sexuality Reader*, New York and London: Routledge, 378–91.

Stein, E. (1992) *Forms of Desire*. New York and London: Routledge.

Steinberg, D. L., Epstein, D., and Johnson, R. (1997) *Border Patrols: policing the boundaries of heterosexuality*. London: Cassell.

Stocking, G. (1993) The turn-of-the-century concept of race. *Modernism/Modernity*, 1, 4–16.

Stone, S. (1997) The Empire Strikes Back: a post-transsexual manifesto. First published in J. Epstein and K. Straub (eds), *Body Guards: the cultural politics of gender ambiguity*, New York: Routledge, 1971. Repr. in K. Conboy, N. Medina and S. Stanbury (eds), *Writing on the Body: female embodiment and feminist theory*, New York: Columbia University Press, 337–60.

Stone, S. D. (1995) The myth of bodily perfection. *Disability and Society*, 10, 4, 413–25.

Tannen, D. (1994) *Gender and Discourse*. New York: Oxford University Press.

Taylor, C. (1985) Interpretation and the sciences of man. In C. Taylor, *Philosophy and the Human Sciences*, Cambridge: Cambridge University Press, 17–41.

Theweleit, K. (1987), *Male Fantasies*, vol. 1: *Women's Floods, Bodies, History*, Cambridge: Polity.

Theweleit, K. (1989), *Male Fantasies*, vol. 2: *Male Bodies: psychoanalyzing the white terror*, Cambridge: Polity.

Thomas, C. (1999) *Female Forms: experiencing and understanding disability*. Buckingham: Open University Press.

Thompson, C., with Mullally, P. (1952) *Psychoanalysis: evolution or development*. London: Allen & Unwin.

Thompson, R., with Sewell, K. (1995) *What Took You So Long? A girl's journey into manhood*. London: Penguin.

Tong, R. (1989) *Feminist Thought: a comprehensive introduction*. London: Unwin Hyman.

Tremain, S. (2000) Queering disabled sexuality studies. *Journal of Sexuality and Disability*, 18, 4 (Winter).

Vance, C. (ed.) (1984) *Pleasure and Danger: exploring female sexuality*. London: Routledge.

Van den Wijngaard, M. (1997) *Reinventing the Sexes: the biomedical construction of femininity and masculinity*. Bloomington: Indiana University Press.

Vogel, L. (1981) Marxism and feminism: unhappy marriage, trial separation or something else? In L. Sargent (ed.), *Women and Revolution*, London: Pluto Press, 195–217.

Vogel, L. (1984) *Marxism and the Oppression of Women*. London: Pluto Press.

Wahid, A. (2000) Women's bodies in northern Nigeria. Lecture. Hull Centre for Gender Studies, March.

Walby, S. (1986) *Patriarchy at Work*. Cambridge: Polity.

Walby, S. (ed.) (1988a) *Gender Segregation at Work*. Milton Keynes: Open University Press.

Walby, S. (1988b) 'Segregation in employment in social and economic theory.' In S. Walby (ed.), *Gender Segregation at Work*, Milton Keynes: Open University Press, 14–28.

Walby, S. (1989) Theorising patriarchy. *Sociology*, 23, 2, 213–44.

Walby, S. (1992) Post-post-modernism? Theorizing social complexity. In M. Barrett and A. Phillips (eds), *Destabilizing Theory: contemporary feminist debates*, Cambridge: Polity, 31–53.

Walker, A. (1982), *The Colour Purple*. London: The Women's Press.

Wallace, M. (1979) *Black Macho and the Myth of the Superwoman*. London: John Calder.

Ware, V. (1992) *Beyond the Pale: white women, racism and history*. London: Verso.

Warner, M. (1993) Introduction. In M. Warner (ed.), *Fear of a Queer Planet: queer politics and social theory*, Minneapolis: University of Minnesota Press.

Watney, S. (1987) *Policing Desire: pornography, AIDS, and the media*. London: Methuen/Comedia.

Webster, F. (2000) The Politics of Sex and Gender: Benhabib and Butler Debate Subjectivity. *Hypatia*, 15, 1, 1–22.

Weedon, C. (1987) *Feminist Practice and Poststructuralist Theory*. Oxford: Blackwell.

Weedon, C. (1999) *Feminism, Theory and the Politics of Difference*. Oxford: Blackwell.

Weeks, J. (1977) *Coming Out: homosexual politics in Britain from the nineteenth century to the present.* London: Quartet.

Weeks, J. (1981) *Sex, Politics and Society: the regulation of sexuality since 1800.* London and New York: Longman.

Weeks, J. (1985) *Sexuality and its Discontents: meanings, myths and modern sexualities.* London and New York: Routledge.

Weeks, J. (1986) *Sexuality.* London: Tavistock.

Weeks, J. (1987) Questions of identity. In P. Caplan (ed.), *The Cultural Construction of Sexuality*, New York and London: Routledge.

Weeks, J. (2000) *Making Sexual History.* Cambridge: Polity.

Weiss, G. (1999) *Body Images: embodiment as intercorporeality.* New York and London: Routledge.

Welton, D. (ed.) (1998) *Body and Flesh: a philosophical reader.* Oxford, Blackwell.

Wendell, S. (1996) *The Rejected Body: feminist philosophical reflections on disability.* London: Routledge.

Westwood, S. (1990) Racism, black masculinity and the politics of space. In J. Hearn and D. Morgan (eds), *Men, Masculinities and Social Theory.* London: Unwin Hyman.

Weymour, W. (1998) *Remaking the Body: rehabilitation and change.* London: Routledge.

Whitford, M. (1991) *Luce Irigaray: philosophy in the feminine.* London and New York: Routledge.

Whitford, M. (ed.) (1992) *The Irigaray Reader.* Oxford: Blackwell.

Wilkinson, S., and Kitzinger, C. (eds) (1995) *Feminism and Discourse.* London: Sage.

Willis, P. (1977) *Learning to Labour: how working class kids get working class jobs.* Farnborough: Saxon House.

Wilson, E., with Weir, A. (1986) *Hidden Agendas, Theory, Politics and Experience in the Women's Movement.* New York and London: Tavistock.

Wilson, E. O. (1978) *On Human Nature.* Cambridge, Mass.: Harvard University Press.

Wilton, T. (1996) Which one's the man? The heterosexualisation of lesbian sex. In D. Richardson (ed.), *Theorising Heterosexuality*, Buckingham: Open University Press, 125–42.

Winnicott, D. (1964) *The Child, the Family and the Outside World.* Harmondsworth: Penguin.

Wittig, M. (1976) *The Lesbian Body.* Trans. P. Owen. New York: Avon.

Wittig. M. (1980) The straight mind. *Feminist Issues*, 1, 103–10.

Wittig, M. (1981) One is not born a woman. In H. Abelove, M. A. Barale and D. M. Halperin, *The Lesbian and Gay Studies Reader*, New York and London: Routledge, 103–9.

Wittig, M. (1992) *The Straight Mind.* New York: Beacon.

Wollheim, R. (1971) *Freud*. London: Fontana.

Women's Studies Group CCCS (1978) *Women Take Issue*. London: Hutchinson.

Wood, N. (1985) Foucault on the history of sexuality: an introduction. In V. Beechey and J. Donald (eds), *Subjectivity and Social Relations*, Milton Keynes: Open University Press, 156–74.

Wright, E. (ed.) (1992) *Feminism and Psychoanalysis: a critical dictionary*. Oxford: Blackwell.

Young, I. (1981) Beyond the unhappy marriage: a critique of dual systems theory. In L. Sargent (ed.), *Women and Revolution*, London: Pluto Press, 43–69.

Young, I. M. (1990a) The Ideal of Community and the Politics of Difference. In L. J. Nicholson (ed.), *Feminism/Postmodernism*, London: Routledge, 300–24.

Young, I. M. (1990b) *Throwing Like a Girl and Other Essays in Feminist Philosophy and Social Theory*. Bloomington and Indianapolis: Indiana University Press.

Young, I. M. (1995) Gender as seriality: thinking about women as a social collective. In L. Nicholson and S. Seidman (eds), *Social Postmodernism: beyond identity politics*, Cambridge: Cambridge University Press, 187–215.

Young, I. M. (1998) *Throwing Like a Girl: twenty years later*. In D. Welton (ed.), *Body and Flesh: a philosophical reader*, Oxford: Blackwell, 286–91.

Index

bisexuality
  and gay and lesbian movement 96,
    146
  and Oedipal crisis 45, 51, 59
  and rejection of 'femininity' 46–8
Blachford, G. 148–9
black rights movement 153–4, 222, 226–7
Bleier, R. 20
Bly, R. 135, 136
body 9–10
  and body image and imaginary bodies
    10, 171–8, 181, 188, 193, 194, 198–9,
    208, 211
  in Butler 9–10, 97, 112–13, 165–6,
    168–71, 198
  control over female bodies 70, 111, 116
  and disability 77–8, 89, 169–70, 179–80
  disciplining of 87, 107, 167–8
  female 17, 18–19, 164, 167–8, 178–80,
    184–5, 186–8
  and femininity 17, 18–19, 163, 167–8,
    179
  and identity 10–11, 36–8, 50–1, 165,
    171–8, 196, 206
  intersex 30–1
  male 18, 132, 160, 187
  and masculinity 18, 168, 181
  and materiality 9–10, 168–71, 177, 179
  and sex differences as natural kinds
    18–19
  and subjectivity 165–81, 184–6, 188–9,
    198, 207
  and transcendence 185, 189
  and transsexuality 10, 166, 206–8, 209,
    211, 214, 218
  see also biology
Bollas, C. 57
borderlands
  concept of 10–11, 201, 207, 210, 216,
    219
  and postcolonialism 212–14
Bordo, S. 236
Boys Don't Cry 128, 237
Bracewell, W. 184
Braidotti, R.
  and gender studies 5, 191–2, 193,
    197–8, 200
  and sexual difference 4, 10, 186, 187,
    189, 196
  and subjectivity 233

brain
  and genetics 22
  and sex differences 23–5, 32, 115, 134
Brando, M. & Lindsay, R. 12–14, 16, 20,
  21
Bristow, J. 52, 114
Brittan, A. 138
Brod, H. 131, 141
Brown, W. 231
buddy system 127
Butler, J. 9, 93, 94–113
  on being/having the phallus 53
  Bodies that Matter 168–9
  and the body 9–10, 97, 112–13, 165–6,
    168–71, 176, 198
  and discourse theory 7, 10, 94–113,
    202, 223
  Excitable Speech 109
  and gender as real 101–3
  and gender studies 5
  Gender Trouble 94, 95, 104, 108, 128,
    166, 205
  and hegemonic masculinity 142–3, 162
  and heterosexual matrix 96, 101, 127,
    200
  and identity 105–8, 127, 217, 234
  and iterability 103–5, 109–10
  and political agency 108–10, 230–2,
    234–6
  and politics of identity 9, 11, 227–30
  and queer theory 95–6, 106, 168, 205,
    214, 223–4, 227
  and sex and gender 96–7, 127
  and sexual difference 4, 10, 194,
    196–200
  and sexuality 9, 118, 126–9
  and subjectivity 107–8, 109, 165–6, 197,
    227, 230–1, 239
  see also performativity

Califia, P. 122
'camp' 148
Canaan, J. E. and Griffin, C. 131–2
capitalism
  and consumerism 237
  and equality of opportunity 183
  and gender divisions 69
  and masculinity 136–7
  and patriarchy 2, 69–72, 74, 86, 89
  and sexuality 120

274 *Index*

Hennessy, R.
  and discourse theory 90–1, 111
  and feminism 221
  and identity politics 228, 236–8
  and materialism 8, 88–9
Herdt, G. 26, 205
hermaphrodites 30
heterosexuality
  in Butler 97–8
  compulsory 97–8, 100, 111, 118–20,
    127–8
  and discourse theory 116
  and gender 118, 128
  and hegemonic masculinity 140–3, 144,
    148, 150
  and infantile sexuality 47
  in Lacan 54
  and language 82–4, 90
  as natural 14, 114, 117, 120, 132
  as normative 76–7, 82–4, 95–6, 110,
    115, 117–19, 127, 200, 228
  and oppression of women 72
  as socially constructed 120
Holland, J. et al. 117
home
  dangers of 209–12
  and identity 10–11, 104–5, 127, 207–9,
    213, 214, 216–18
homophobia 9, 125, 126, 132, 143–5, 146,
    156, 163
  and race 152–3
homosexuality
  and the brain 23, 24, 32, 115
  and 'butch' 148, 149
  and Foucault 82, 146–7
  as natural 95–6, 120
  as 'other' 200
  and psychoanalytic theory 48–9, 95,
    115
  and queering 95–6
  and racism 149–50
  as resistance to heterosexuality 76–7,
    100, 146
  as subordinated masculinities 141, 146–9
  as unnatural 14, 114–15
  visibility of 95, 228, 236–7
  see also desire, same-sex; gay and lesbian
    movement; lesbianism
Hondagneu-Soleto, P. and Messner, M. A.
  135

hooks, b. 106–7, 153–4, 178, 180, 208–9,
  225
Hopper, E. 175
Horney, K. 50, 241 n.1b
Hull Centre for Gender Studies 1–2, 3
Humphries, M. 148
hypermasculinity 135, 141, 148, 149, 154
hypothalamus, and sexual difference 23–4,
  32

identity
  and behaviour 34–6
  and belonging 215–16, 219
  bisexual 45, 46–8, 51, 59
  and the body 10–11, 36–8, 50–1, 165,
    171–9, 196, 206
  and borderlands 201, 210, 212–14, 216
  in Butler 105–8, 127, 217, 228
  and class 76, 78
  and culture 43, 56, 64, 87, 101, 111–12
  decentring of 54–5, 81
  in discourse theory 85–6, 98, 105,
    223–4, 235
  gay 146–7, 226
  multiple 55, 107, 127, 147, 219, 235
  and Oedipal crisis 42–6, 51
  as performative 11, 98–9
  and race 106–7, 177
  and sexual difference 4, 47, 64, 187,
    197
  and sexuality 117, 126, 146
  shared 106, 208, 222–5, 228, 233
  as socially constructed 121, 204–5
  as style 78, 145, 166, 217, 226
  and the symbolic 52–3, 193
  and the unconscious 39–41, 48, 61–2
  see also politics, of identity
ideology
  and discourse 90–1
  and Marxism 69, 80, 84
  and patriarchy 71–2
  and sexuality as natural 114–15
  and social construction of gender 79–80,
    84, 127, 140
imaginary, the 165–81, 208, 217
  in Butler 10, 198–9, 211
  in French feminism 56
  in Irigaray 10, 56, 180, 188, 189–90,
    193, 194, 199
  in Lacan 52, 65, 175–6

and femininity 1, 4, 26–7, 50, 66
and ideology 79–80, 84, 90
and masculinity 1, 4, 26–7, 66, 131–2,
    136–7, 153–4, 159–60, 165–6
sex, gender and social roles 64–7
and sexuality 115–17, 120–4, 127, 226
and social role theory 66–7
see also Butler, J.; discourse theory;
    materialism; performativity
social relations, in materialist feminism
    67–8, 72–4
social role theory 66–7, 137–9
socialization *see* social constructionism
sociobiology 13, 20–2, 29, 134–6
Soper, K. 223
speech, hate speech 109
Spivak, Gayatri 7, 87, 169, 194–7, 230
sport, and femininity 163, 164
Squires, J. 222, 223, 232
Stacey, J. 66
Staples, R. 131, 152
Star, H. J. 203
stare, and the disabled 77
Stefano, C. di 221
Stocking, G. 19
Stone, S. 203, 204, 205, 209
style, and identity 78, 145, 166, 217, 226
subjectivity
    and belonging 215–16, 219
    and the body 8, 47, 64–5, 165–81,
        184–6, 188–9, 198, 207
    in Butler 107–8, 109, 165–6, 197, 227,
        230–1, 239
    female 52–4
    and gender 3, 8, 13, 61–2, 79–80, 140,
        168, 199, 205
    and identity politics 220–2
    and ideology 80, 84
    and language 51–3, 55, 62, 81–2, 84,
        85–6, 88, 96, 99, 107–8, 189
    and race 107
    and sexual difference 8, 47, 64–5, 184,
        197
    shared 224–5, 233
    as temporal 174, 217
    and the unconscious 62
subordination
    and black masculinities 149–55
    and gay masculinities 141, 146–9, 226
    of women 2, 50, 67, 117; and black

masculinities 152, 154; and capitalism
    69; and male pleasure 121–2; and
    patriarchy 70–4
superego, and the father 43, 47
Symbolic, the 57, 239
    in Irigaray 55, 188–90, 193, 194
    in Lacan 52–3, 55, 62–3, 85, 99–100,
        142, 159, 184

Taylor, C. 34
testosterone 19
Theweleit, K. 131, 137
Thomas, C. 78
Tong, R. 69, 122, 183
transcendence, in de Beauvoir 185, 189
transgender narratives 10, 210, 212
    and queer theory 6, 204–6, 207
transsexuality
    and the body 10, 166, 181, 206–8, 209,
        211, 214, 218
    and concept of 'home' 207–9, 210, 214,
        216–18
    female-to-male 128, 160–1, 203, 204,
        210, 218
    and feminism 2, 125, 202–4, 218
    male-to-female 96, 202–3
    and naturalism 31–2
    and queer theory 204–6
    and realness of gender 181, 206–9, 210,
        214, 216
transsexual theory 166, 201, 206

UN Women's Conference, Beijing 232–3
unconscious
    and gender formation 8, 44–6, 61–2, 64,
        155–6, 239
    and identity 39–41, 48
    in Lacan 53, 55, 65, 99
understanding, and behaviour 34–6
universalism
    feminist 3, 6, 33–4, 158, 194–5, 220–1,
        225
    in gay movement 226
    materialist 73, 74, 75
    psychoanalytic 158, 175, 230

Van der Wijngaard, M. 30–1
Vance, C. 121, 123–5
violence, male 61, 70, 121, 157, 223
visibility, queer 228, 236–7

Compiled by Meg Davies (Registered Indexer, Society of Indexers).